IMAGES of America

NEW GLARUS

On the Cover: This group of farmers is no doubt happy with the new steam-powered threshing machine they are using. Machines such as this one made grain farming much easier. Before threshing machines were available, all the grain had to be hand cut. The kernels of grain had to be knocked off the plant stems with the use of handheld flails, which was very hard and tedious work. (Courtesy of Jane Greene.)

IMAGES
of America

NEW GLARUS

Kim D. Tschudy

ARCADIA
PUBLISHING

ISBN 978-1-4671-1303-8

Published by Arcadia Publishing
Charleston, South Carolina

Printed in the United States of America

Library of Congress Control Number: 2014940533

For all general information, please contact Arcadia Publishing:
Telephone 843-853-2070
Fax 843-853-0044
E-mail sales@arcadiapublishing.com
For customer service and orders:
Toll-Free 1-888-313-2665

Visit us on the Internet at www.arcadiapublishing.com

To Elda and Linda Schiesser, whose decades of contributions to New Glarus leave us with a very deep body of understanding of who, what, and why we are the community we are. They have given two lifetimes of making New Glarus a better and much more interesting place to live. Their volunteer work in the documentation of New Glarus history, events, and the arts is nothing short of amazing.

Contents

ACKNOWLEDGMENTS

Without the help, knowledge, and wise counsel of so many people, this book on New Glarus would not have happened. It is impossible to thank everyone who had a part in this project; you've all been great to work with. This book has been the most emotional one I have done. Memories of so many people in our collective past played heavily as the book progressed. The children of World War II veterans stirred the deepest of these emotions as they shared their mothers' and fathers' stories.

Al Lienhardt was especially helpful with his sharing of his father Fred Lienhardt's personal papers, from the years when Fred was selling farms to the newly arriving Amish. Those papers gave a true voice to his father, who had a strong conscience, which showed when he stood up for the Amish. It was not easy for Fred to take an unpopular stand. Thankfully, he did.

Jay, Esta, and Louise Kramer were wonderful in sharing their reflections of coming to New Glarus as young Amish children. Memories of the early May night, when we sat at your kitchen table, under the hissing warmth of the gas lantern, sharing your stories of being the only Amish children to go to public school will remain forever—thanks!

Also, a big thank-you to my friend Terry Goetz, who so graciously volunteered to do the proofreading for me. Your reader's eye really made this project turn out better. Thanks, Terry, for all the time you put into this book.

And to the computer guru, Troy Gempeler, who on many occasions saved me from wanting to run screaming from the writer's hovel in distress from computer overload. Your tech skills were, as always, a lifesaver.

Elda and Linda Schiesser are so much more than just friends who have similar interests. Any time a question was asked on historical matters, Elda and Linda always had the answer or the knowledge of where to begin the search for the answer. This mother-and-daughter pair has become so much more than friends. Elda and Linda have become like an adopted mother and sister. For that I am forever grateful.

Last but not least, thank you to Jacel Egan and Liz Gurley from Arcadia Publishing. Both of you are great to work with. And, as always, I extend a big thanks to John Marty from the New Glarus Historical Society. The history conversations with John are always a much-anticipated time of good sharing.

All photographs, unless otherwise noted, are from the author's collection.

INTRODUCTION

The Oglala Sioux holy man Black Elk once said, "You have noticed that everything an Indian does is in a circle, and that is because the Power of the World always works in circles, and everything tries to be round. Even the seasons form a great circle in their changing, and always come back again to where they were. The life of a man is a circle, from childhood to childhood, and so it is in everything where the power goes."

The months of writing this book about the Village and Township of New Glarus in the 36 square miles locals call home, where six generations of families have been birthed, were times of deep introspection. Many cold February nights and early mornings gave pause to how difficult the ancestors' early years in New Glarus were.

The area's forefathers' first farming endeavor was growing wheat. Wheat gave them food and the necessary money to pay off their 20-acre farms. As times got better, they added more land and wheat. But, the wheat farming played itself out. Without nutrient-rich animal manure to apply to their fields, within two decades the wheat wore out the soil.

With the failure of wheat crops, these small-acreage farmers tried dairying. Their hard work brought them success. Soon, their acreage doubled to 40-acre and then 80-acre farms. Barns were built and added on to as their success grew. By the turn of the 20th century, many of the small vernacular houses of utilitarian design gave way to new and bigger farmhouses that reflected their successful dairying endeavor.

Four decades ago, nearly every barn had the lights on, early in the morning and late into the evening, as the twice daily milking was done. These former 20-to-40-acre farms had grown into 160-acre farms that were the economic powerhouse for the businesses of New Glarus. Farm-implement shops, car dealers, hardware stores, feed mills, plumbers, and electricians were all kept busy keeping these farms working.

Today, the barns, with the exception of 12, are all empty. The cows are long gone. The days of the 40-cow family farms are gone. Main street is no longer the vibrant hub of locally generated commerce with farmers coming into town after morning milking to pick up parts for the combine, grind a load of feed, pick up some fence boards at the lumber yard, and make a stop for a quick Huber's beer before returning home to begin cultivating the recently planted corn.

There was a sense of community in spirit and action—and not just empty words. Several farmers would go together to purchase a hay bailer, combine, or whatever other piece of critical, expensive machinery that was much needed but used for only a few days each year. Threshing days were always eagerly anticipated. Several neighboring farmers would gather and work from farm to farm to combine the oats and eat a hearty dinner cooked by the farmers' wives. The next day, they moved on to the next neighborhood farm, repeating the previous day's work, until all the neighboring farmers had the oats safely stored in the granary.

The area has changed, just as its people have. Today, residents live with the memories of the vibrancy these many small farms brought to New Glarus for 13 decades. People have enjoyed the good times and proved resilient with the bad times. Land once lush with hay and corn now grows houses for commuters working in nearby cities.

Gone also are, with the exception of one family, the 50 to 70 Amish families that settled in the quiet valleys in the mid-1960s. These humble people of the land, with their Protestant Christian roots as deeply planted in Switzerland as the rest of the population's own protestant Christian ancestors, are missed. They became good friends, neighbors, customers of the local businesses, and well-respected farmers.

The Amish are gone, but they left their mark on our community. A long, multistate legal battle over compulsory education laws was finally settled with a US Supreme Court case, Yoder vs. Wisconsin, which finally resolved, once and for all, the issue of freedom of religion. This case began in our school district. Popular myth states that the Amish left New Glarus because our school district filed truancy charges against five of our Amish neighbors, but that was not the case. "The New Glarus Amish left because they couldn't get along with each other. Yoder vs. Wisconsin had nothing to do with us leaving," said the son of one of the early New Glarus Amish.

In the late 1950s, the face of New Glarus changed forever. Highway 69, which used to wind through downtown New Glarus, was relocated to the east edge of town, bringing with it a new commercial district "down on the highway." Gas stations quickly sprung up to capture the gas dollars and chance to sell some locally made sodas (Squirt, Hires Root Beer, and strawberry soda), a bag of chips, and a candy bar to the traveling public. Soon to come were banks, specialty shops, fast food shops, and mini malls.

The 1970s brought with it many changes. The Milwaukee Road railroad that served New Glarus since 1887 announced that it was going to abandon service from Brodhead to New Glarus. In 1972, the Wisconsin DNR purchased the right-of-way and converted it to a four-season recreational trail. During its first 10 years, the Sugar River State Trail attracted over 500,000 visitors to the area. The old New Glarus train depot was remodeled as the trail headquarters.

The 1980s saw yet more changes in New Glarus. The Chalet Landhaus motel opened on Highway 69, and Poplar Grove, the last cheese factory with a New Glarus address, closed. Disch Furniture, a longtime business, closed in 1982. The following year saw Stuessy's Grocery store sell out to Dennis and Toots Hoesly. But the big news of the year was the arrival of cable television. Over the balance of the decade, New Glarus Woods State Park expanded by 260 acres. The Wilhelm Tell Pageant celebrated its 50th year, and a Winterfest event was started. Swiss Valley Orchard opened for business and quickly became the biggest fall tourist draw for New Glarus.

The 1990s again were years of changes. Earth Day saw the beginning of a recycling program in New Glarus, Dr. Marty began a well-deserved retirement, Swiss Church began mission trips to Central America, New Glarus's Edelweiss Gegenseitige Unterstuezings Gellschaft Germania Ladies Society Local No. 11 disbanded after having been formed in 1923. Switzerland celebrated its 700th birthday with nearly 100 New Glarus residents going to Switzerland to help them celebrate. In 1995, New Glarus celebrated its sesquicentennial with 13 days of events and many relatives visiting from Switzerland.

Fred Lienhardt was the New Glarus realtor who sold most of the newly arrived Amish their farms. These farm sales created a lot of concern from the local business community. The New Glarus Businessmen's Association summonsed Lienhardt to a meeting to answer their concerns about the Amish. He was asked the question, "What reasons you can give that their (the Amish) presence will be beneficial to the community?"

Lienhardt's answer set a course for the future of New Glarus. He said, "Our community can only prosper by growth and understanding. We cannot prosper by having empty farms surround us; we cannot prosper unless we welcome all kinds of people regardless of color, creed, or religion to our community."

As the town closes in on its 170th anniversary, New Glarus is a changed place. When the area's ancestors first arrived here, the Swiss were, in the minds of the Winnebago people (whose land this was for centuries), the minority. Today, the population is much more diverse and, with that diversity of African Americans, Hispanics, Asians, Sikhs, and LGBT residents, the citizens are the stronger and more prosperous community Fred Lienhardt hoped for.

One

The Early Years

New Glarus was not born of dreams. New Glarus was birthed of desperation and hope for a better future—somewhere, elsewhere. The town's ancestors had nothing but hope to guide them to America and eventually to the Little Sugar River Valley in Green County, Wisconsin. It was here that the first settlers' hopes of a better future began. Their beginning here was difficult, very difficult. The settlers arrived in mid-August 1845. The growing season was drawing to a close. Food and shelter was needed for the advancing fall and winter.

The warming ground of spring served as a harbinger of better times ahead. Better times that had, for their last few years in their homeland, eluded this group of hearty new immigrants. Food crops were planted. More and better shelters were constructed. Livestock was purchased to provide both meat and milk. The winds of the much better days ahead were beginning to blanket the valley in which they chose to make their new home. To be sure, those first years were better than those they left behind, but it was several years until the growing settlement began to set its taproots deep into the place they named New Glarus, a quiet reminder of the ancestors' namesake homeland: Glarus, Switzerland.

This chapter tells, to some degree, the story of the beginning of New Glarus through 1925. The late 1920s marked the end of the arrivals of new emigrants from Switzerland. And, with that ending, it marked to some degree the end of the evolution of the Swiss language, as it is still on occasion spoken in New Glarus.

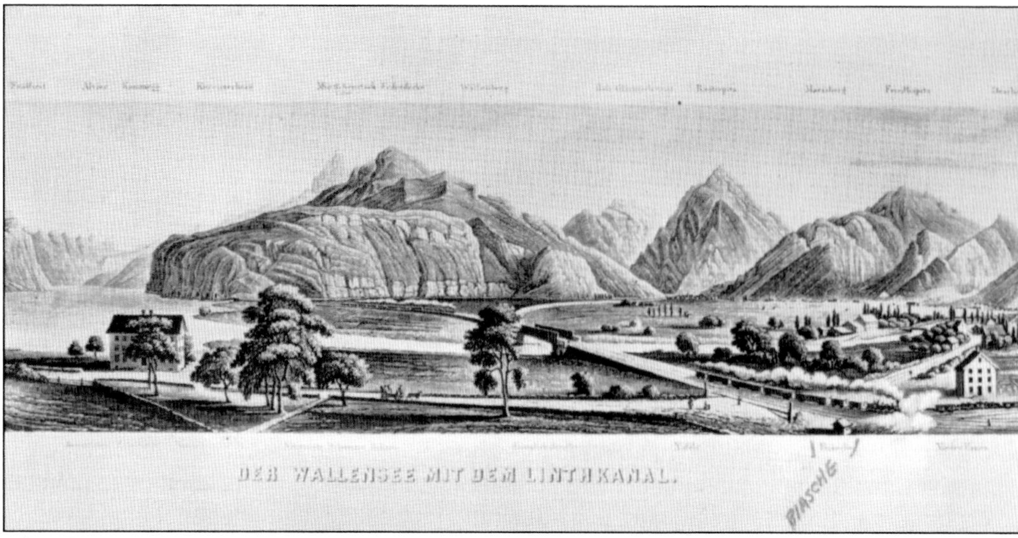

This drawing depicts the point where the first Swiss settlers in New Glarus started the long journey from their home in Switzerland to their new home in America. The night before they left here, 53 other Swiss decided to join them in the trip to America, leaving Switzerland on April 16, 1845, and arriving in what was to become New Glarus on August 15, 1845, with only 62 miles of this arduous journey made by land.

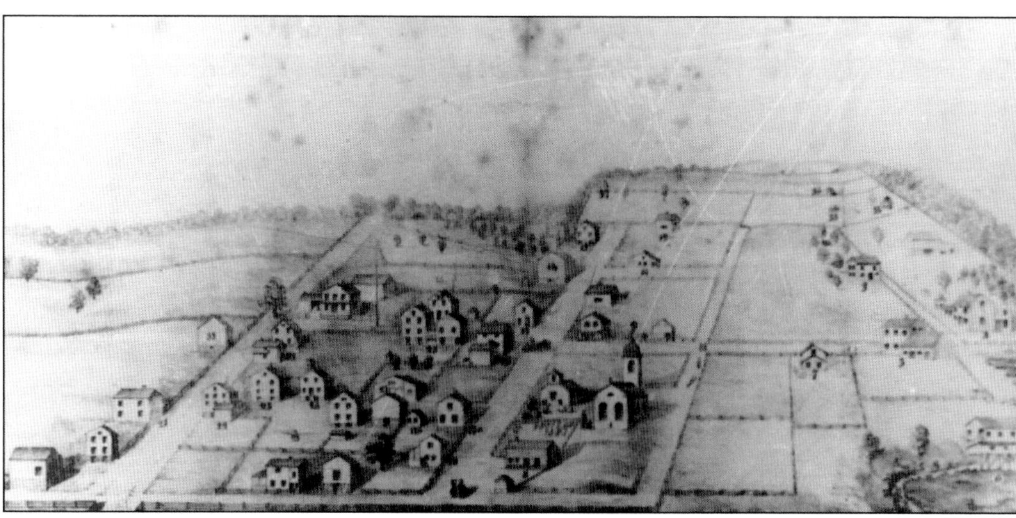

The year 1859 shows a village that has grown considerably since the first cabin was built just 14 years earlier. Several of the buildings shown in this drawing still exist today and serve as personal residences.

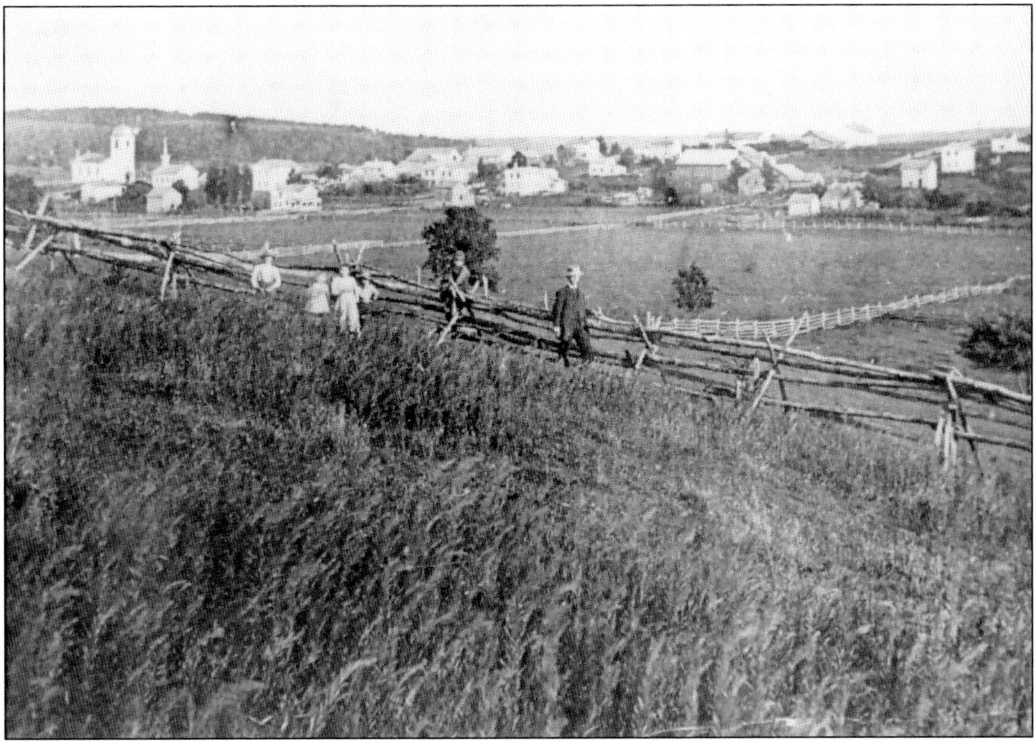

This early view of New Glarus was taken from the northwest corner of the village looking southeast toward the Little Sugar River. Farm fields are now clearly defined with simple fences of small logs. The photograph was taken some time between 1858 and 1880.

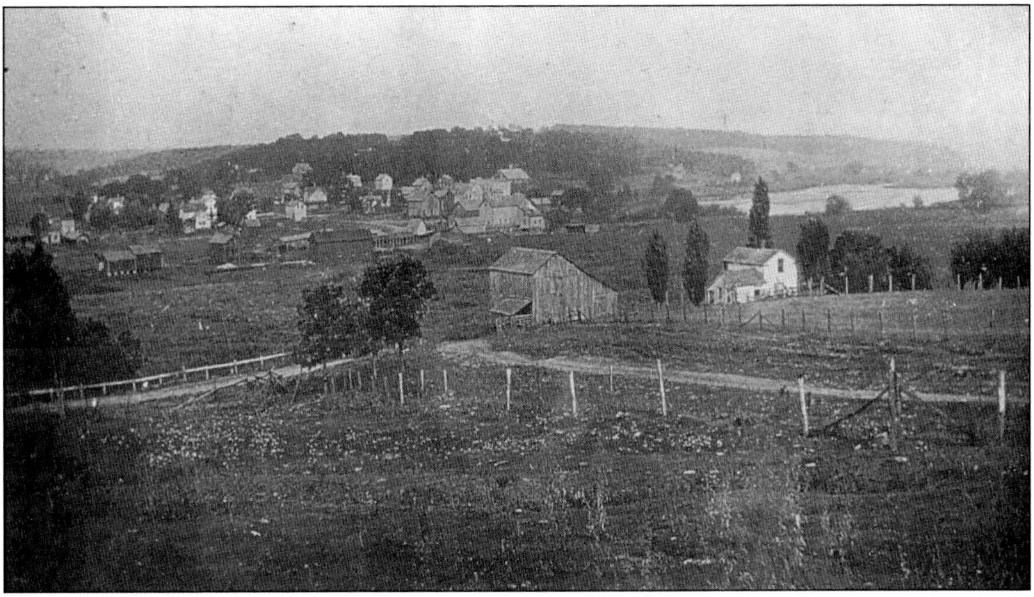

Looking northwest from County Highway W gives a view of the millpond built by Joshua Wild to power his mill. The small white house on the Harold Hoesly farm was located on the east side of the Little Sugar River. When being torn down in the 1970s, an original log cabin was found underneath the home.

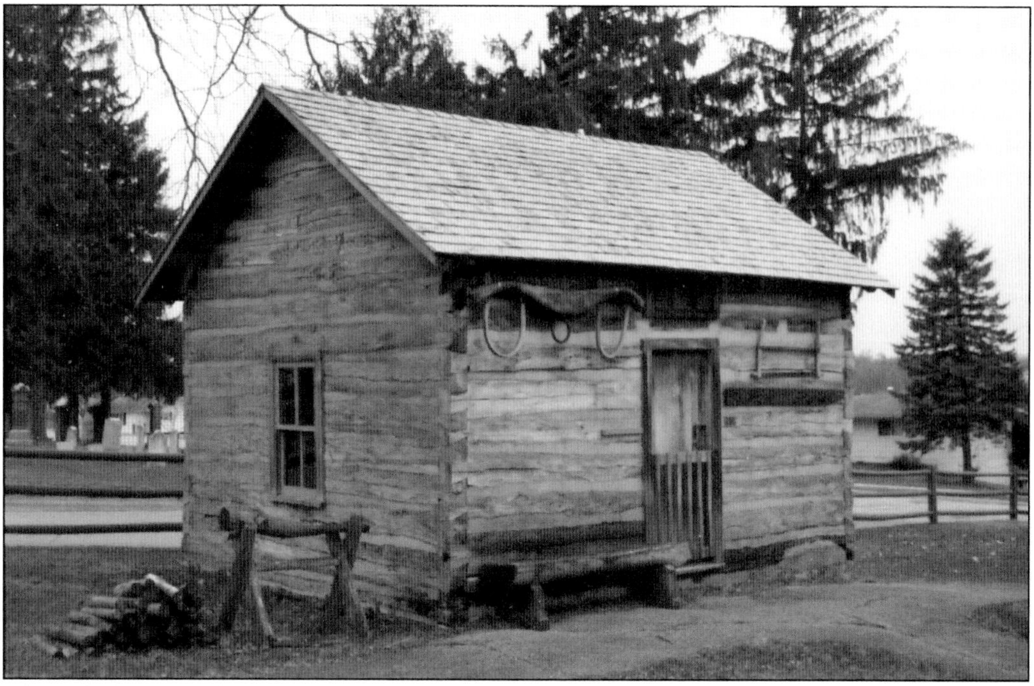

This is the log cabin found inside the house in the previous photograph. The cabin was disassembled and moved to the Swiss Historical Village and rebuilt. Today, it serves as a living history reminder of how the first-generation ancestors lived their first few years in America.

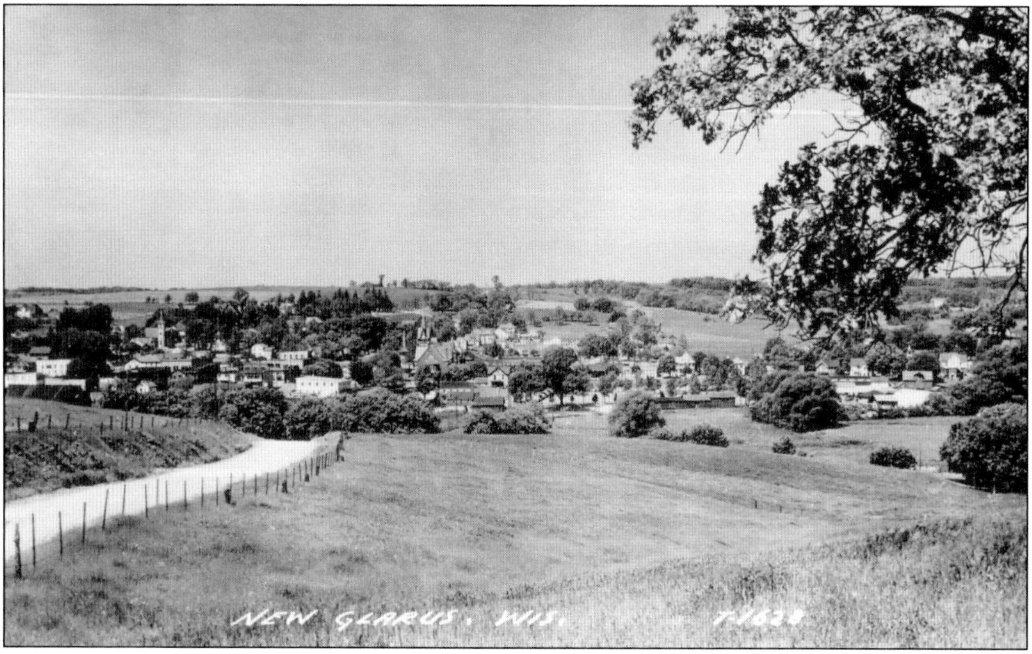

Around 1950, Highway W is still a narrow, dusty gravel road that leads to the Town of Exeter. The first row of buildings in town was along the railroad right-of-way. The Harold Hoesly farm is just out of the photograph to the right. This site is now Brennan's Market warehouse.

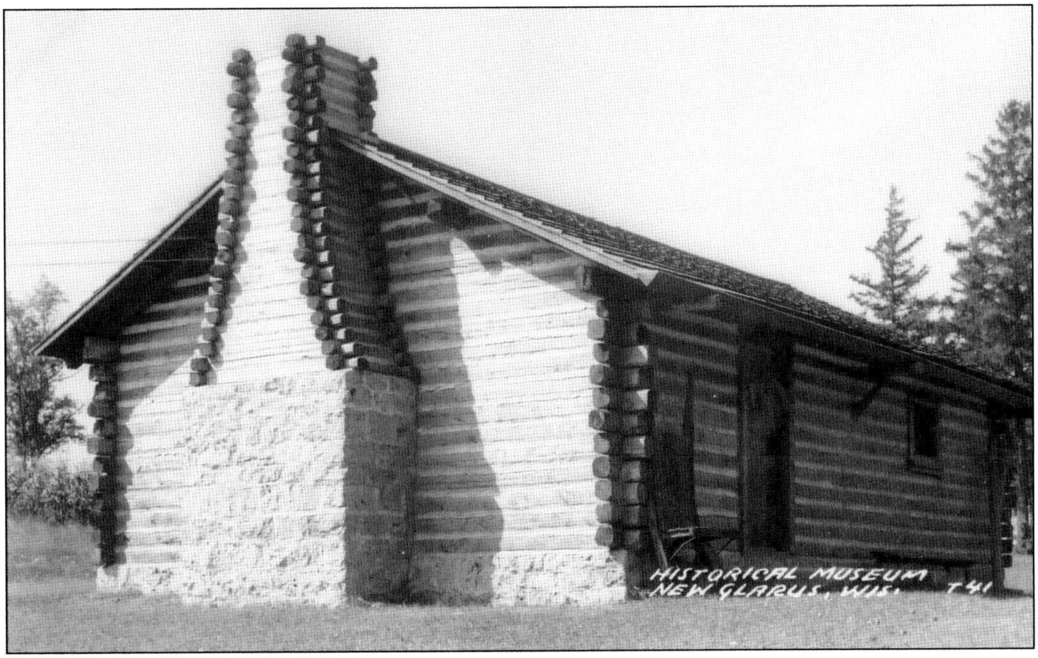

The Swiss Historical Village erected this replica log cabin as the first of the many buildings now in the village. The land for the village was donated by the S.A. Schindler family of New Glarus. The Swiss Historical Village is open daily from May through mid-October.

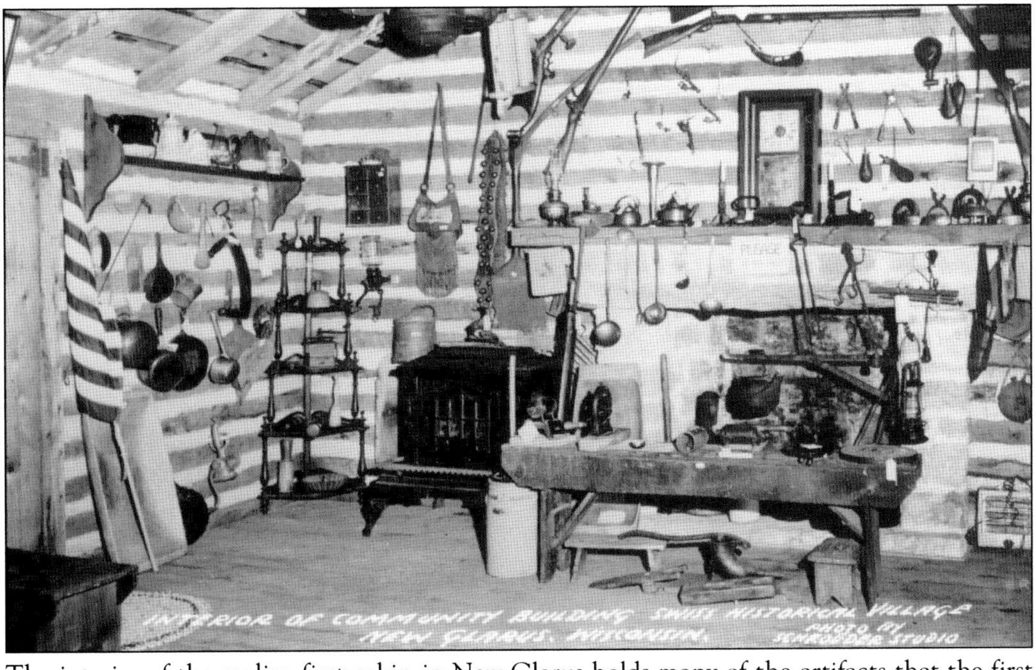

The interior of the replica first cabin in New Glarus holds many of the artifacts that the first settlers used in their daily lives. They did their cooking, living, and sleeping all in this very small space. Many times, these log cabins held families of four or more living in close quarters.

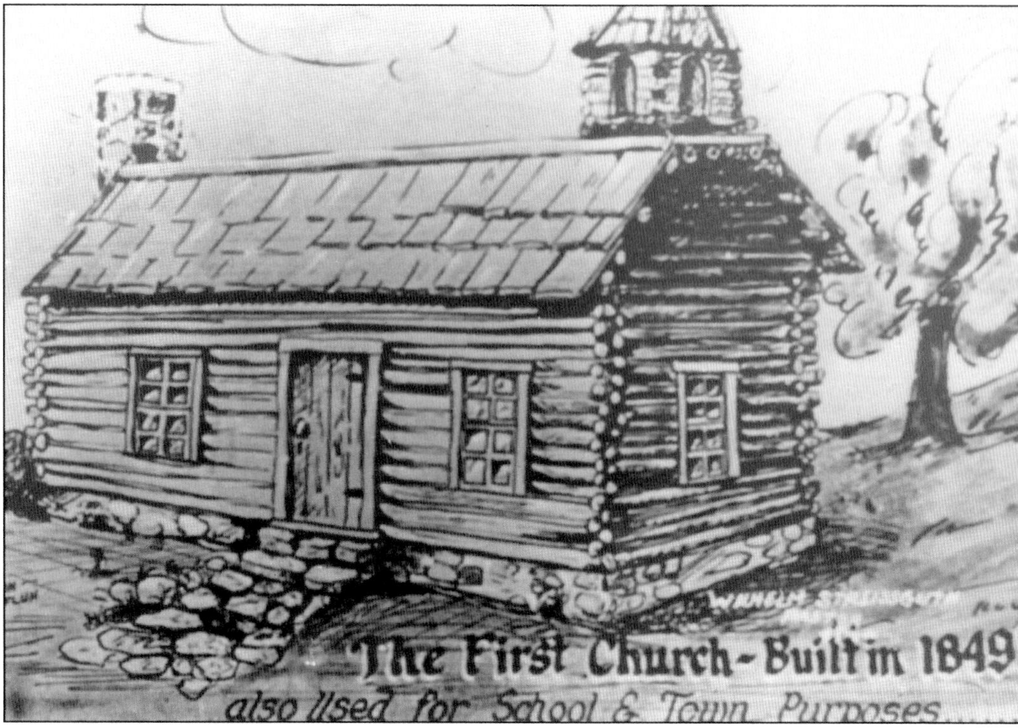

This drawing represents what the first church in New Glarus looked like. In addition to housing the church, the building served as the first school and location for town meetings where decisions guiding the future of the new community were made.

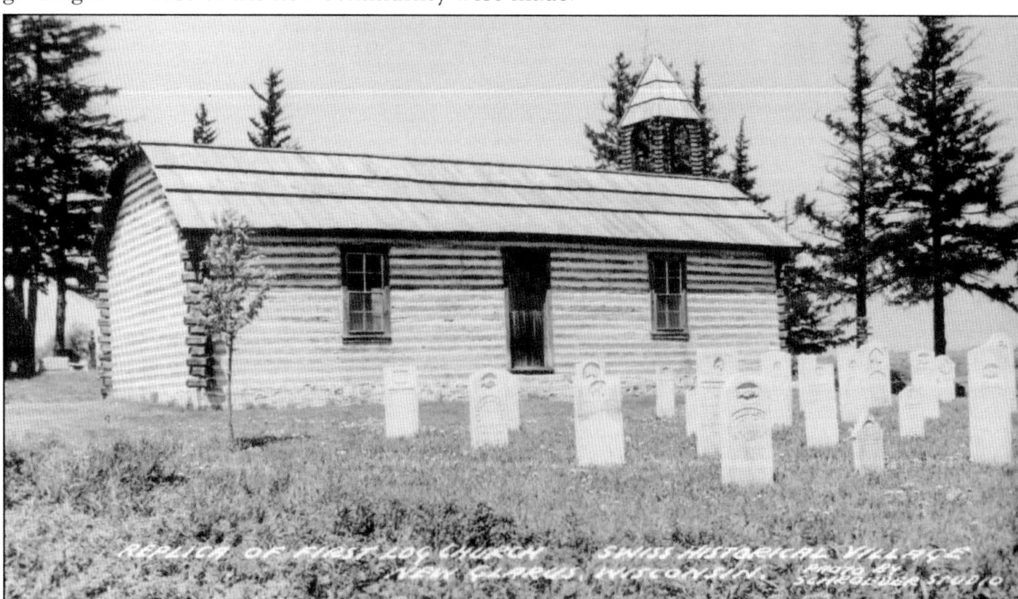

Since 1959, this replica log church on the grounds of the Swiss Historical Village has, on the Saturday closest to August 15, hosted a First Settlers church service. At each of these church services, the descendants of the first settlers are asked to rise and be recognized. Weddings have been held in the church.

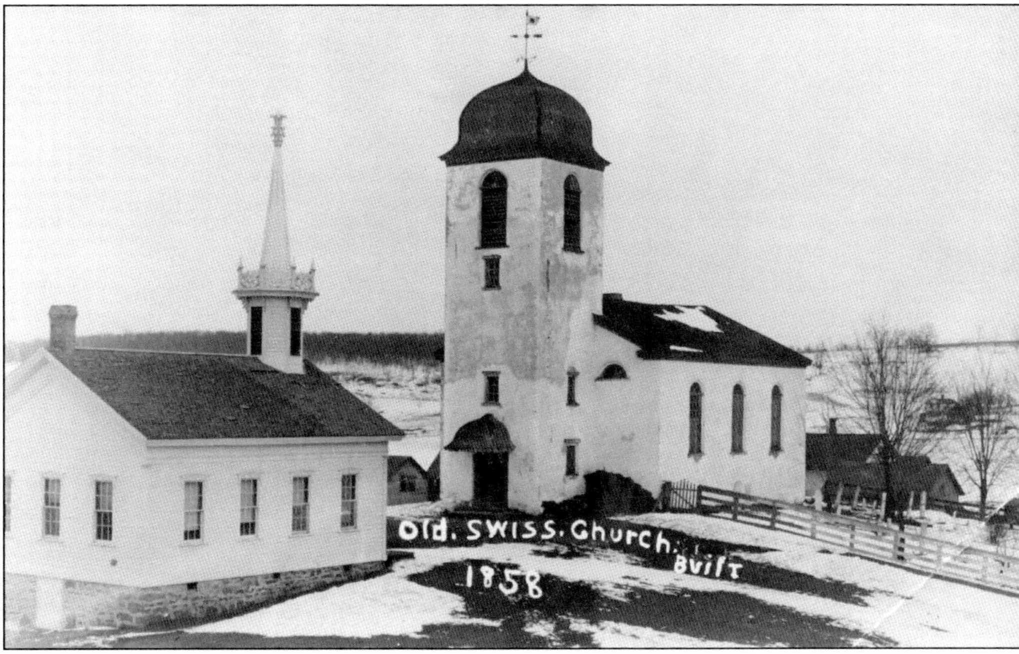

The building on the left is the Zwingli House, where community meetings and dinners were held. On the right is the second church to stand on this site. Built of native limestone in 1858, it was torn down in April 1900. The current church was dedicated on March 24, 1901. The early cemetery still exists on the south hill of the church grounds, but the headstones have been removed.

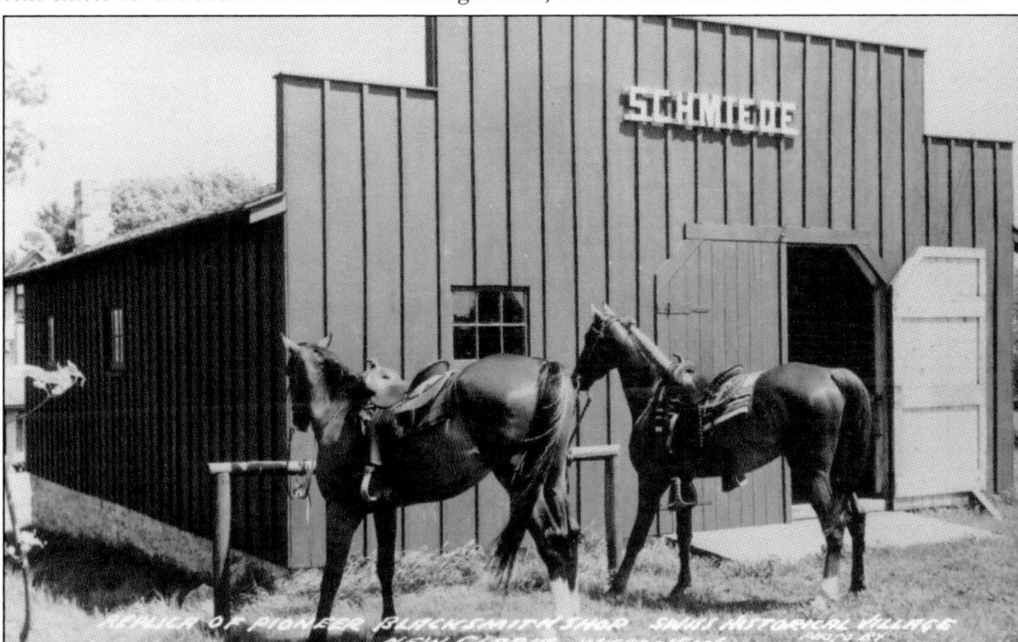

Every town had one or more blacksmith shops. The blacksmith was the person who could often fix anything, and his work included shoeing horses. One New Glarus blacksmith, Fred Haldiman, was still shoeing horses into the last years of the 1950s in his small shop behind his home on Fourth Avenue.

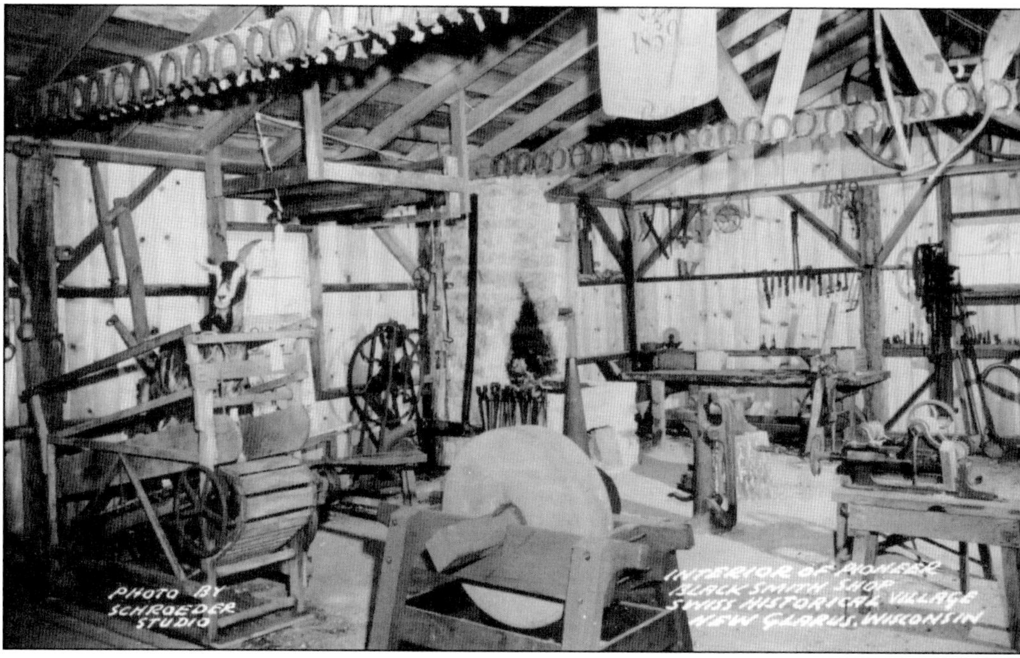

Once each year, this replica blacksmith shop at the Swiss Historical Village comes alive with the smell of blacksmithing coal in the forge, heating the metal to make ornamental ironwork. If one has the good fortune to grow up near a blacksmith shop, the clang of the hammer hitting red-hot steel and the smell of the forge bring back memories from well over half a century ago.

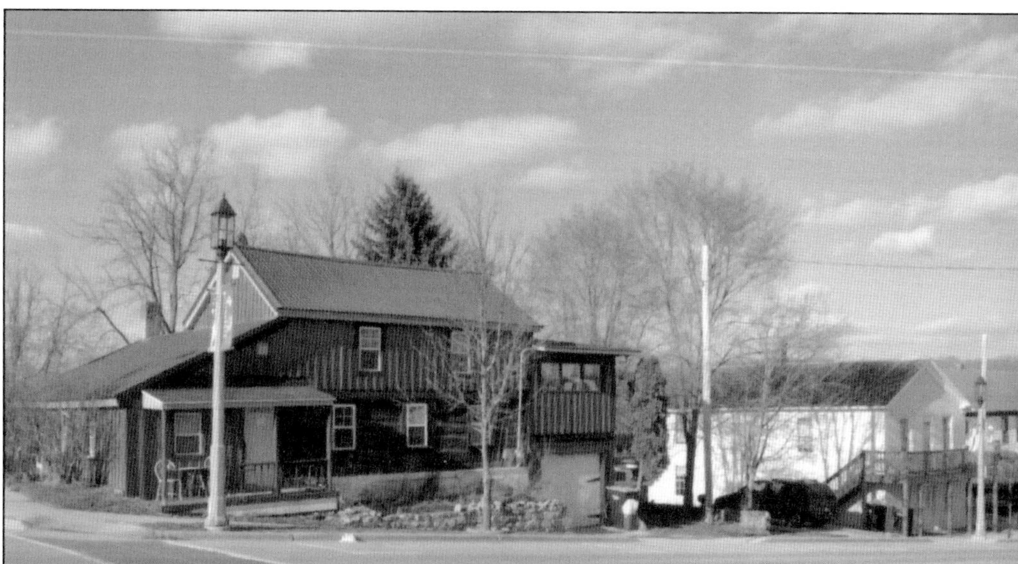

The two buildings pictured here are among the early structures in New Glarus. The white building on the right, listed in the National Register of Historic Places, was a tinsmith shop, which later became Dr. Blumer's office. The building on the left was originally a shoemaker shop and residence. The log cabin portion of the building was uncovered several years ago.

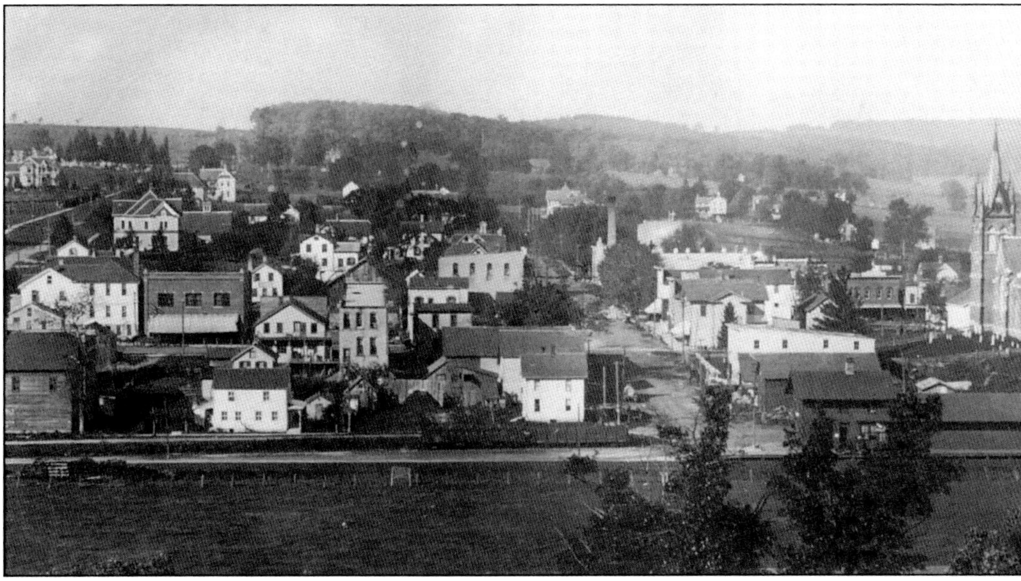

This view of New Glarus was taken from Grossenbacher's Hill looking west. The second building on the left in the second row is the Levitan and Steussy general merchandise building. The small white building in the center foreground is the home of Robert Streiff, the local liveryman who hauled freight from the depot to local businesses.

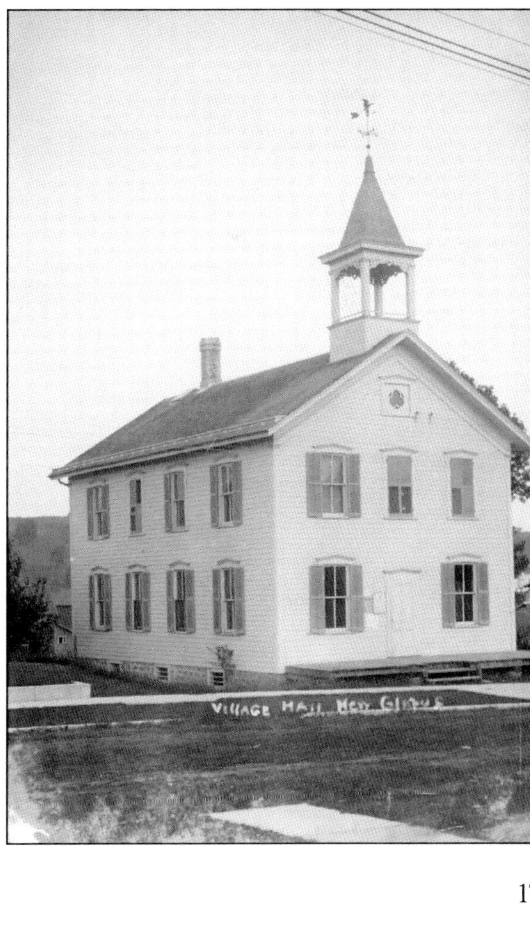

The New Glarus Town Hall, built in 1888, housed the Town of New Glarus government until the late 1990s. The basement still houses the first New Glarus jail, now used for storage. The second floor of the building was utilized by the Ancient Order of United Workmen. Many civic groups used the building for their meeting place. The town hall is now listed in the Wisconsin and National Register of Historic Places.

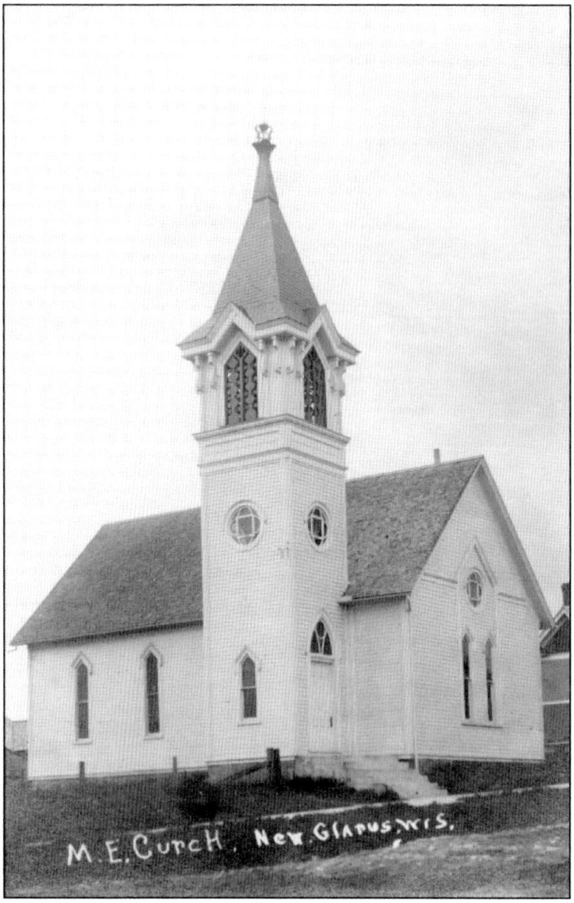

The last church service in the Evangelical United Brethren Church was held on May 26, 1968. The congregation disbanded, and members joined a number of other area churches. The local Masonic and Eastern Star Lodges purchased the building for their permanent home.

Family reunions were always an eagerly awaited for event each summer. The reunions meant a chance to see relatives who had long ago moved away from New Glarus and returned home once again for a couple of days. This photograph shows a Wild family reunion being held at the Shooting Park Barn.

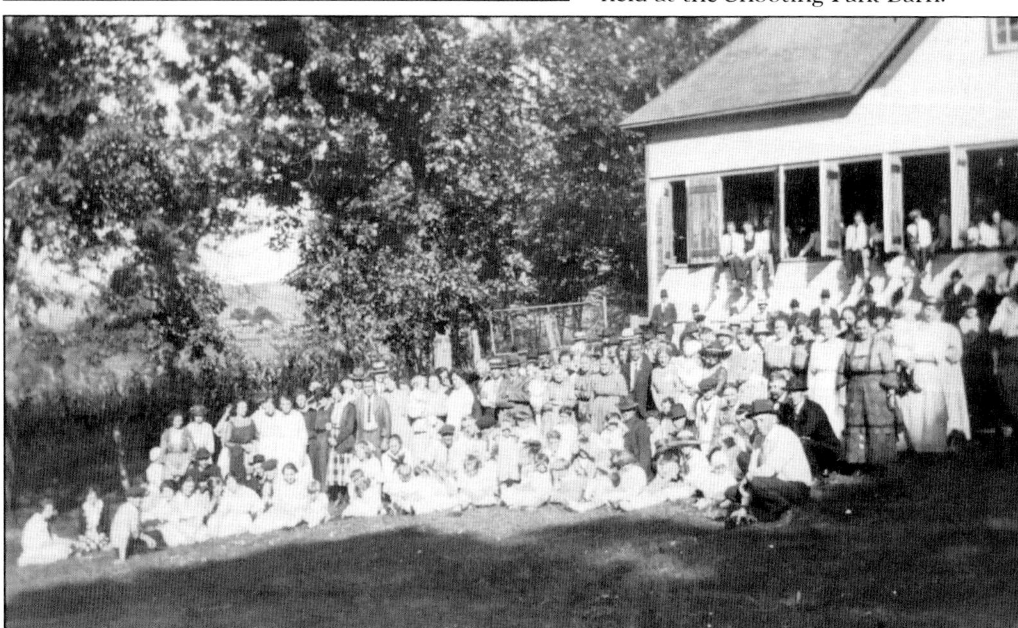

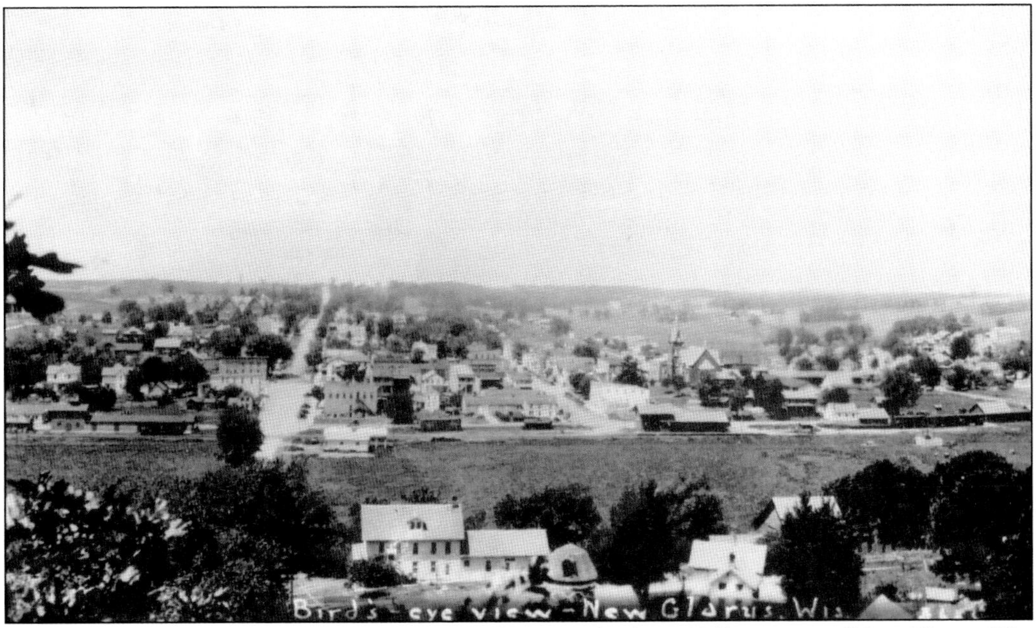

This overview of New Glarus is from the top of Grossenbacher's Hill just east of New Glarus. The large white building in the foreground was constructed as a railroad hotel but never opened as such because the railroad was located on the west side of the Little Sugar River instead of the east side. The depot can be seen in the right center with several boxcars to the north of the depot.

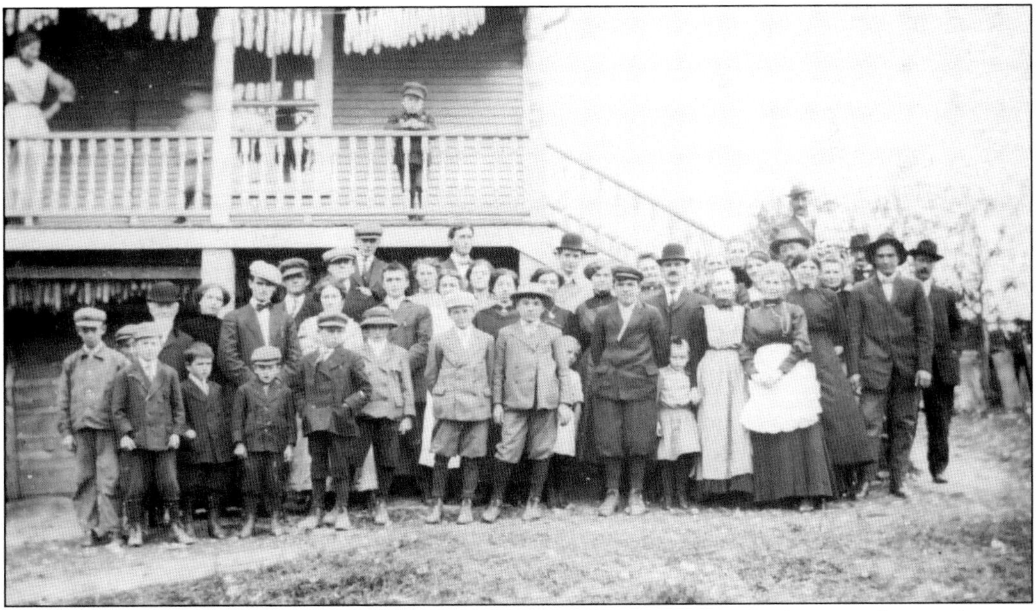

The young people's singing group depicted here in an undated photograph is standing in front of the south end of the railroad hotel. A note on the back indicates that this is a group gathered at Baltz Hefty's, where they performed. This building was probably constructed in 1887.

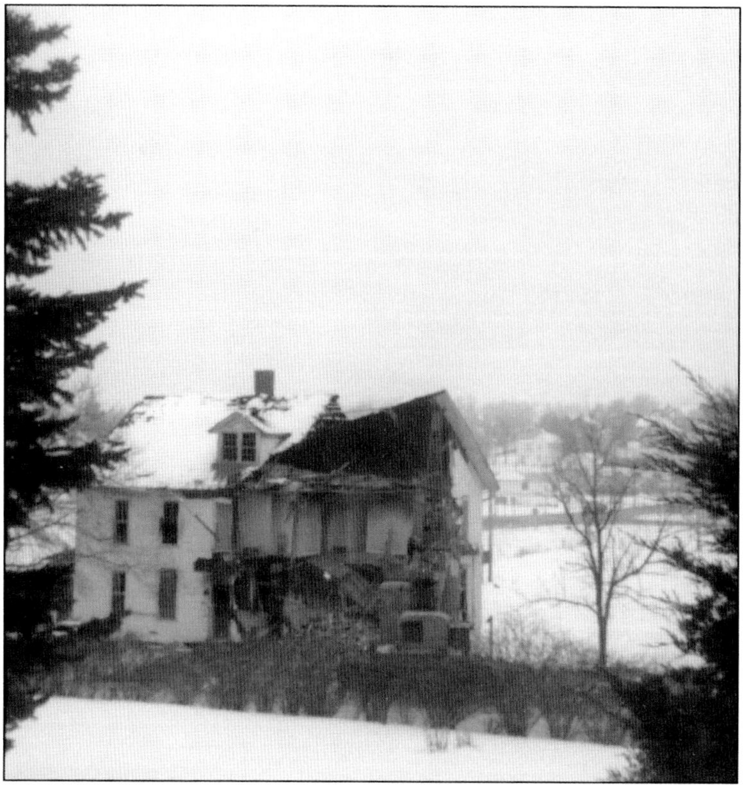

A disastrous January 6, 1972, fire gutting the railroad hotel led to the building being demolished. This structure served for many years as a multi-unit apartment house. The Don Zuber family that owned the building reconstructed a new home on the site. (Mike Zuber collection.)

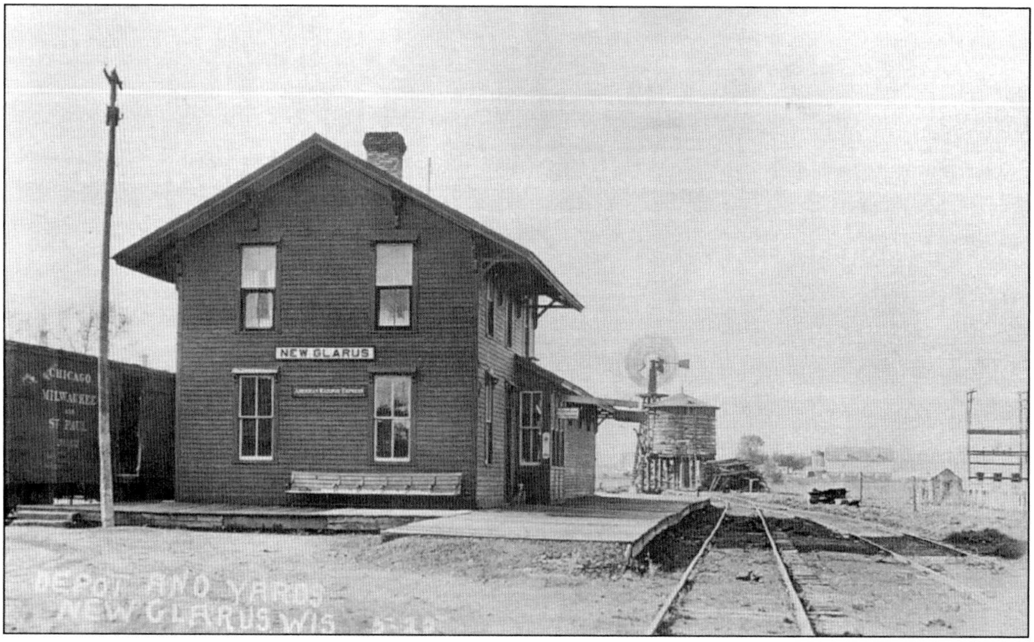

The New Glarus Milwaukee Road railroad depot is shown here in 1925. In 1887, New Glarus was the last community in Green County to get rail service. The depot, which was entered into the National Register of Historic Places, was restored around 2004 in an effort led by the New Glarus Depot Preservation Society.

Two

Century Farms

Wisconsin author Ben Logan, in the introduction to his book *The Land Remembers*, wrote, "Once you have lived on the land, been a partner with its moods, secrets, and seasons, you cannot leave. The living land remembers, touching you in unguarded moments, saying, I am here. You are a part of me. That land is my genesis. I was born there, cradled by the land. I cannot leave the land. How can I when a thousand sounds, sights, smells, tell me I am part of it?"

Those few words of Logan's tell the story of the land—land the owners of these Wisconsin Century Farms hold dearly in their hearts and minds. The Wisconsin Century Farm recognition program began as a part of Wisconsin's centennial, held in 1948. Each year since 1948, during the August Wisconsin State Fair, the previous year's group of newly named Wisconsin Century Farms owners is recognized. Wisconsin has over 7,300 recognized century farms.

More than just an honor for 100 years of family ownership, the metal sign each century farm receives is a testament to the tenacity farm families have shown for over a century. These people have stood the test of time with their ownership and careful stewardship of the land.

The family memories are etched deeply into these sometimes fourth-, fifth-, or sixth-generation family owners as they care over land that in many instances would have provided them with a lifelong bank account by having sold the family land. Instead, they chose to live on and protect the land that provided their early ancestors with a way to a better life.

Several of these New Glarus century farms ownerships reach back to the 1840s and 1850s. One farm in particular stands out, the Hefty Blum homestead farm. This farm was entered into the National Register of Historic Places in the late 1990s, making it the first National Historic Register homestead farm district in Green County.

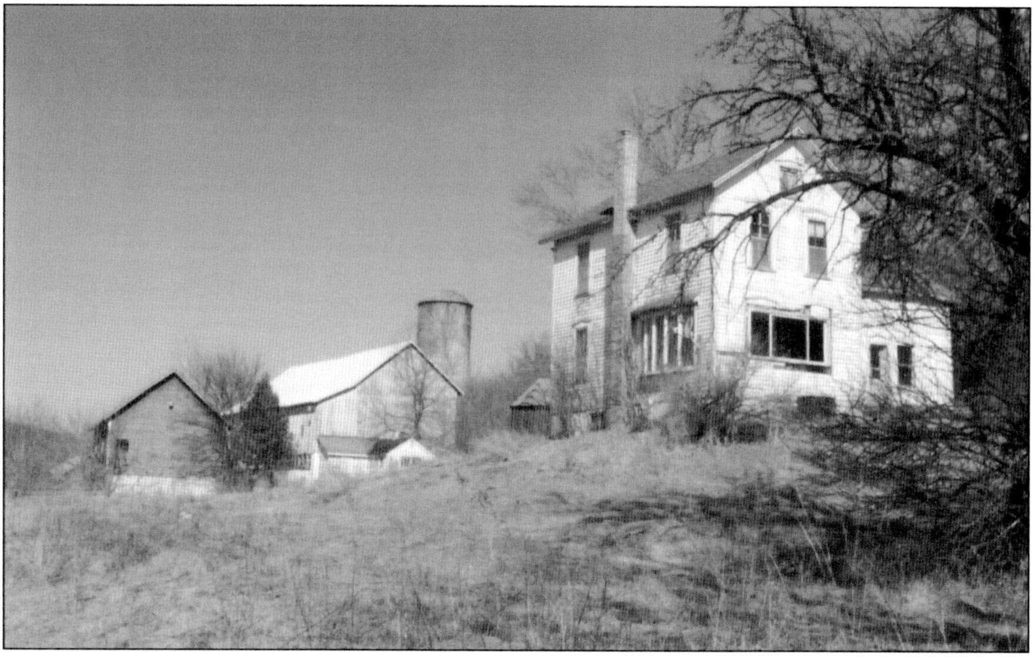

The former Delmar and Betty Zentner farm in the Town of New Glarus was founded in 1845 and was listed as a Wisconsin Century Farm in 1953. Delmar and Betty were very active in the Wilhelm Tell Pageant from its inception in 1937. The Zentners sold their farm in the mid-1960s to an Amish family.

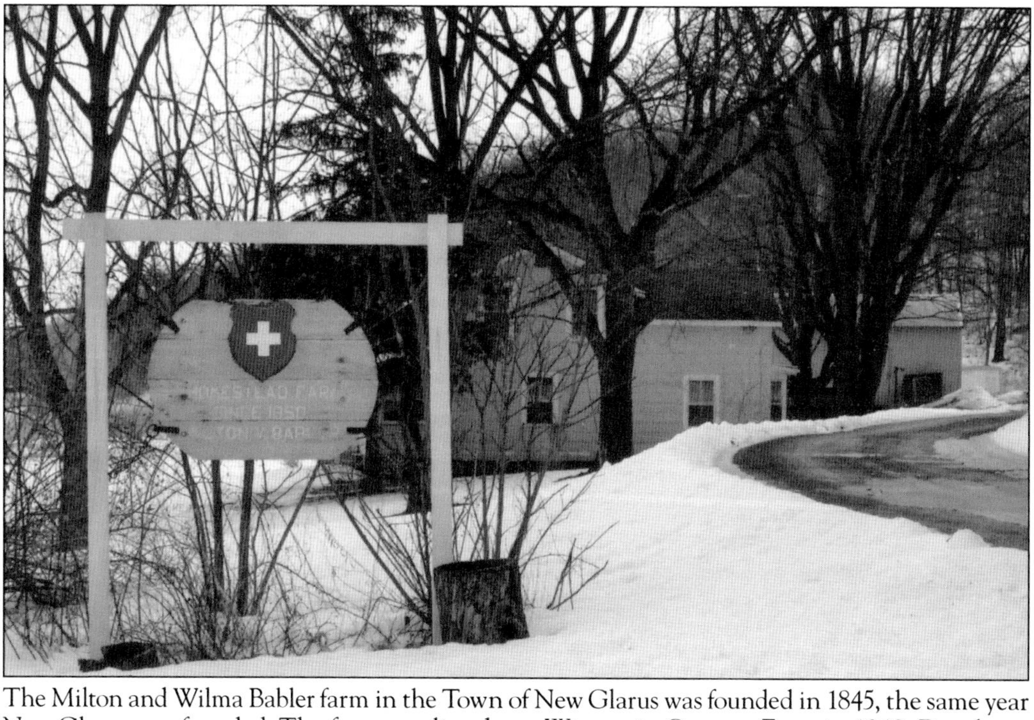

The Milton and Wilma Babler farm in the Town of New Glarus was founded in 1845, the same year New Glarus was founded. The farm was listed as a Wisconsin Century Farm in 1948. Daughters Muriel and Rhoda still own the farm but live elsewhere.

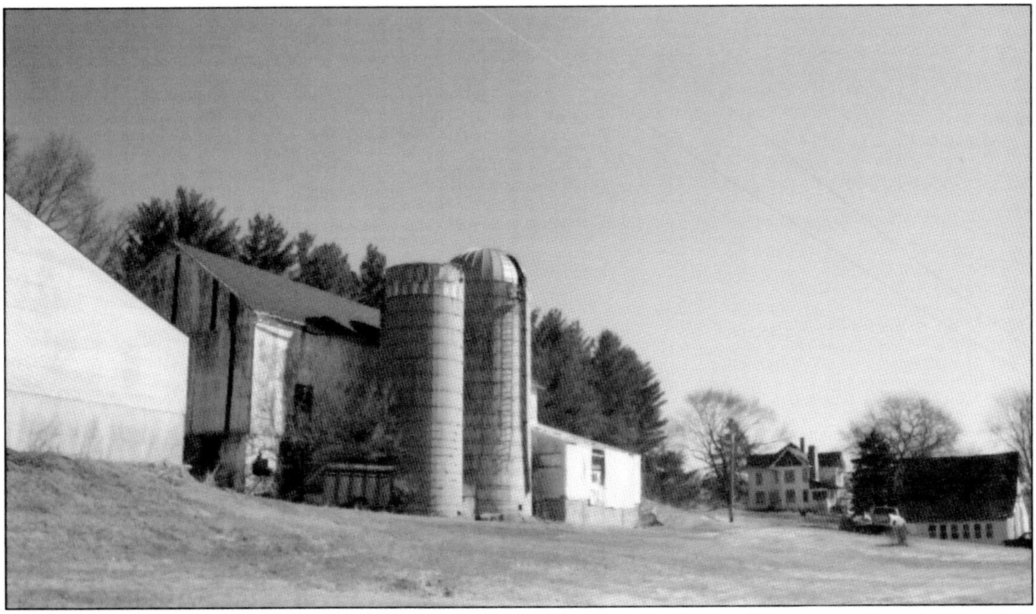

The Nic Zentner-Gilbert and Hilda Duerst farm in the Town of New Glarus was founded in 1845 and listed as a Wisconsin Century Farm in 1946. After retiring from farming, Gilbert and Hilda took over ownership of the local A&W root beer stand. For the kids who grew up in the 1960s, a trip to the A&W was always known as going down to Gibby and Hilda's.

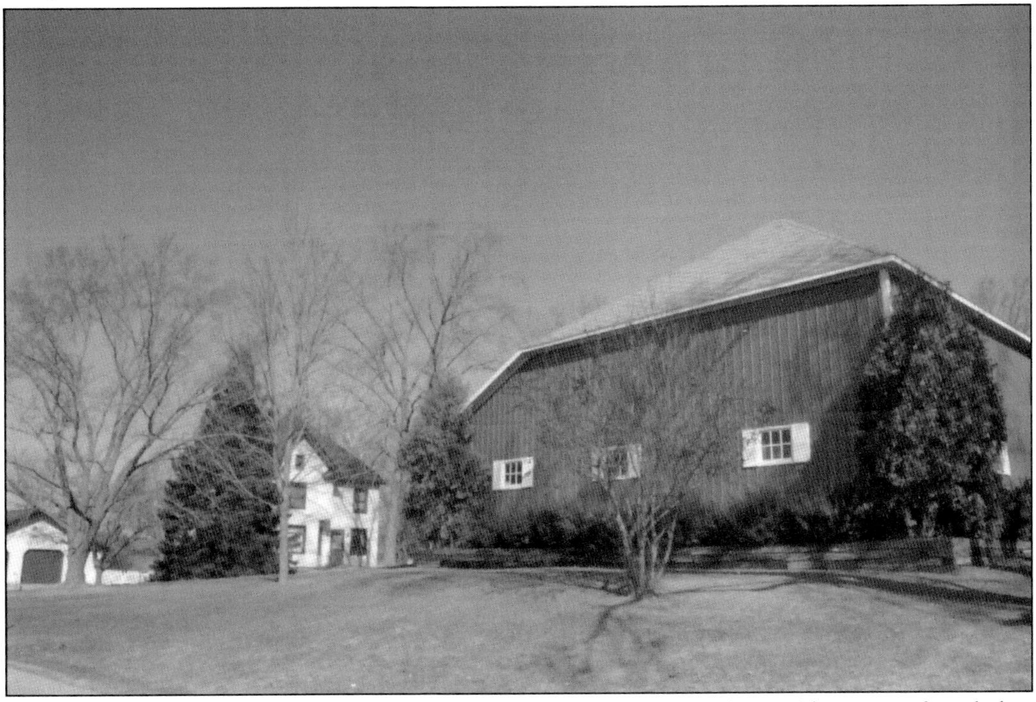

The Willis Zwicky farm, which lies in both the Village and Town of New Glarus, was founded in 1845 and listed as a Wisconsin Century Farm in 1948. The Stanley Kittleson family resided here for a number of years. During the ownership of Delmar and Kathy Naef, the barn burned. The current owners have lovingly restored the interior of the house to its original look.

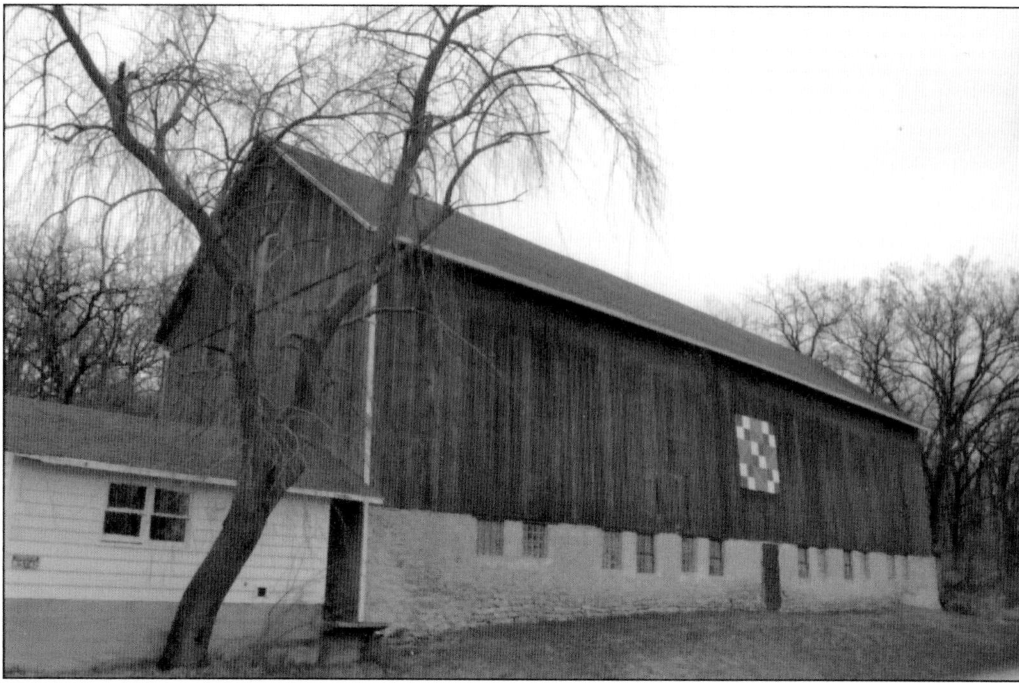

The Nic Elmer farm, founded in 1847, was listed as a Wisconsin Century Farm in 1948. This photograph, taken on County H one mile southwest of New Glarus, shows one of approximately 250 barn quilts that grace barns throughout Green County.

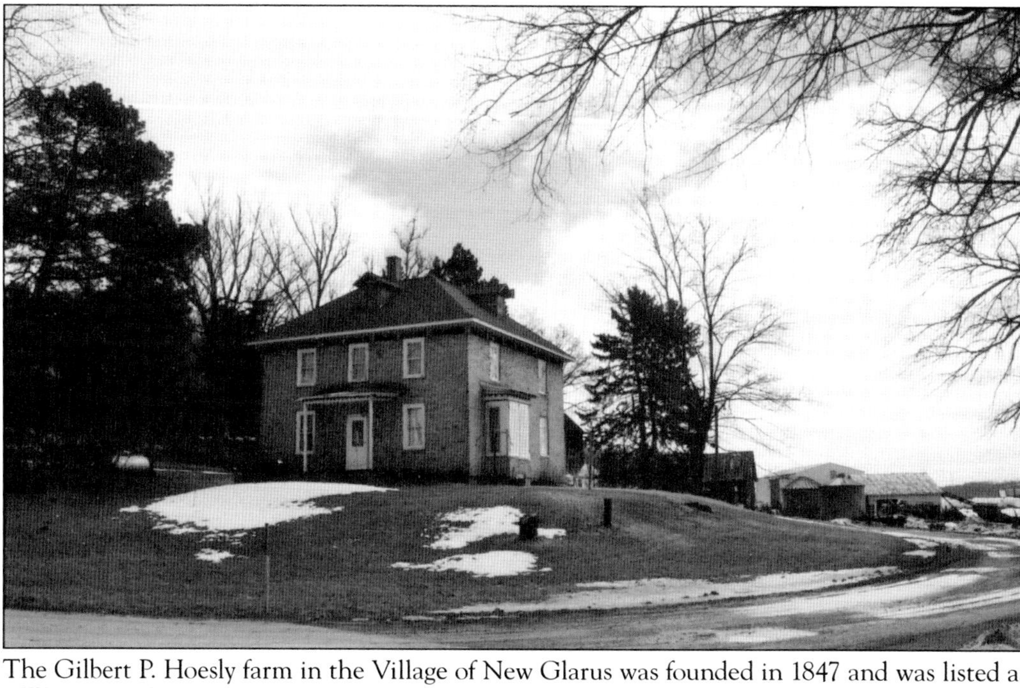

The Gilbert P. Hoesly farm in the Village of New Glarus was founded in 1847 and was listed as a Wisconsin Century Farm in 1948. Gilbert Hoesly served several terms as New Glarus village president in the 1950s. The Bill and Kay Kummer family have owned the farm for many years and are active dairy farmers.

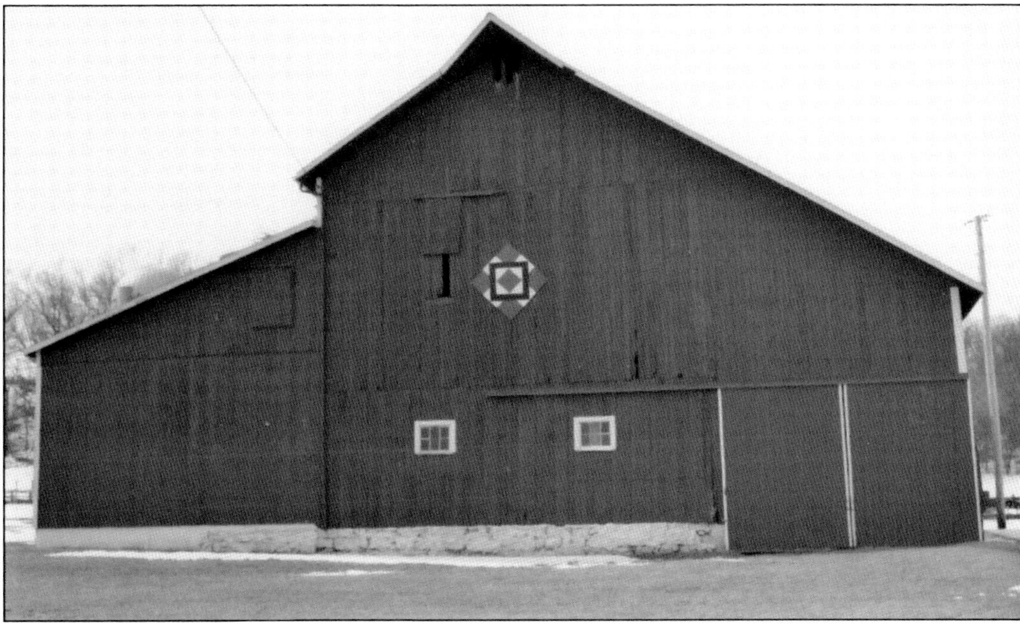

The Elmer Hoesly homestead farm in the Town of New Glarus was founded in 1847 and was listed as a Wisconsin Century Farm in 1948. Like many former dairy farms, the dairy barn, probably built in the 1880s, was torn down, but a smaller barn remains in use. The quilt on the barn was done by the Green County Barn Quilt Project. Hoesly's son Dwight and his wife, Janis, live on the farm.

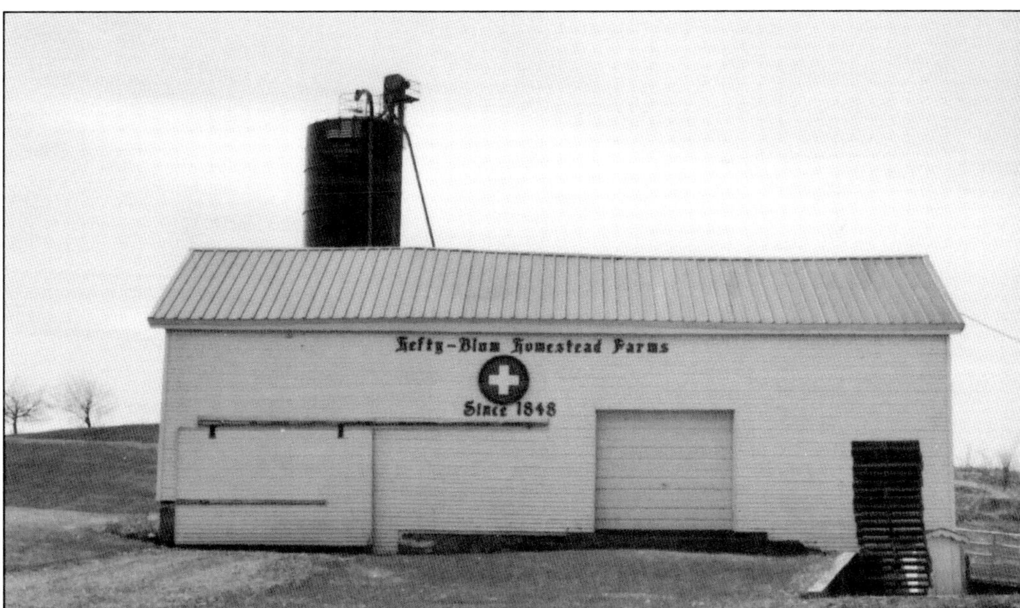

The Fred and Miriam Hefty Blum homestead farm in the Town of Washington was founded in 1848 and was listed as a Wisconsin Century Farm in 1998. The farm is in the National Register of Historic Places. Many of the buildings have been restored. The most recent restoration was the c. 1881 cheese factory that now houses a mail-order cheese business. Three generations of the Hefty Blum family live in homes on the farm.

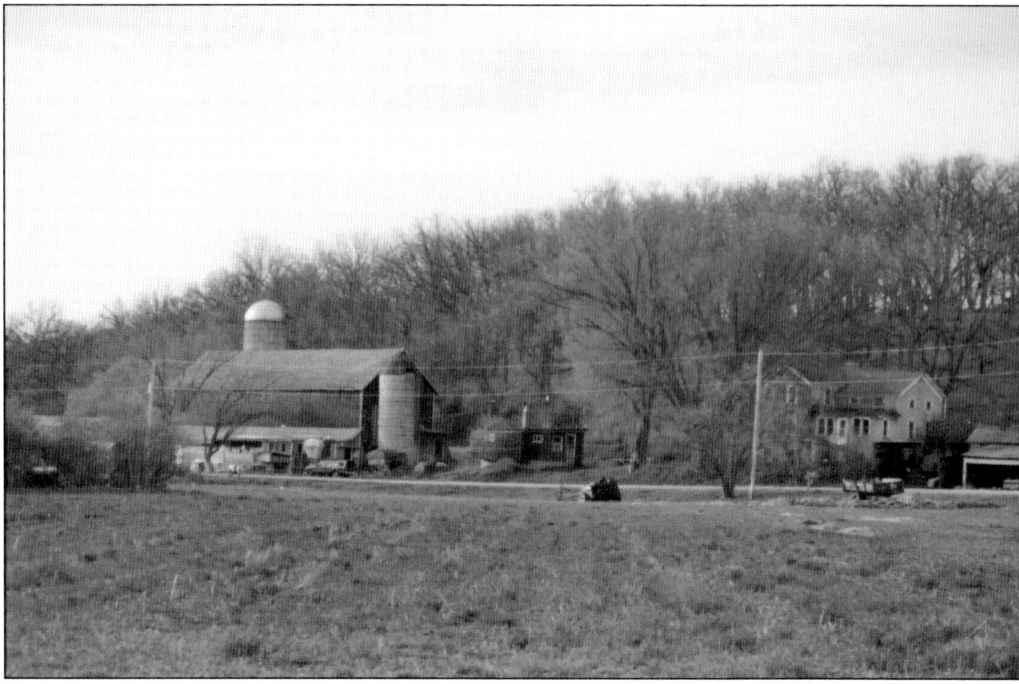

The Lawrence and Joan Hefty farm in the Town of New Glarus was founded in 1851 and listed as a Wisconsin Century Farm in 2001. The Heftys are actively farming, and each September they provide goats for the annual Wilhelm Tell Pageant held near New Glarus.

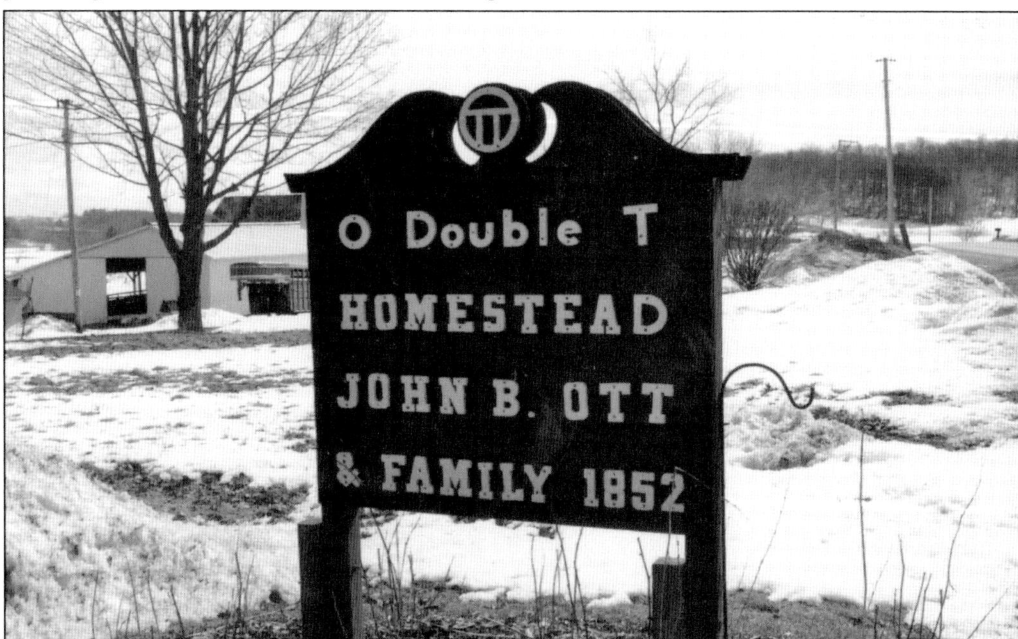

The John and Mary Ott homestead farm in the Town of New Glarus was founded in 1855 and listed as a Wisconsin Century Farm in 1971. John is still actively farming, although he is not dairying. He was the third generation of his family to be the manager of the Farmer's Coop Stockyard in New Glarus, which has since closed.

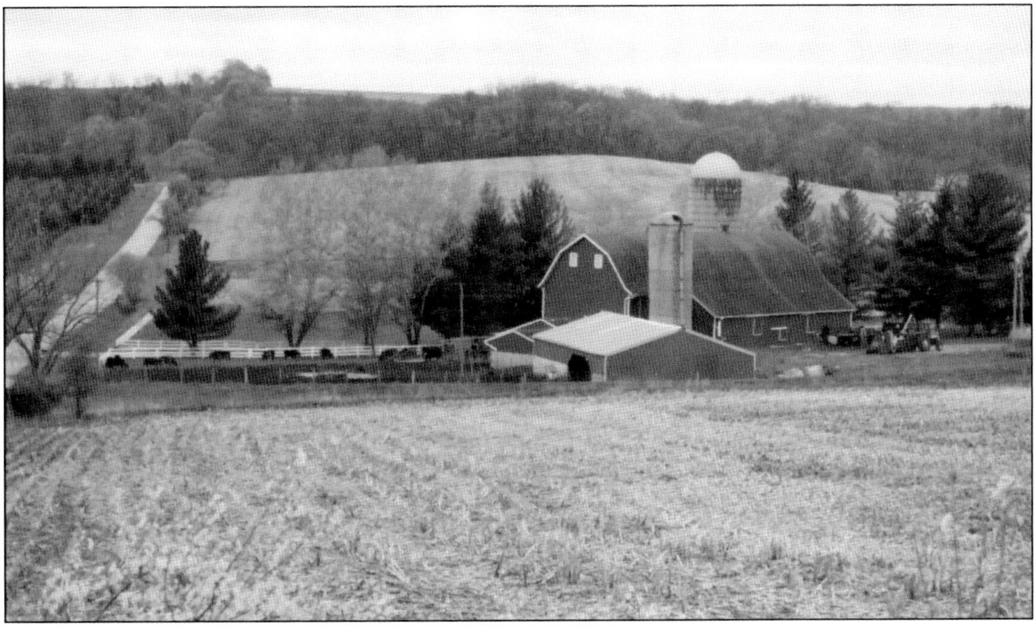

The Nic and Alda Kubly farm in the Town of New Glarus was founded in 1855 and listed as a Wisconsin Century Farm in 1963. The Kublys' son Herbert, who was raised on this farm, was the first of his family to go to college. After graduation, Herbert went on to write for *Time*, *Life*, *Vogue*, *Atlantic*, and *Esquire* magazines. He retired from the University of Wisconsin—Parkside as a much-loved and -revered English professor.

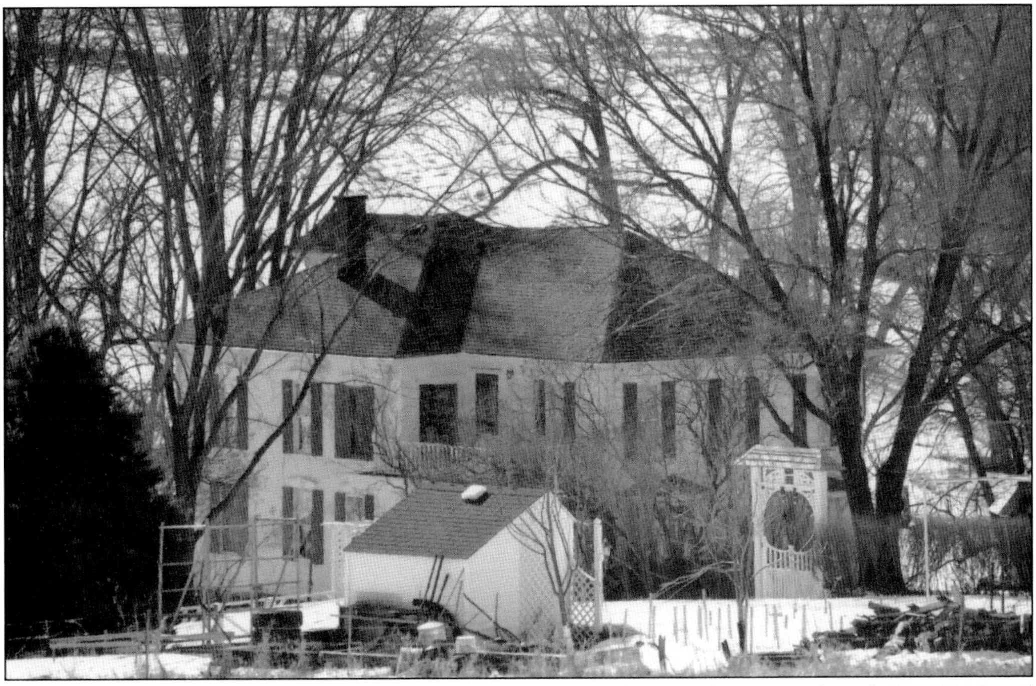

The Ernest "Red" and Hilda Zentner farm in the Town of New Glarus was founded in 1866 and listed as a Wisconsin Century Farm in 1967. Red was one of the members of the Edelweiss Stars, a New Glarus Swiss singing group that entertained all over the United States and Switzerland.

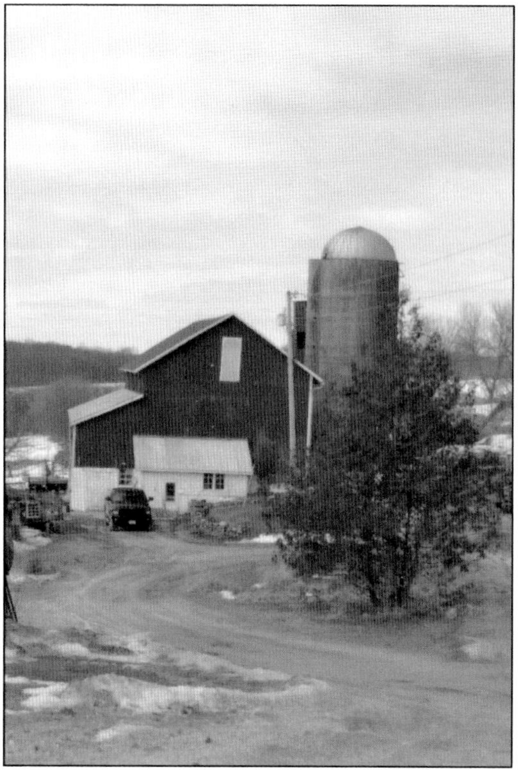

The Harold and Joan Legler farm in the Town of New Glarus was founded in 1868 and listed as a Wisconsin Century Farm in 2002. Harold has operated the family farm since his graduation from New Glarus High School. His father, Robert, is still active in farm operations and each year enters the annual Wilhelm Tell Swiss yodeling contest.

This hay pyramid was built on the Robert Legler farm in late September 1966 and was seen in the *Cleveland Press* on October 25, 1966. Legler had to build this pyramid because the haymow in his barn was already full with the first two crops of hay from earlier that summer, which is a sign of a good season.

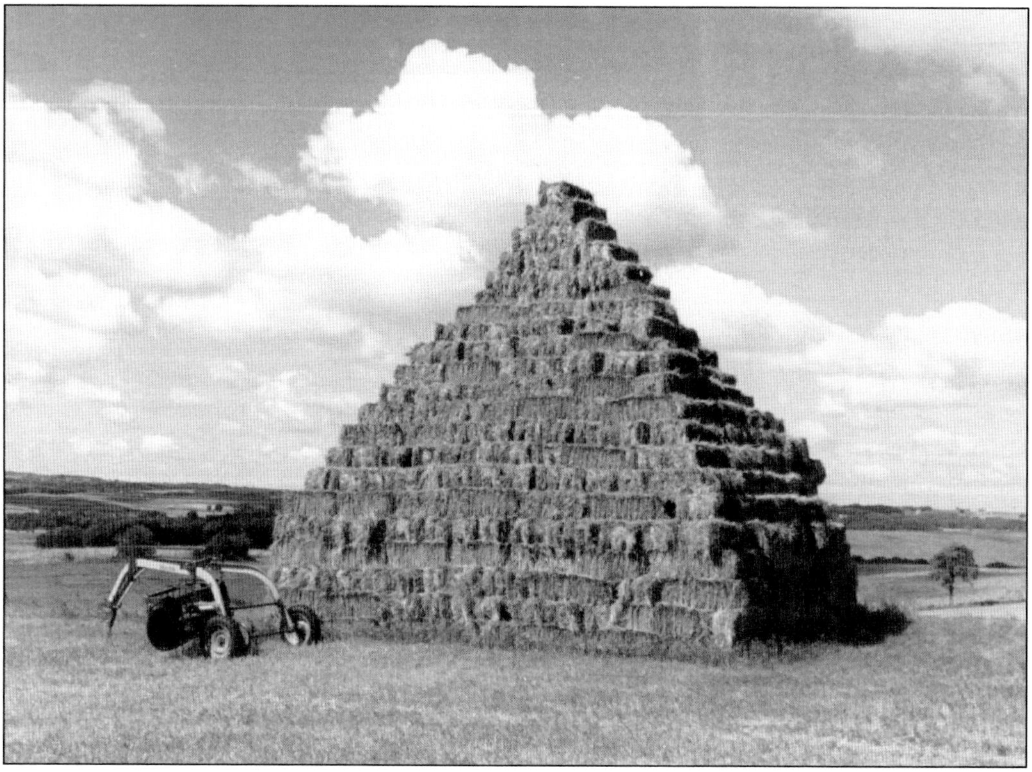

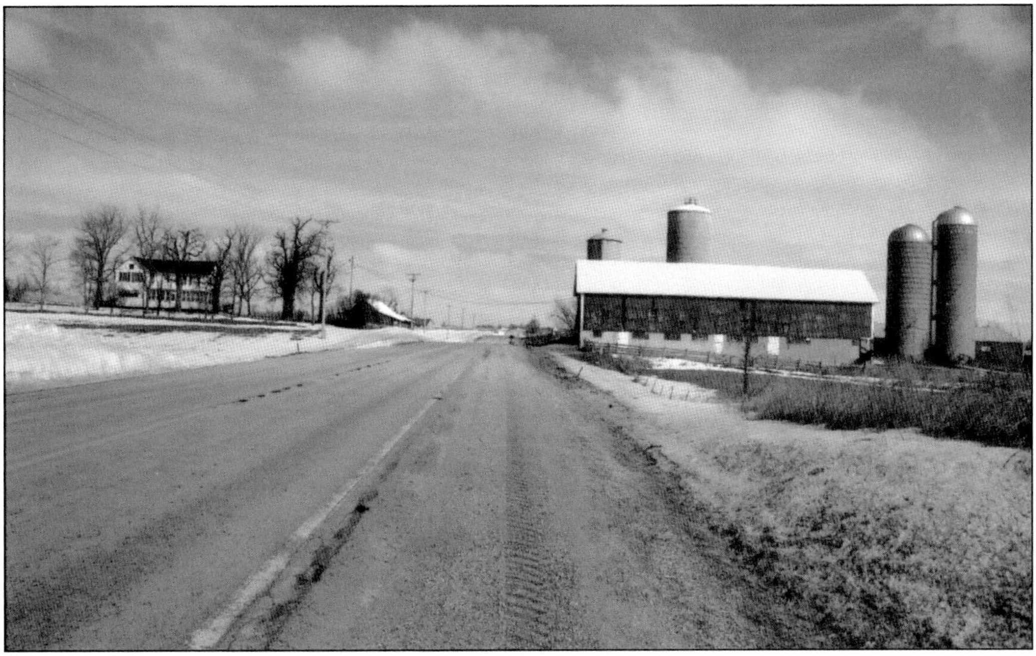

The Larry and Zenda Klassy farm in the Town of Adams was founded in 1872 and was listed as a Wisconsin Century Farm in 1975. The house on this farm was designed by noted Monticello architectural firm Steinmann Architects and built by New Glarus builder Waldo Altman. Altman, during his building career, constructed many of the early New Glarus homes.

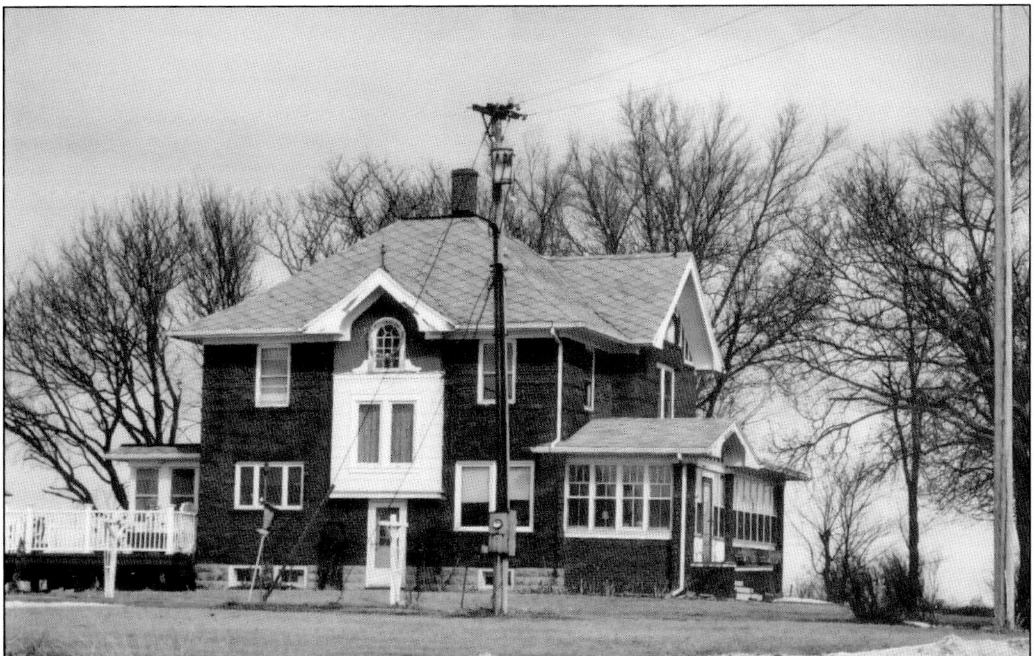

The Larry and Zenda Klassy farm in the Town of York was founded in 1874 and listed as a Wisconsin Century Farm in 1975. The house on this farm is built on the same floor plan as the Klassy farm in the Town of Adams.

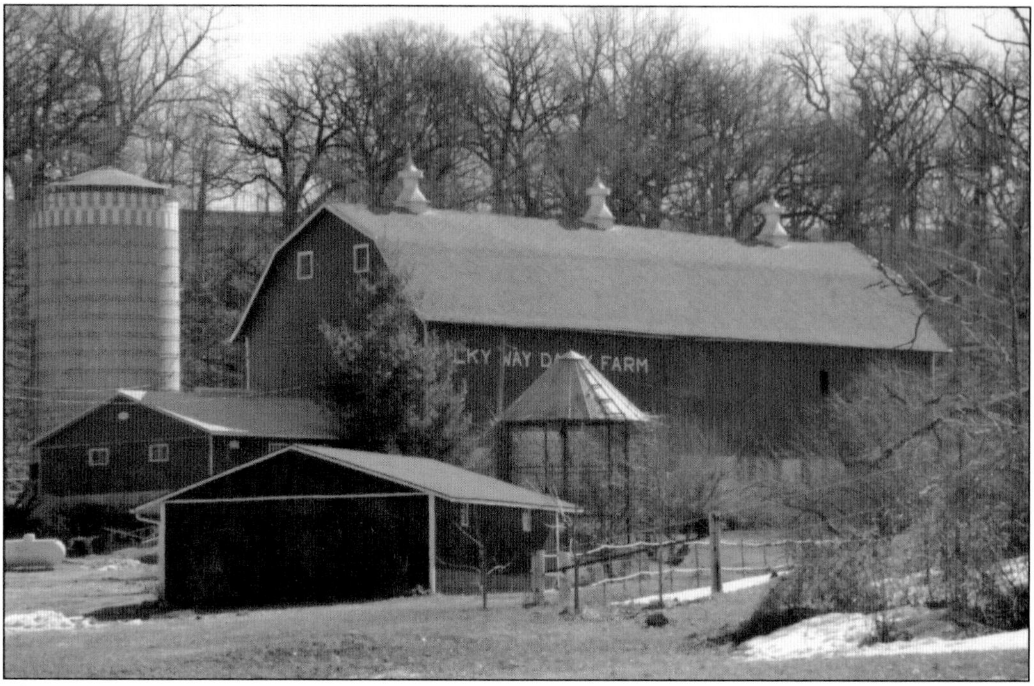

The Delmar and Jean Elmer Arm farm in the Town of New Glarus was listed as a Wisconsin Century Farm on its 100th anniversary in 1978. For many years, the barn was empty, but a new owner is now operating as a cow-calf operation, giving the barn on the farm a new life. This farm was on the cover of *Capper's Farmer* magazine in June 1950.

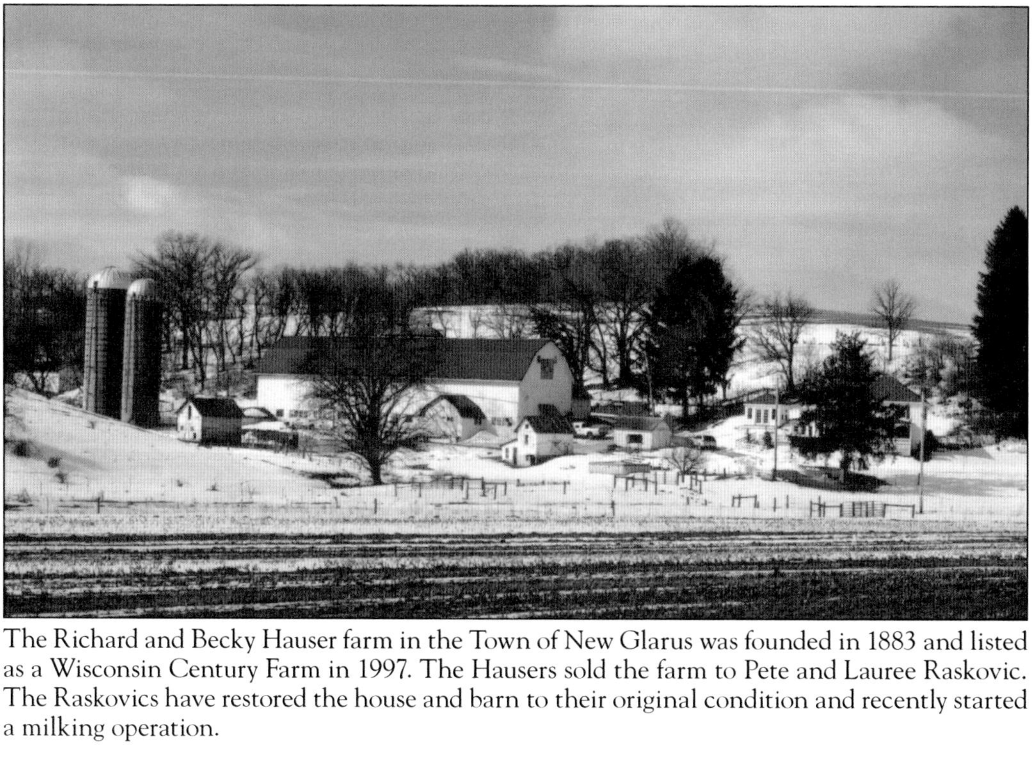

The Richard and Becky Hauser farm in the Town of New Glarus was founded in 1883 and listed as a Wisconsin Century Farm in 1997. The Hausers sold the farm to Pete and Lauree Raskovic. The Raskovics have restored the house and barn to their original condition and recently started a milking operation.

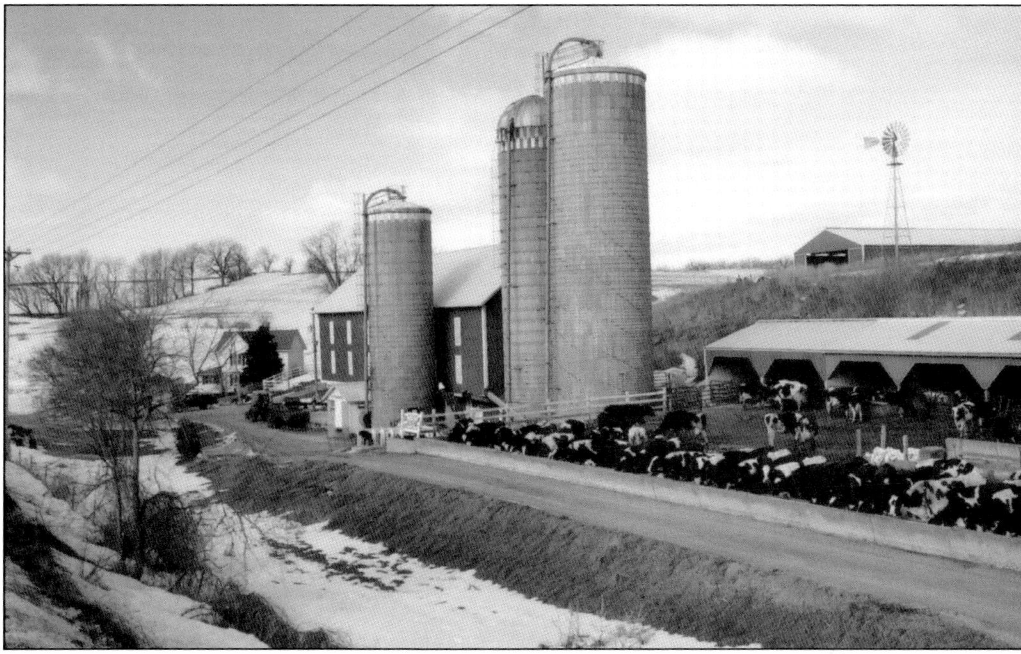

The Don and Jane Elmer farm in the Town of New Glarus was established in 1886 and listed as a Wisconsin Century Farm in 1987. In 2012, the Elmers hosted the annual Green County Breakfast on the Farm day. The louvers on the barn are to help cross-ventilate the haymow to aid in drying the hay. Don and Jane are the fourth generation of the family to operate the farm.

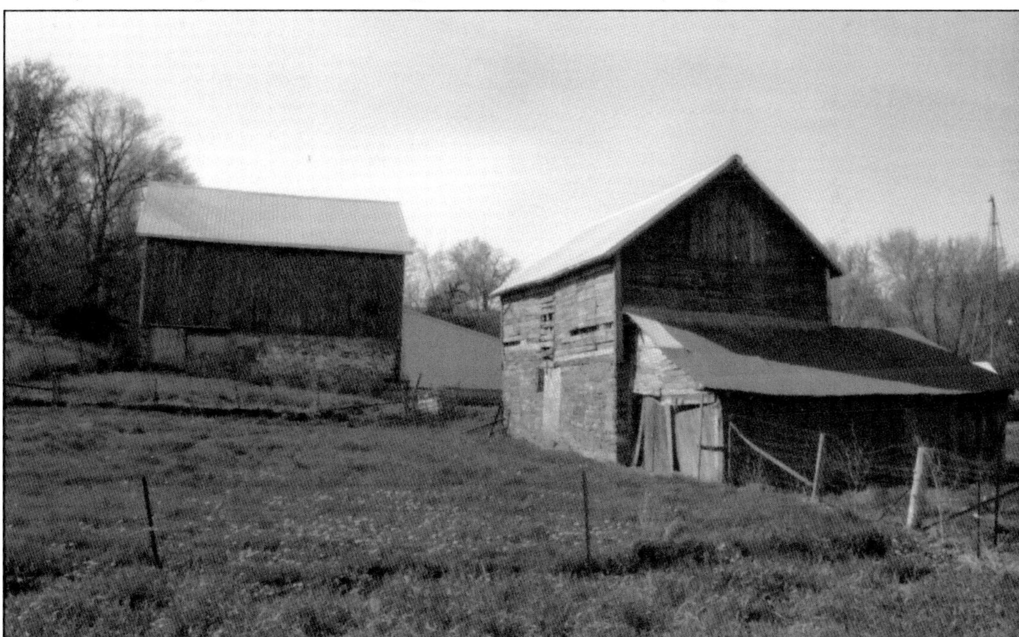

The Silvan and Avis Disch farm in the Town of Exeter was founded in 1887 and listed as a Wisconsin Century Farm in 1987. Silvan and Avis are still engaged in farming vegetables, fruits, and honey, which they market through area farmers markets. They were active in the Dane County Farmers Market for over 30 years. Their daughter Debbie helps them on market days.

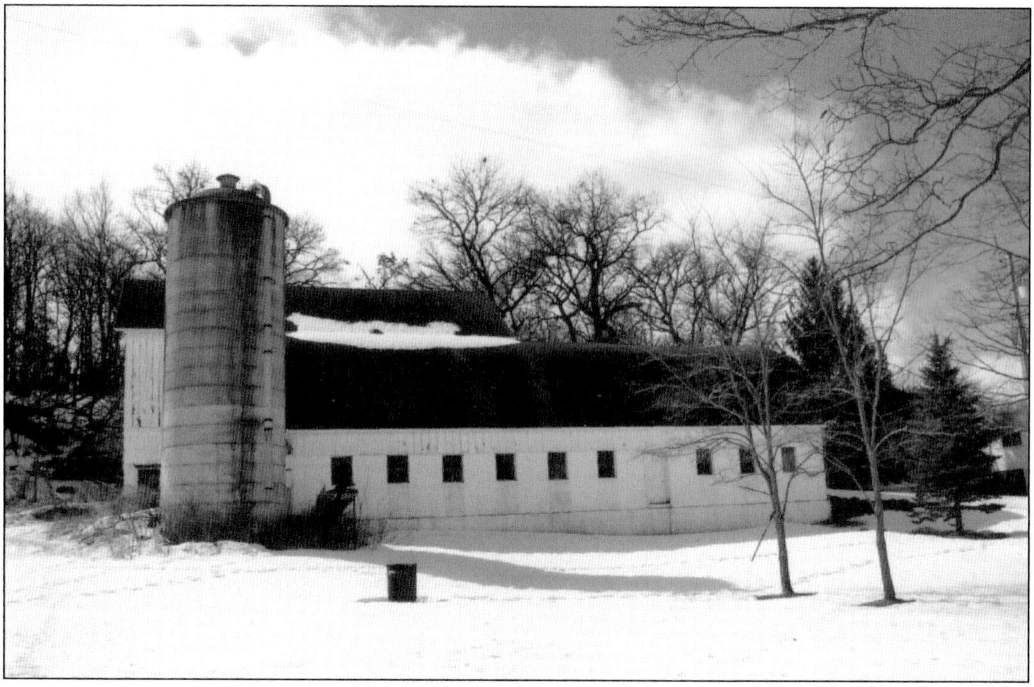

The Bill and Jackie Disch Hustad farm in the Town of Exeter was founded in 1887 and was listed as a Wisconsin Century Farm in 1991. Jackie is the fourth generation of the Disch family on the farm, which is located next to the Silvan and Avis Disch farm.

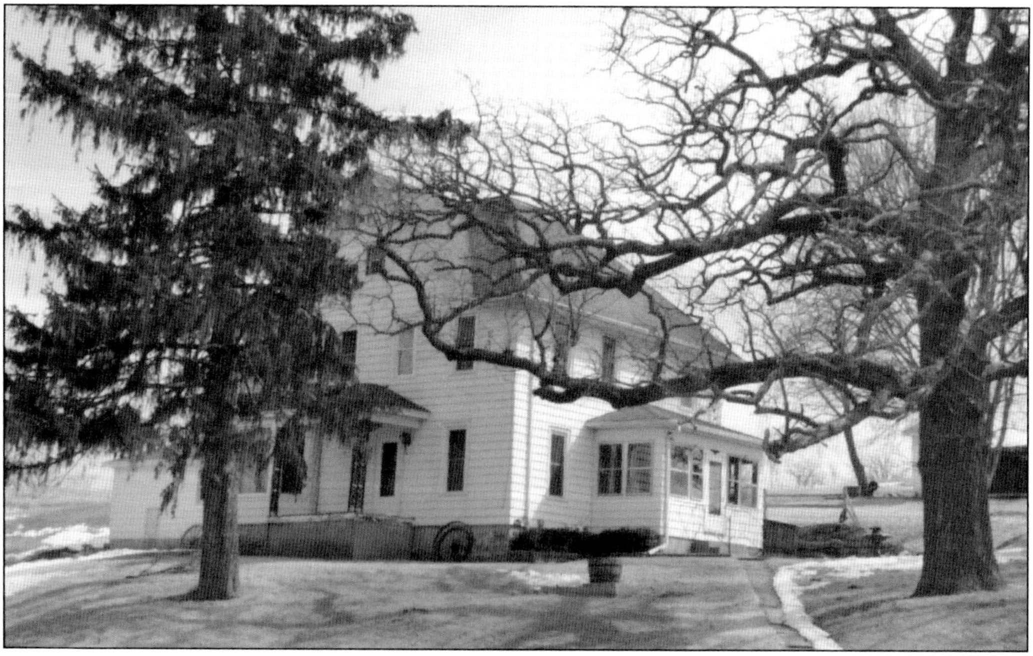

The Rolland and Betty Hustad farm in the Town of New Glarus was founded in 1887 and listed as a Wisconsin Century Farm in 1988. Rolland served for many years as the Town of New Glarus chairman. Rolland and Betty's grandson Jeff Hustad and his family now own the farm and reside there.

Three

Cheese Factories and Country Schools

Early agricultural endeavors in the area, once enough land was cleared, began with raising wheat as a cash crop. Wheat was a good cash crop, but after two decades it began depleting soil fertility. Reduced yields, along with a chinch bug infestation in the Midwest brought wheat farming to an end. Shortly after the conclusion of the Civil War, local farmers switched to dairy farming.

Typically, 5 to 10 neighboring farmers would form a cooperative, build a cheese factory, and hired a cheese maker to operate the factory. All shared in the profits or losses of the factory. Living quarters for the cheese maker and his family were provided on the second floor of these neighborhood factories.

If successful, a second cheese maker would be hired. These men lived at the cheese factory during the cheese-making season from early spring to late fall. During the winter, the cows were not milked. These bachelors would then move into town for the winter, returning to work in spring. During their time off, the bachelors would often stay at the Wilhelm Tell Hotel. If they did not have money to pay for the winter room and board, they were granted credit to be paid off when they returned to work in spring. The men entertained the community with winter Swiss wrestling matches, drawing good crowds.

Country schools dotted the valleys of the area for a century or more. These one-room schoolhouses, in addition to their daytime duty, served as the civic and social center of the school district. One teacher taught all eight grades. Students of these country schools often reflect on their education and feel very strongly that they received an excellent education. The last of the country school districts, within what now makes up the New Glarus School District, closed in the early 1960s.

The biggest event of the country school year was the school Christmas program. Mothers baked and cooked all day in eager anticipation of a few hours away from home, where they could mingle with other women in the neighborhood. For fathers, it was a chance to be picked to be Santa for the students. The schools and cheese factories shown in this chapter all are within what now makes up the New Glarus School District.

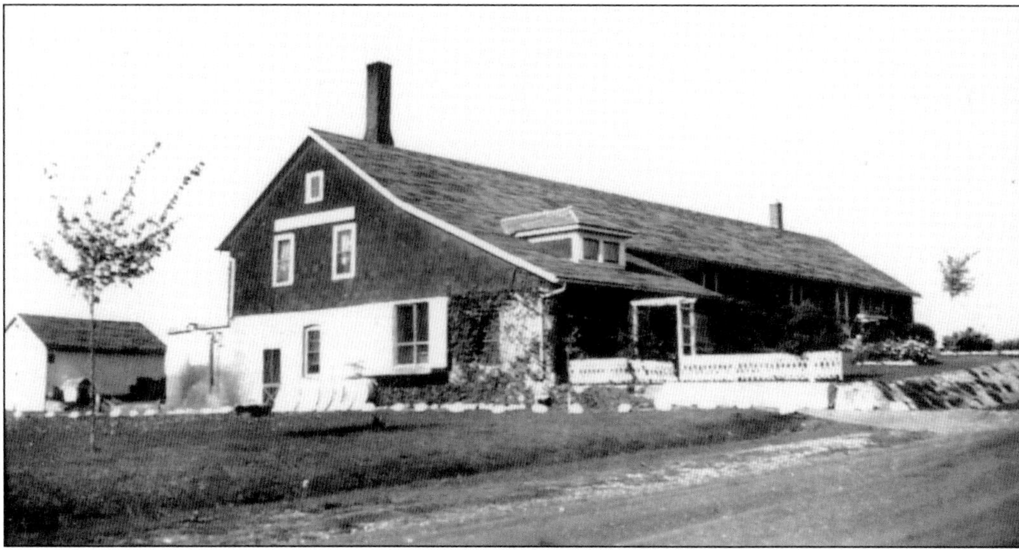

Farmer's Grove cheese factory closed, as many of the remaining small country cheese factories did, in the early 1970s as more milk was being sold to the larger regional factories. The last cheese makers at this factory, the Roy Stettler family, moved their operation to the Brodhead, Wisconsin, area, where their son Steve makes award-winning cheese at Decatur Cheese Factory.

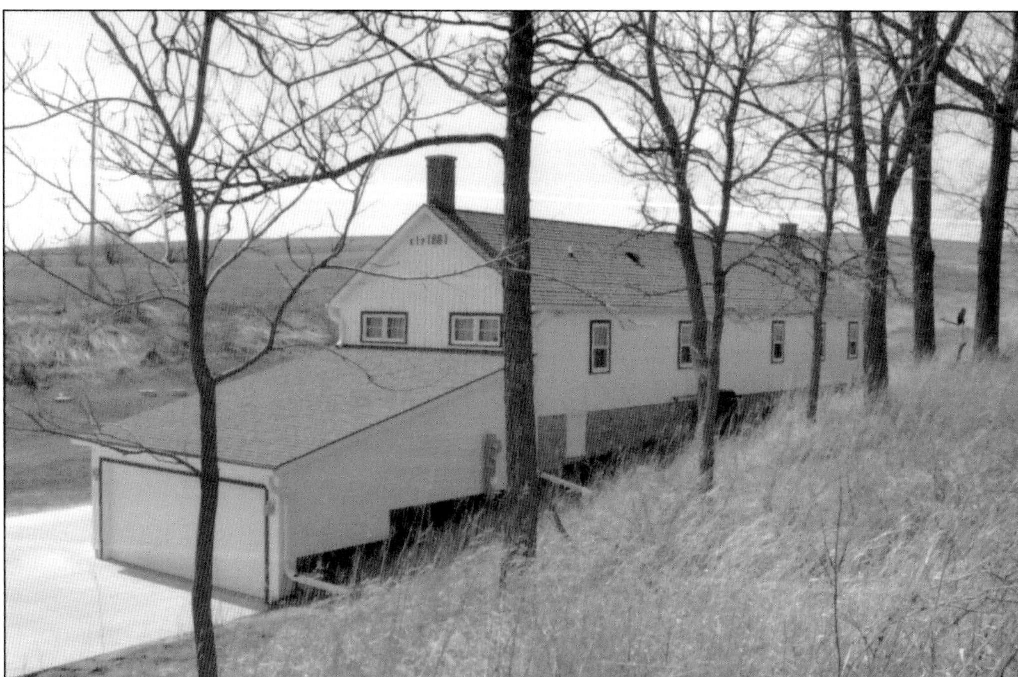

This c. 1881 cheese factory is very unique in that it was a privately owned, on-the-farm cheese factory for the Hefty Blum farm. The factory did take in some milk from neighboring farms. The factory sat empty for over 50 years and was recently restored. Silvan and Jane Blum operate a cheese sales business, Hefti Creek Farm, out of the factory and live on the second floor of the building.

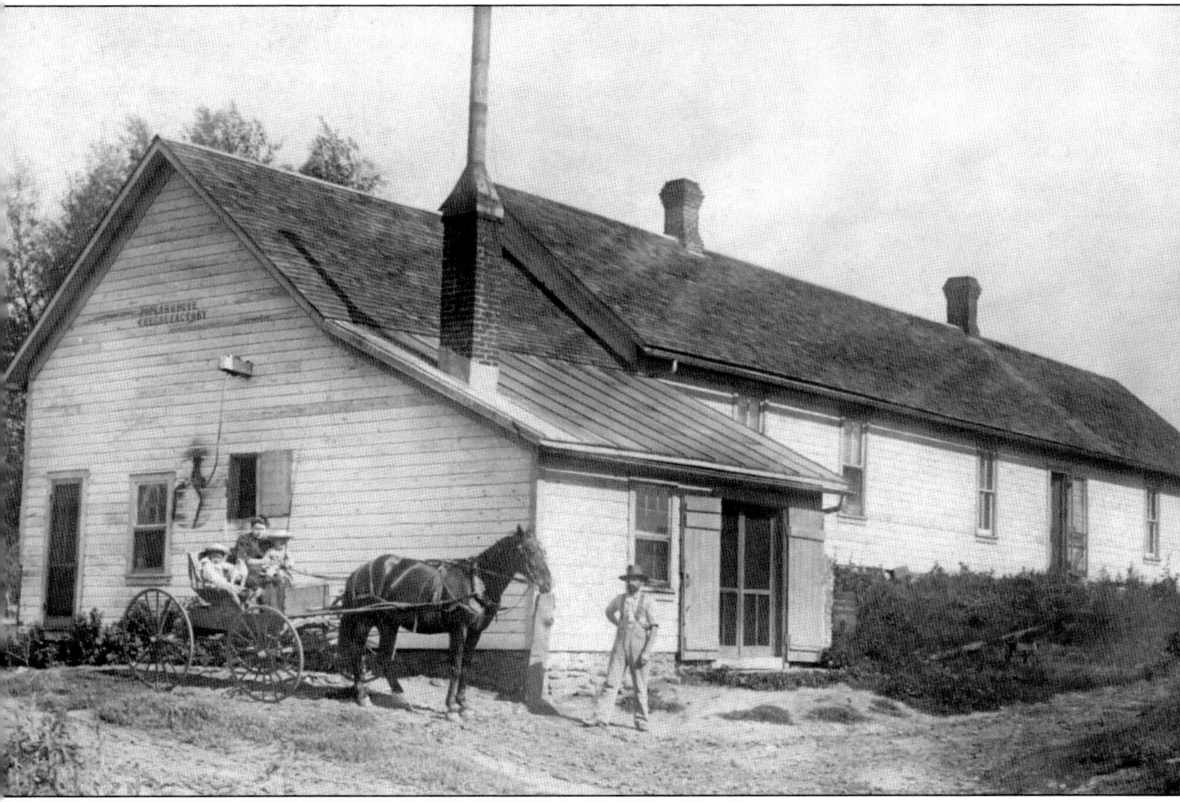

The Poplar Grove Cheese Factory on Highway 39, several miles west of New Glarus, was one of the very last small cooperative factories to operate in Green County. The last cheese maker, Alfred Lehnherr, was known for his excellent brick cheese. Today, the factory is utilized as a home workshop, with the owner occupying the living quarters.

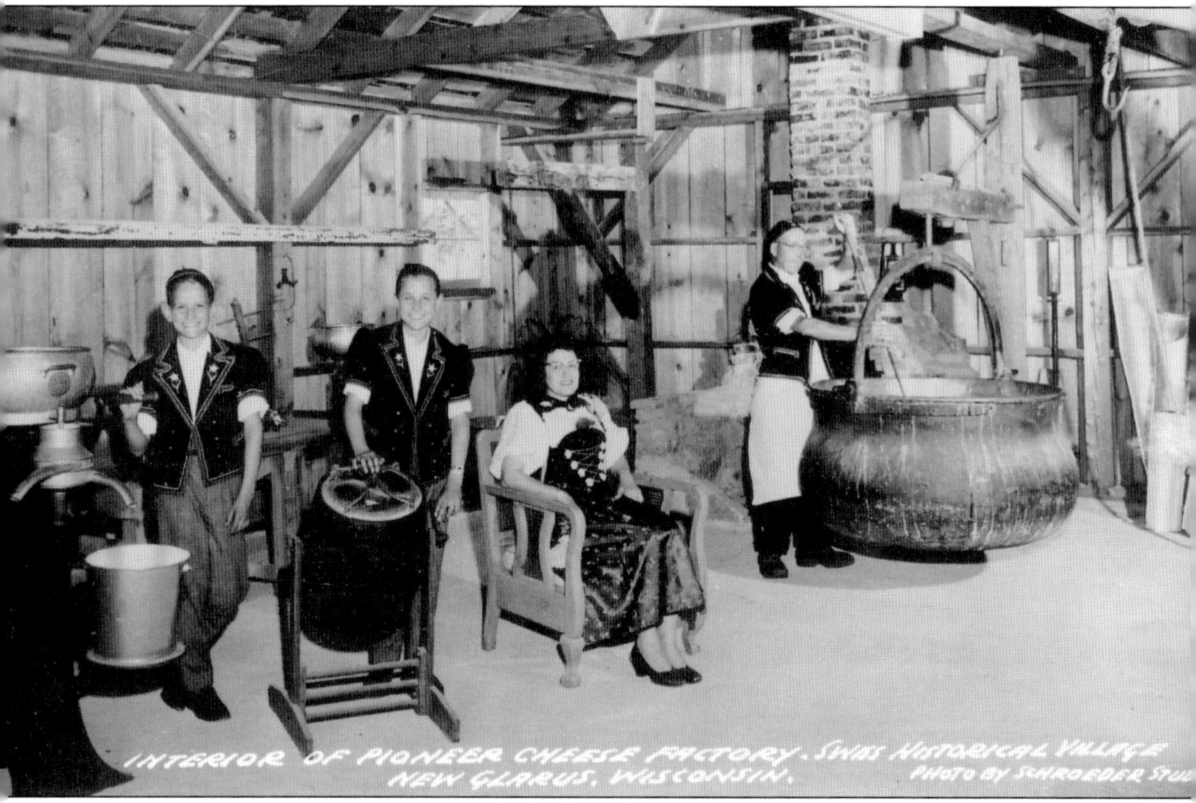

This replica of an early cheese factory is in the Swiss Historical Village in New Glarus. The cheese factory equipment, which is used to make a batch of Swiss cheese once each year, was donated by Carl Marty Sr. of Monroe.

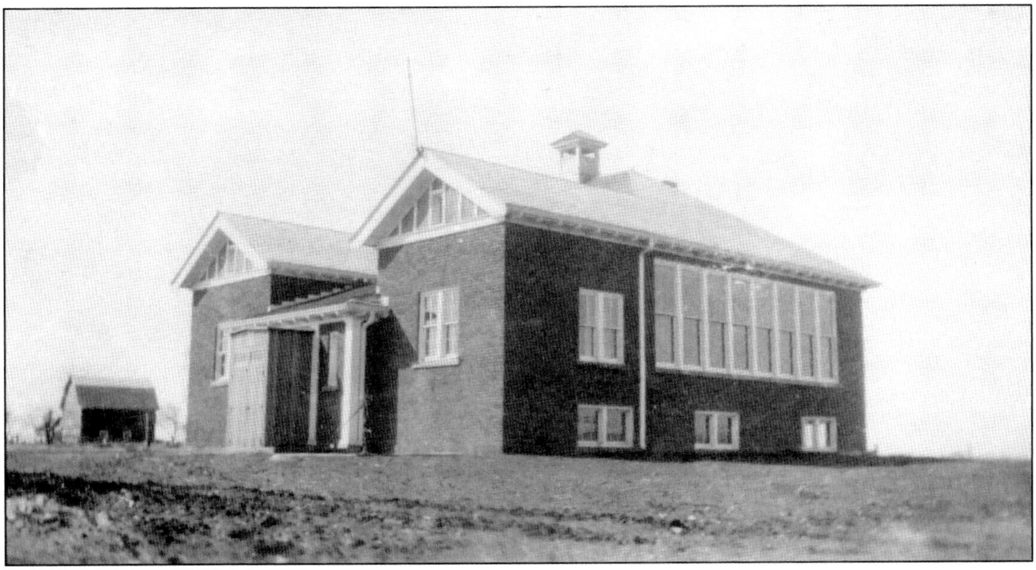

This undated photograph shows the early Postville School, which was replaced by the current brick building. After consolidation into the New Glarus School District, the newer school building was converted into the Postville Bible Church. The congregation outgrew the school building and constructed a new church in New Glarus.

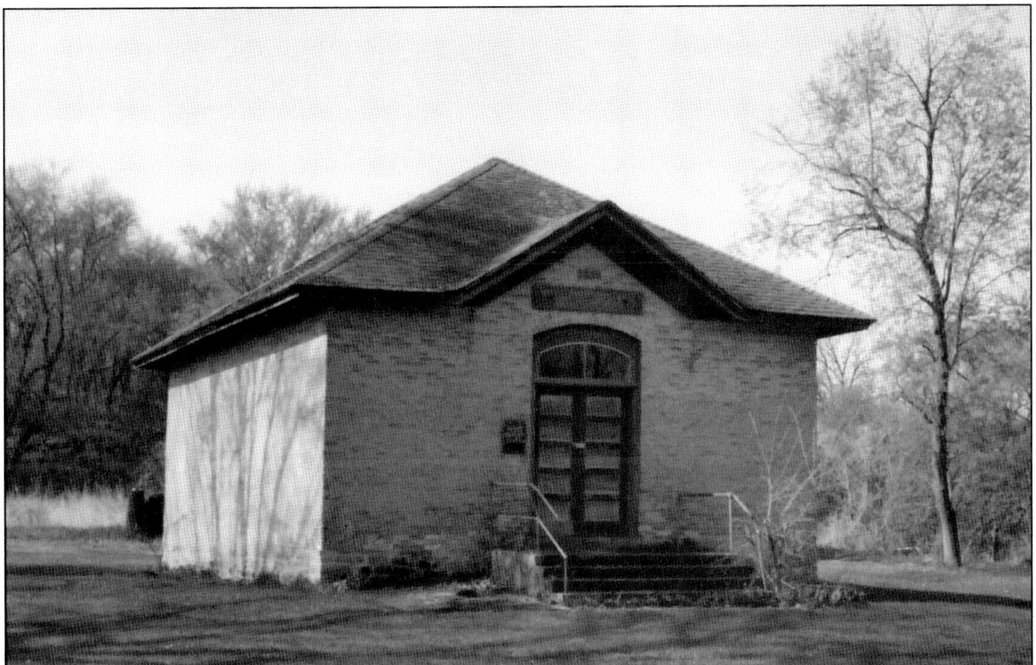

The Wallace School was built in 1891 utilizing Cream City (Milwaukee) brick. Wallace School served the southeast end of the New Glarus School District until it closed and became part of the New Glarus School District. The interior of this building is unique. It is clad with beadboard paneling that instead of being perpendicular floor to ceiling is cut at a 45-degree angle, giving the interior a very unusual look. Wallace School was named for one of the Irish families that lived near the school.

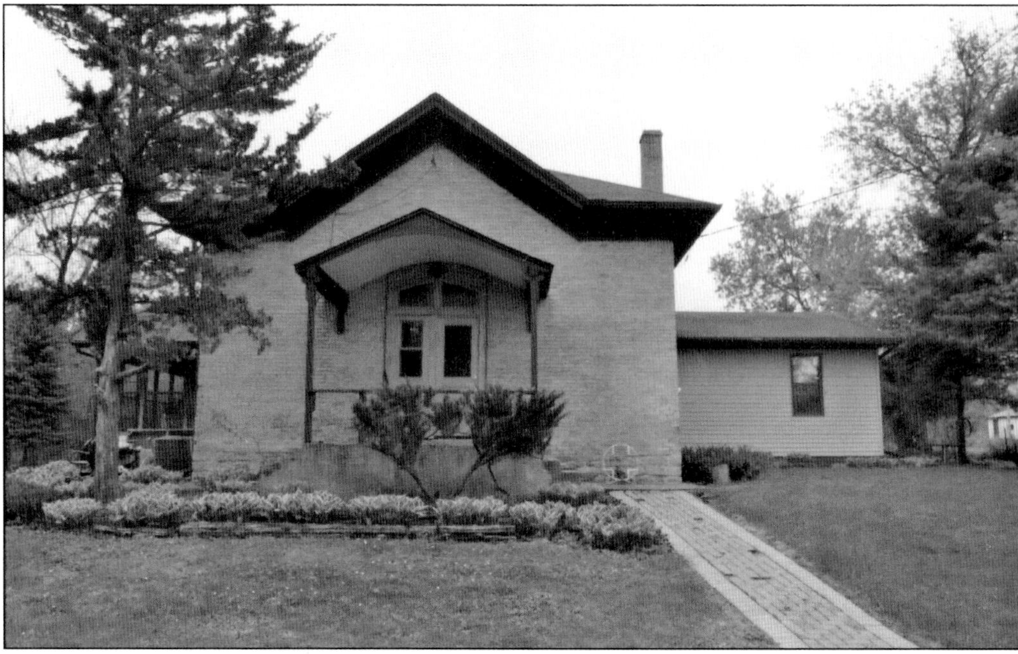

Ross School in the Town of Exeter, located at the intersection of Green County Highway W and Christen Road, served the eastern portion of the New Glarus School District. Ross School was built in the late 1800s and looks very much like Wallace School. Ross School got its name from the very prominent Ross family, who lived across the road from the school. A country railroad stop just east of Ross School, Ross' Crossing, was also named for the Ross family.

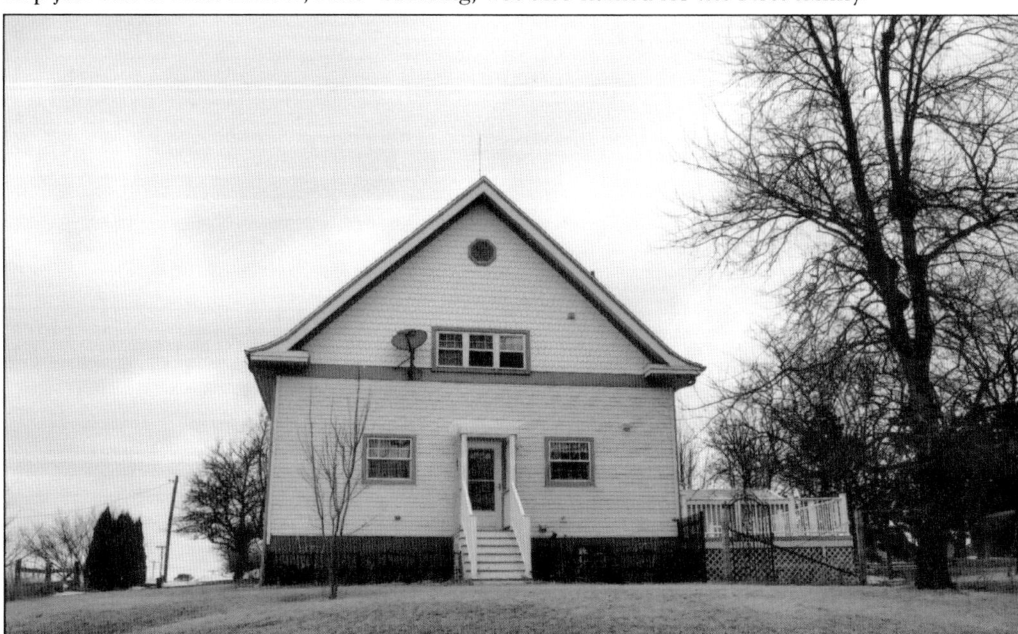

The Dividing Ridge School, located at the corner of Green County Highway J and Dividing Ridge Road, is a spacious building that has been carefully renovated into a beautiful home. Note the still-operable schoolyard swing set on the school grounds on the far right in the photograph.

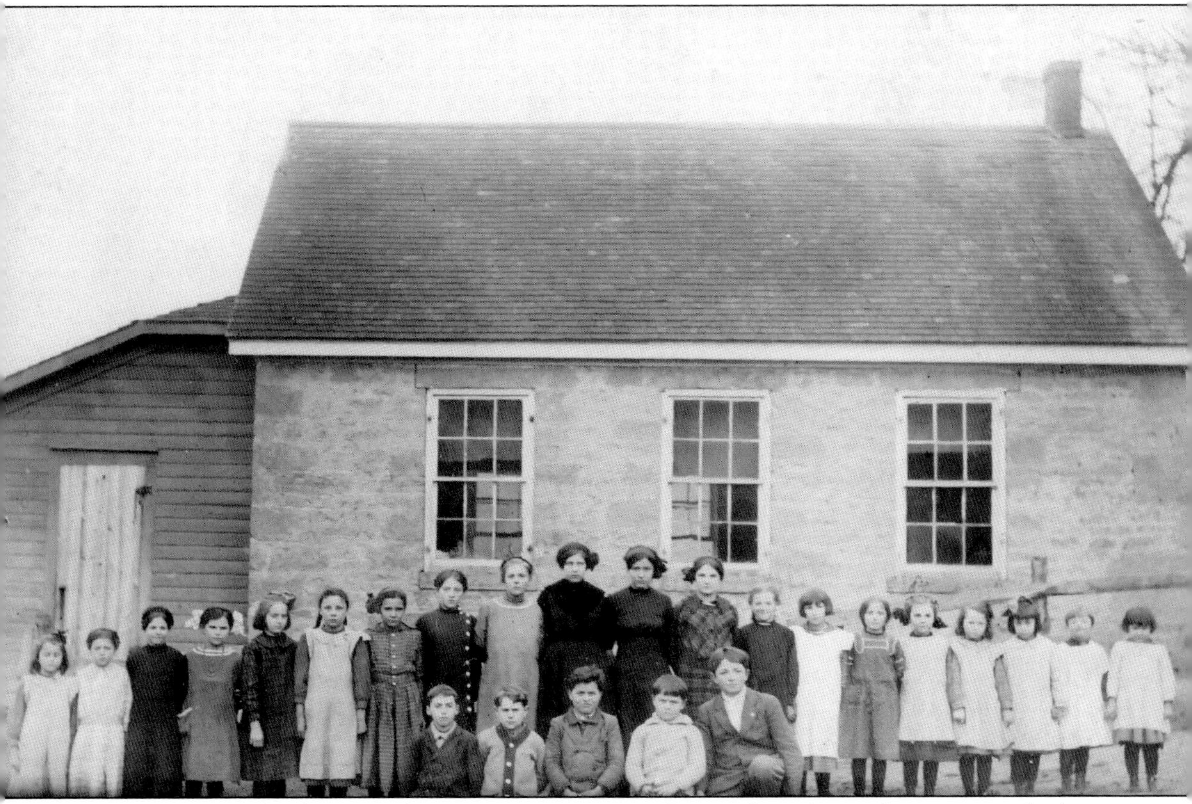

Spring Valley School was on the Green-Dane County line and was located approximately three miles north of New Glarus on Wisconsin Highway 69. After it ceased to operate in June 1961, it was used for a time as living quarters until it was demolished in the late 1960s. Constructed in the 1860s, it was the only stone school built of hand-quarried limestone in what would become the New Glarus School District.

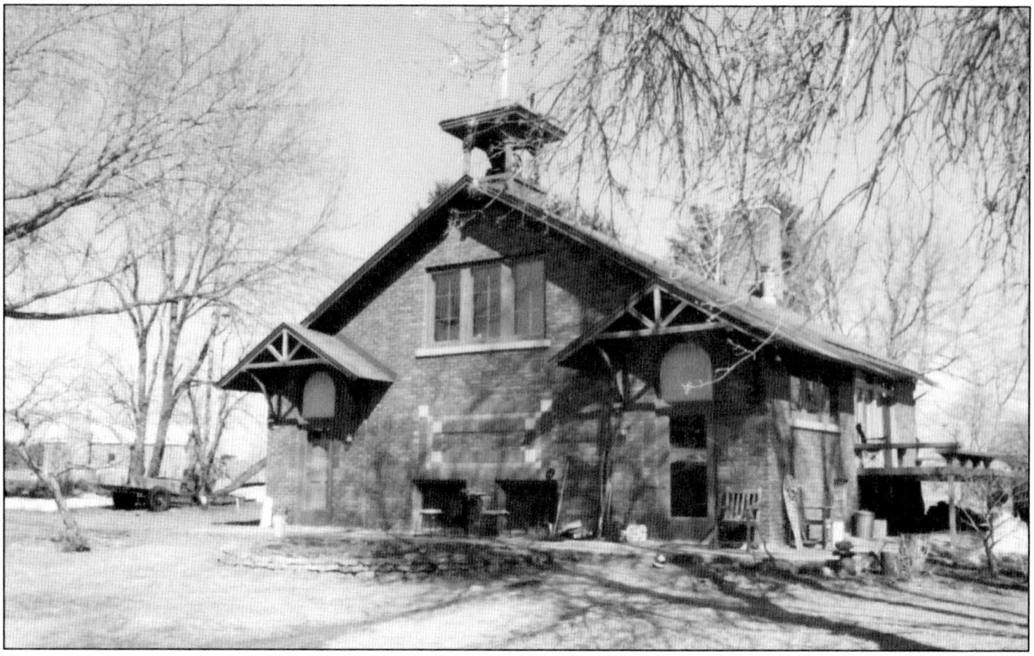

Bowers School is the northern-most school in the New Glarus School District. It is located on Bowers Road just west of State Highway 92 in the Town of Primrose. After the school closed, residents of the township purchased the building to be used as a community center. The school is now a private residence.

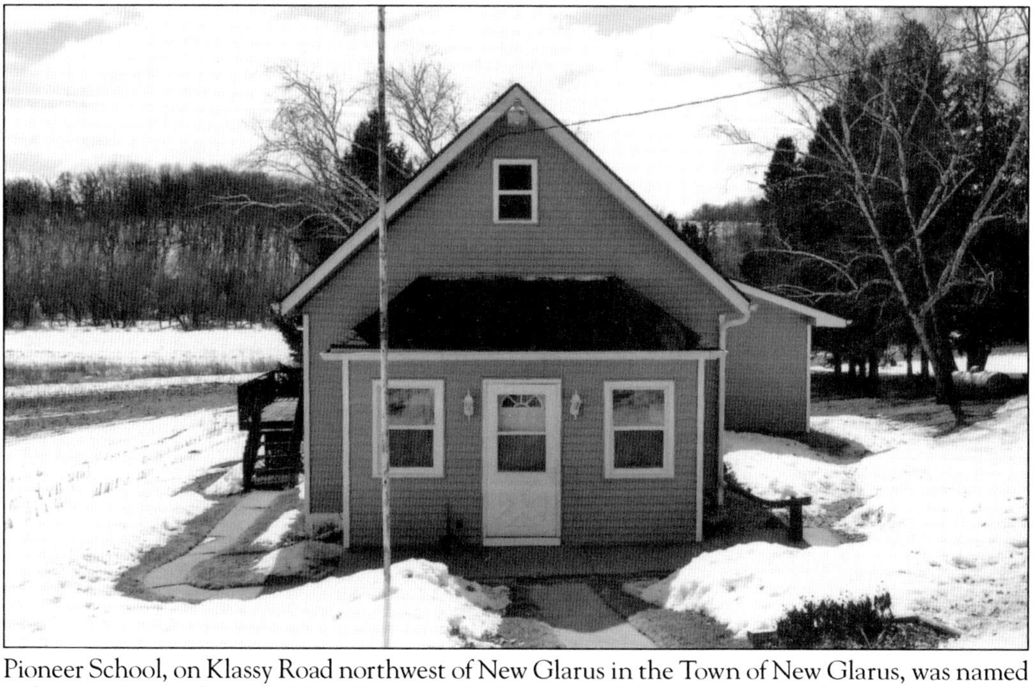

Pioneer School, on Klassy Road northwest of New Glarus in the Town of New Glarus, was named so because it was through this valley that the founders of New Glarus passed on their way from Mineral Point to where they decided to locate the new colony. Pioneer School closed in 1955 and has been used as a private home since.

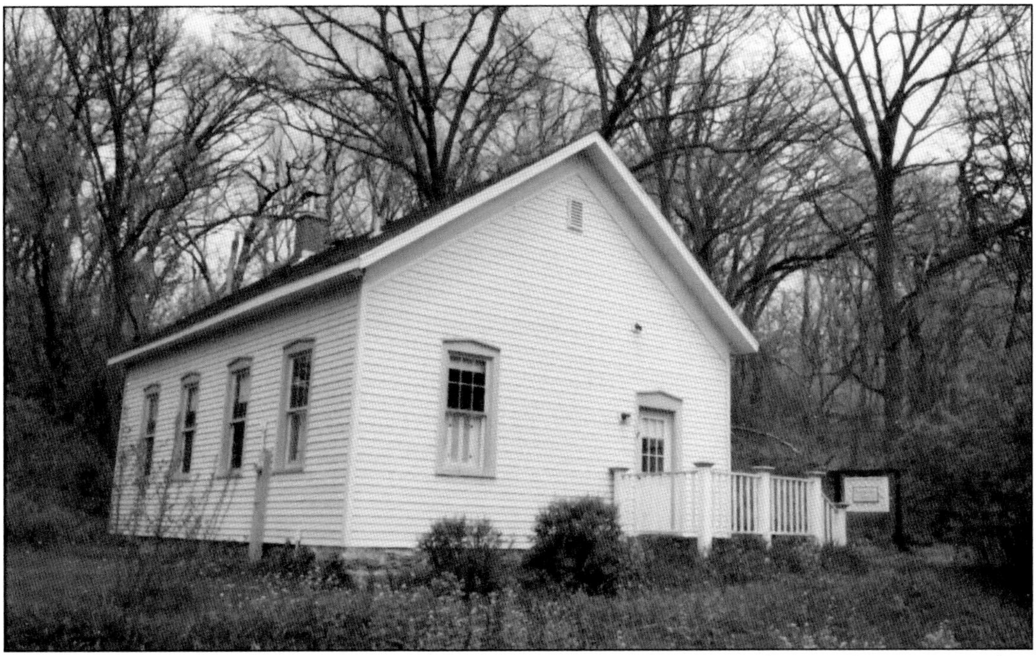

Meadow Valley School is located about two and half miles southwest of New Glarus on Meadow Valley Road in the Town of New Glarus. After the school closed, it was home to a motorcycle club. A number of years ago, the school was restored and became a bed-and-breakfast. Today, the owner uses the school as an art studio.

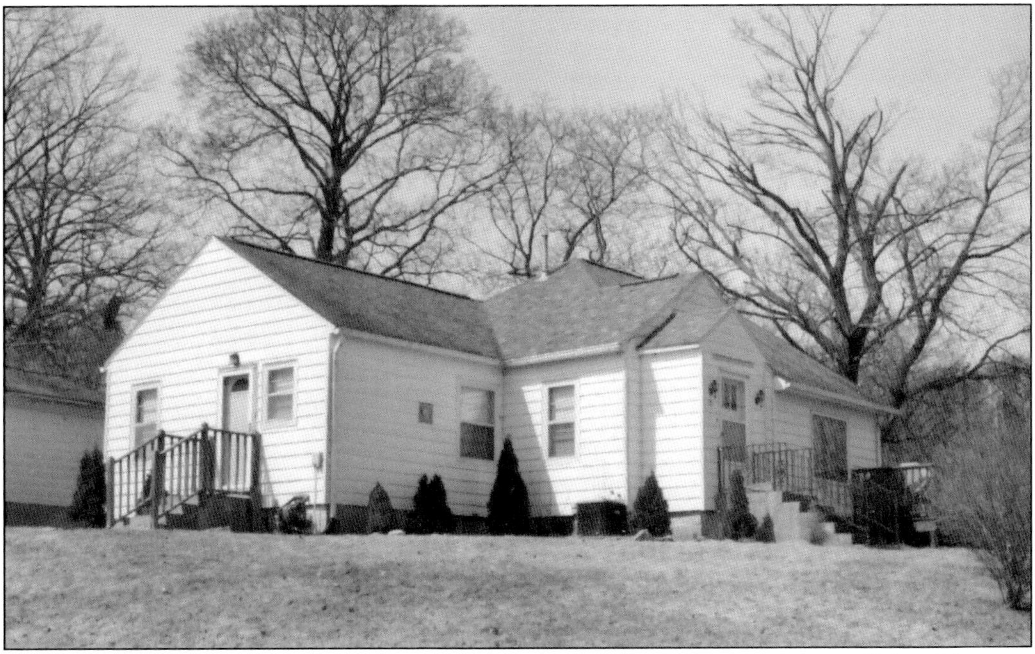

Legler Valley School was located on Legler Valley Road about two miles west of New Glarus in the Town of New Glarus. After closing to students, the building was moved into New Glarus, where it was turned into a very modern looking post–World War II home housing local veteran Harold Ingwell and his wife, Kathleen, and their young family.

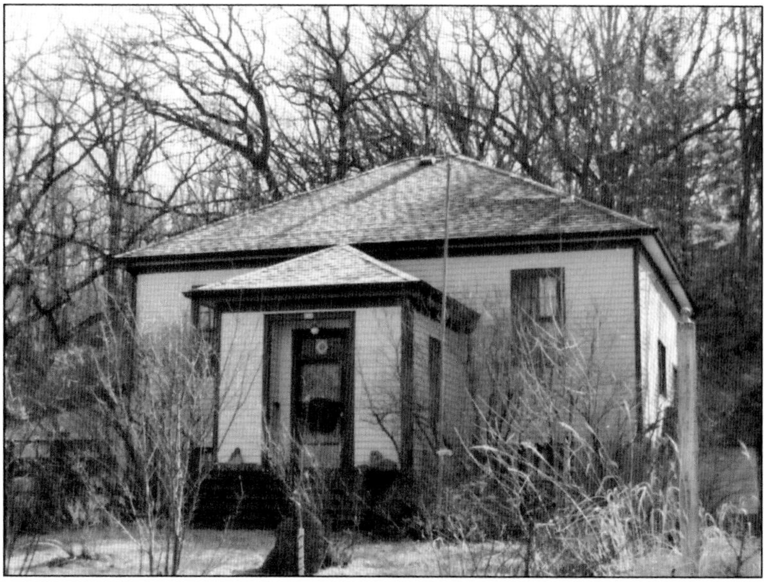

Tyvand School, located on Tyvand Road, is approximately seven miles west of New Glarus in the Town of Perry in Dane County. It was one of the last country schools to close. Tyvand School is located within "the prairie" and today serves as a private home and workshop for a piano tuner and musical instrument repair shop.

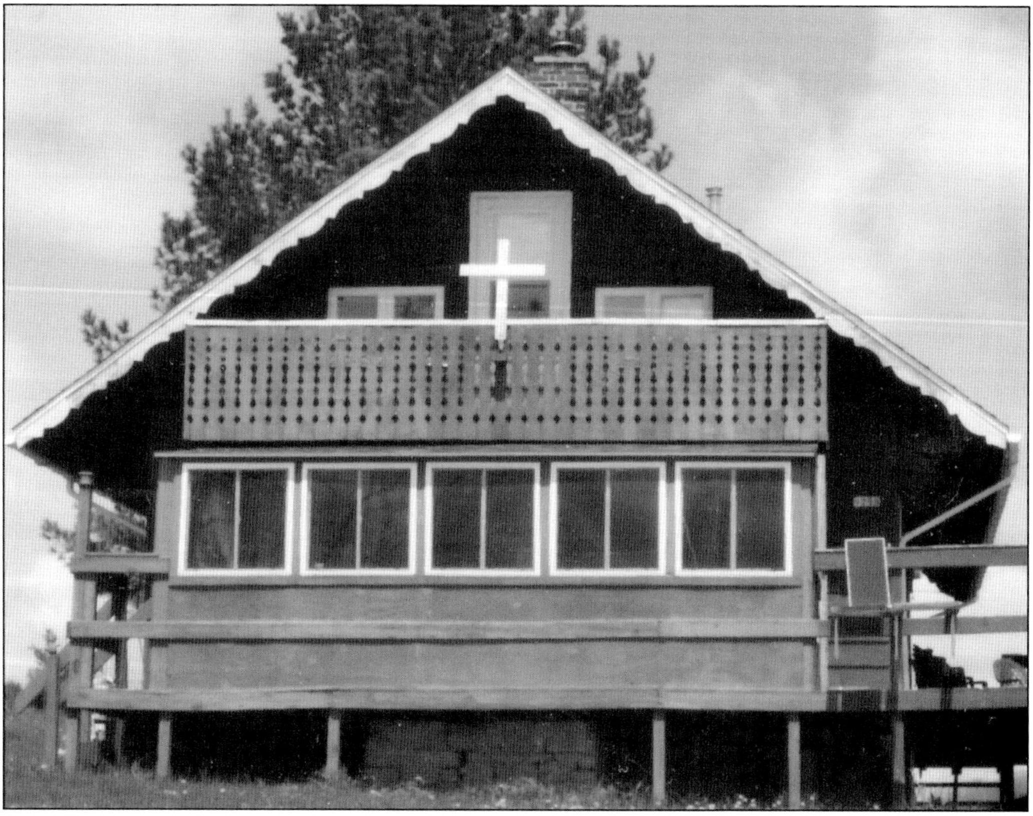

Pleasant View School is located approximately five miles north of New Glarus in the Town of Primrose in Dane County. Robert Arn, a longtime New Glarus businessman, spoke Swiss. His family moved to the Pleasant View School area, but classes were taught in Norwegian. Arn took a lot of teasing for being unable to speak the language. By the time he quit school after fifth grade, though, Arn was fluent in Swiss, Norwegian, and English.

Four

Village Anniversaries

Anniversaries, of both New Glarus and Switzerland, were celebrated with equal earnestness. New Glarus began celebrating anniversaries on July 12, 1885. A gathering was held in a wooded grove on the west edge of town. The year 1891 brought a very different anniversary: the 600th anniversary of Switzerland. Crowds in New Glarus reached 6,000 participants. The Milwaukee Road railroad ran extra trains to get all of the celebrants to New Glarus. Four years later, in 1895, New Glarus once again celebrated; this time, it was the 50th anniversary of New Glarus. The six remaining original colonists were recognized. The special guest speaker for the 70th anniversary in 1915 featured a fellow Swiss: Wisconsin governor Emmanuel Phillip. A striking monument in the churchyard was dedicated to the memory of the founding families.

By 1925, the 80th anniversary, only two of the original settlers remained: Mrs. William Engler Sr. and Oswald Babler. The year 1945 was the centennial for New Glarus. World War II had ended, but most of the young men and women of New Glarus had not yet returned from Europe and the South Pacific war zones. The community held a very subdued centennial observance at the First Settlers Monument. The village would celebrate the community's 100th anniversary one year later. Photographs of that event can be found in Images of America: *The Swiss of New Glarus*.

New Glarus marked the 120th anniversary in 1965. A Hall of History was set up in the village hall. Shop windows around town were filled with residents' displays of collections, hobbies, and crafts. One of the big events was the presentation of the much-loved Swiss story of *Heidi*.

The year 2015 will mark the 50th anniversary of the *Heidi* drama, which coincides with the 170th anniversary of New Glarus's founding.

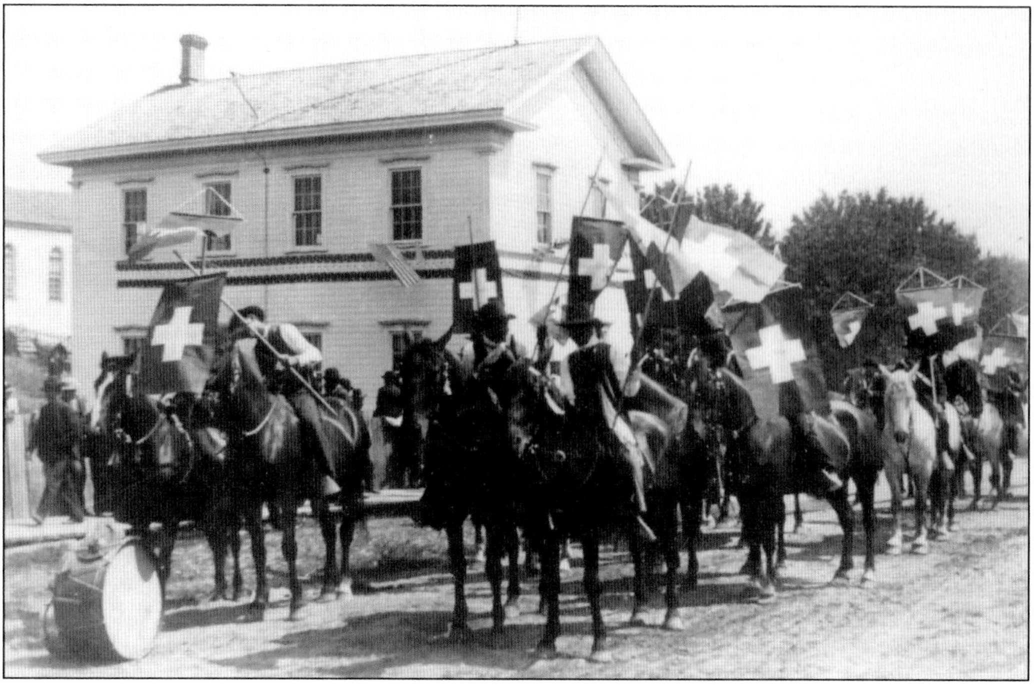

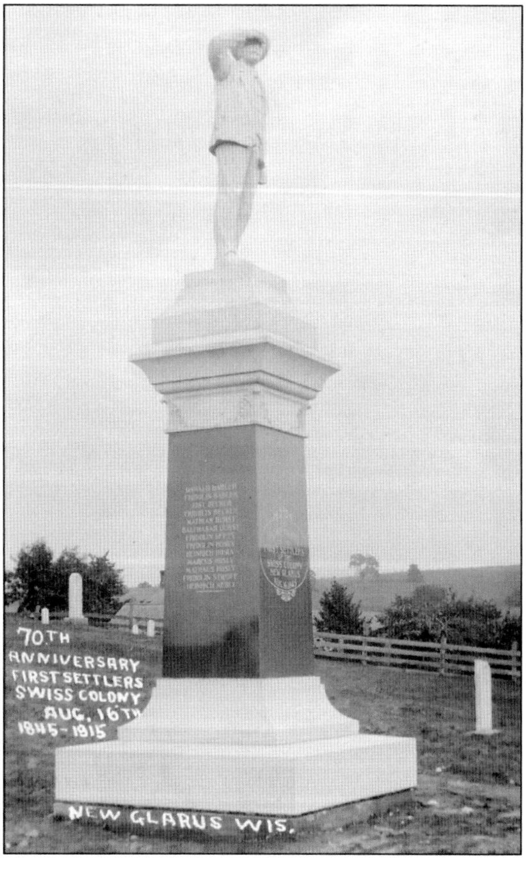

This 1895 photograph is of the 50th anniversary of New Glarus. The building in the foreground was the first true schoolhouse in New Glarus. For many years, it housed a restaurant, barbershop, and pharmacy. It was recently renovated and is now a gift shop. The building to the far left is the second church on that site. This building is located at the corner of First Street and Fifth Avenue.

The year 1915 brought many area people to New Glarus to celebrate the growing community's 70th anniversary. The main event of the festivities was the unveiling of the First Settlers Monument, which was erected in the front yard of the church. In the background are the gravestones of many of the earliest New Glarus settlers.

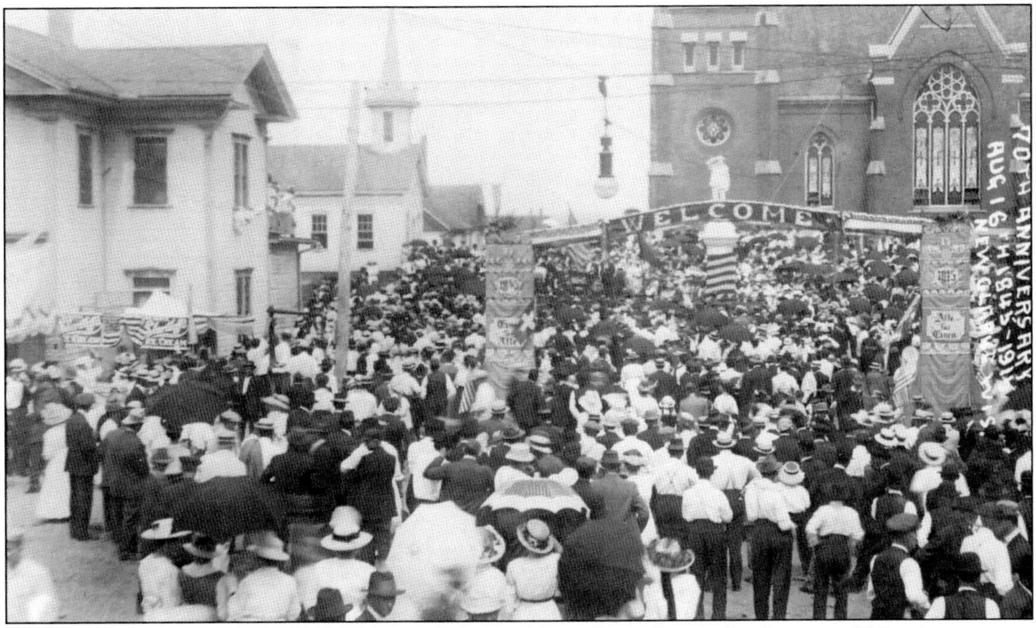

The soon-to-be dedicated First Settlers Monument is draped in red, white, and blue bunting in part to show that the New Glarus Swiss had become very proud American citizens. It was said among the Swiss that one becomes a real American when able to read a newspaper in English.

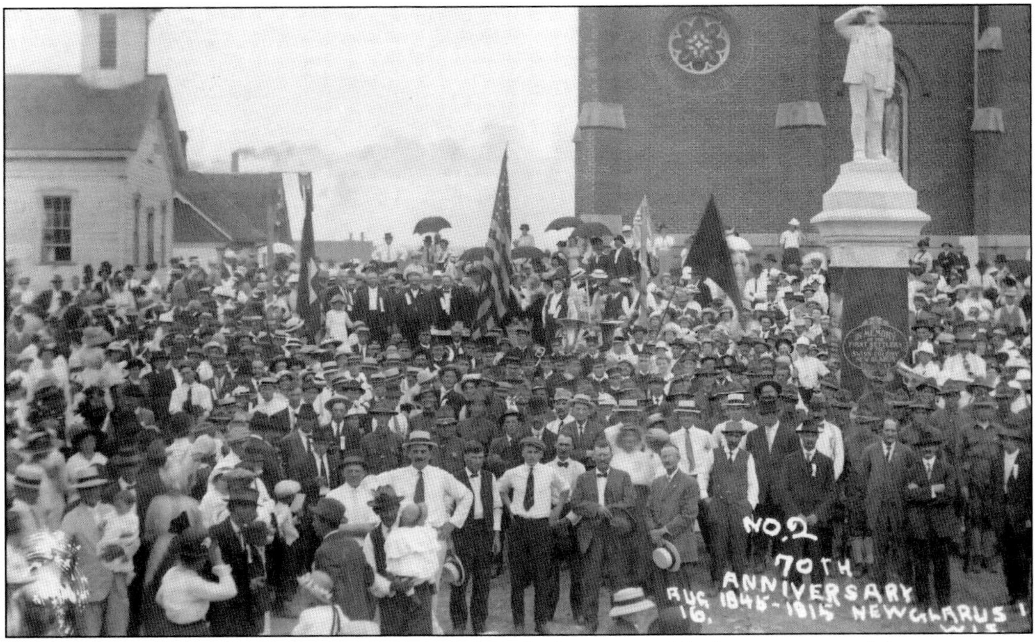

The First Settlers Monument is now unveiled as the large crowd looks on in awe of the monument erected to the memories of their ancestors who two generations before settled in the Little Sugar River valley after a many months journey from poverty and hunger in Switzerland to the country that gave them hope and a new future. A note on the back of the photograph asks, "Can you find Alvin on here?"

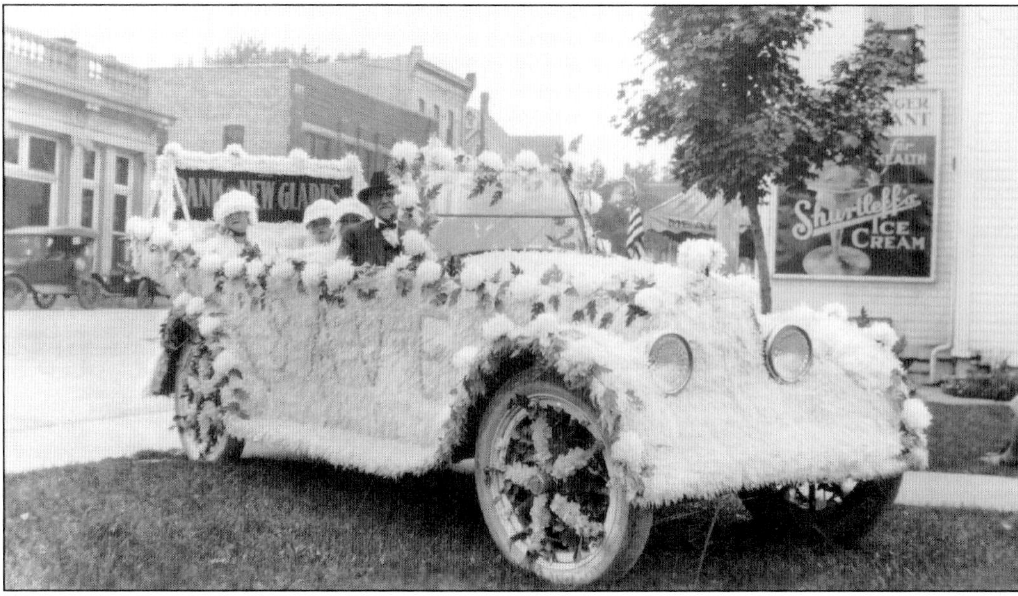

This Bank of New Glarus car is all decked out for the 70th anniversary. The man in the dark suit appears to be Oswald Babler, who no doubt was one of the most esteemed guests of the event. The Bank of New Glarus is on the far left in this photograph. Notice the Shurtleff's ice cream sign on the side of the Luchsinger Restaurant. Shurtleff's ice cream was a real tasty treat.

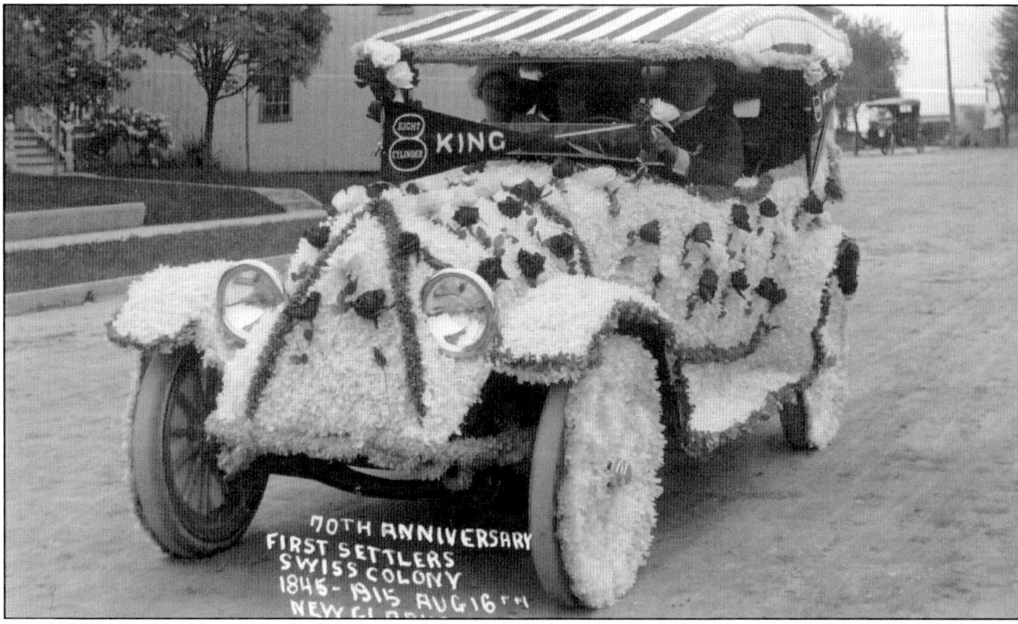

This decorated car float was sponsored by Joe Hoesly's King Auto Dealership, which was located at 109 Fifth Avenue. Hoesly's King Auto building later served as Glaeden's Barber Shop and Fuhrman's drug store. The upper floor held two apartments. In 1980, the building was remodeled, and a Swiss-motif front was added to the building.

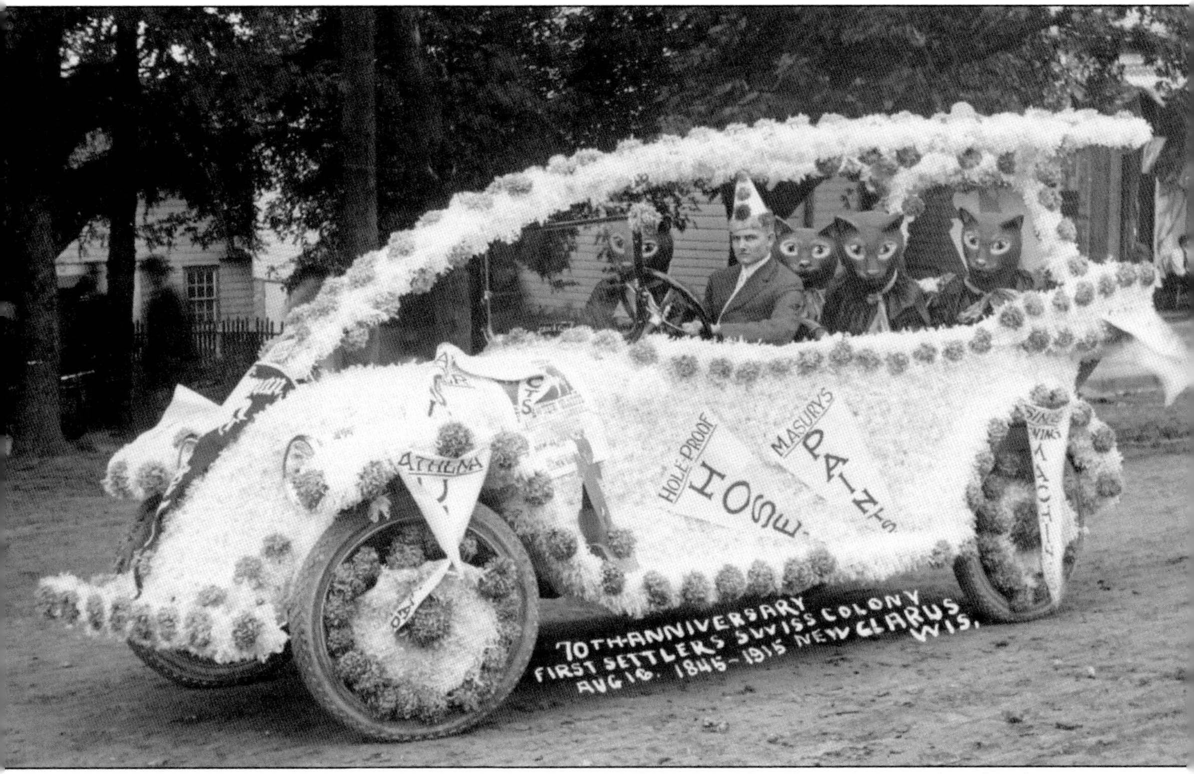

This float appears to be occupied by some rather rough-looking hombres or a traveling landscaping and painting crew staffed by a number of necktie-wearing guys in bear suits. Nothing is known about who sponsored this float or the identity of the driver or the men in the bear suits.

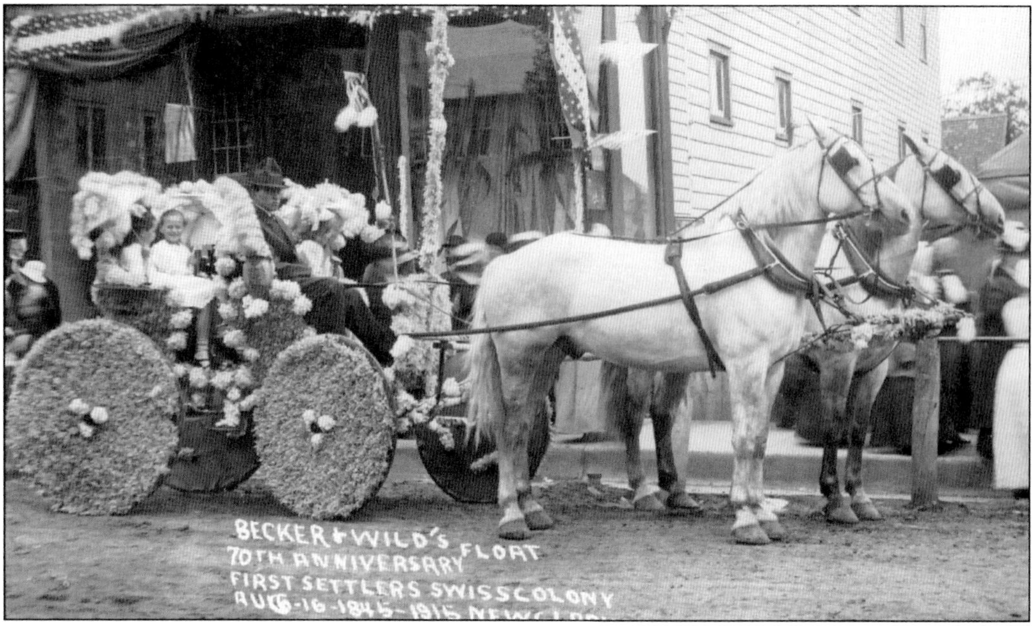

The Becker and Wild horse-drawn carriage is being driven by Melvin Becker. The building in the background appears to be what is currently owned and occupied by Sugar River Shop, located at 108 Fifth Avenue. Longtime New Glarus attorney Ed Willi had his law office in this building for many years.

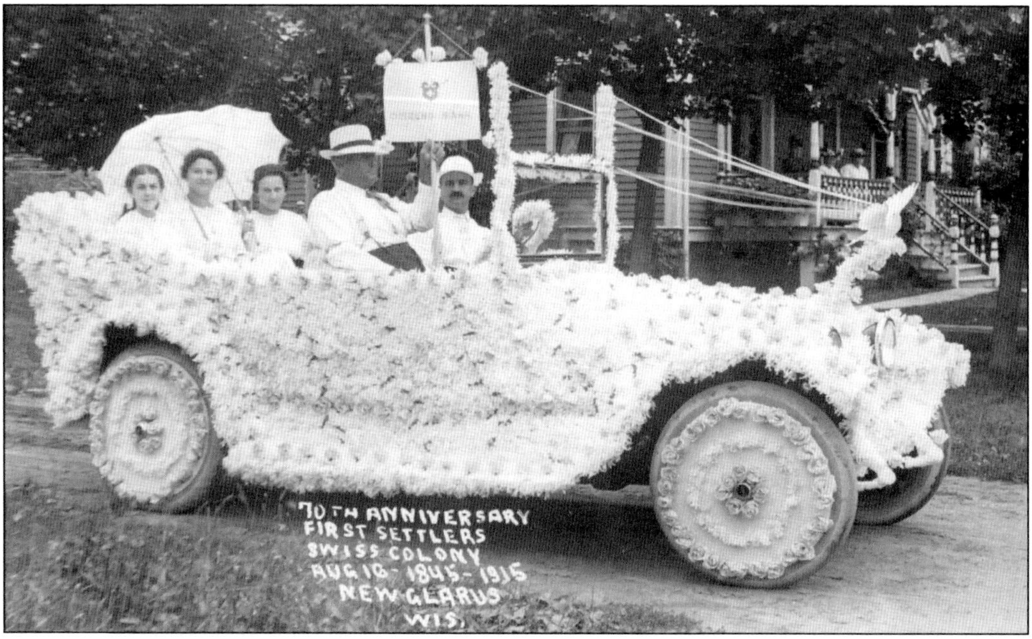

This beautifully decorated float sponsored by the Bank of New Glarus is being driven by J.J. Figy. The Bank of New Glarus was founded in 1893 and during the depression was closed for only one day, and then reopened, because it was found to be very financially sound—unlike many banks during that time.

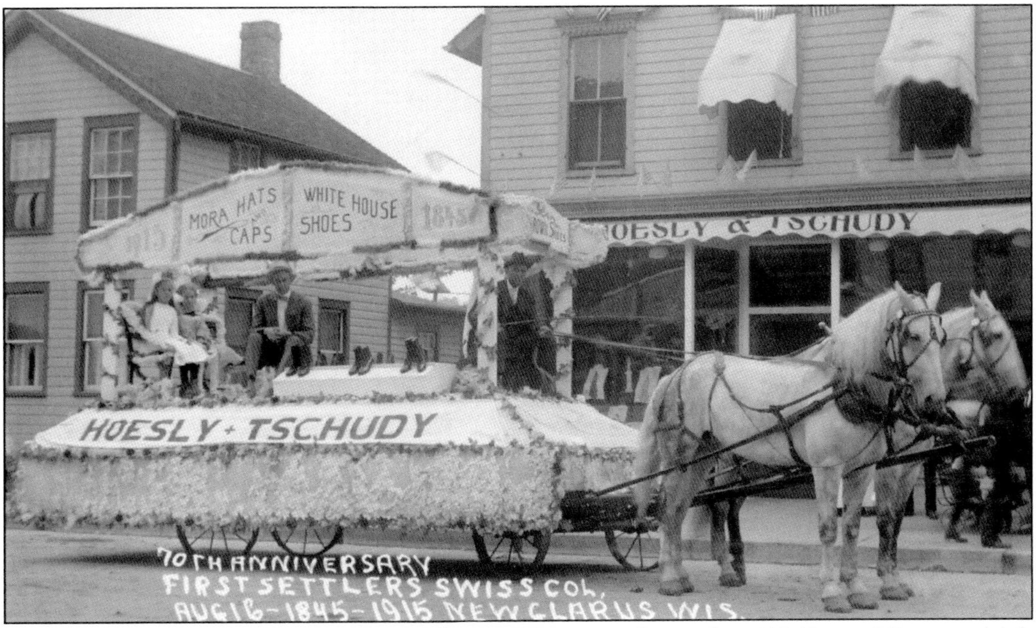

The Hoesly & Tschudy float pauses in front of the store, located at 412 Second Street, which was owned by Henry B. Hoesly and Fred Tschudy. Hoesly sold out to Tschudy, and Hoesly began Hoesly Hardware on First Street, which the family operated until the late 1960s, when the Bank of New Glarus purchased the structure for a major building project.

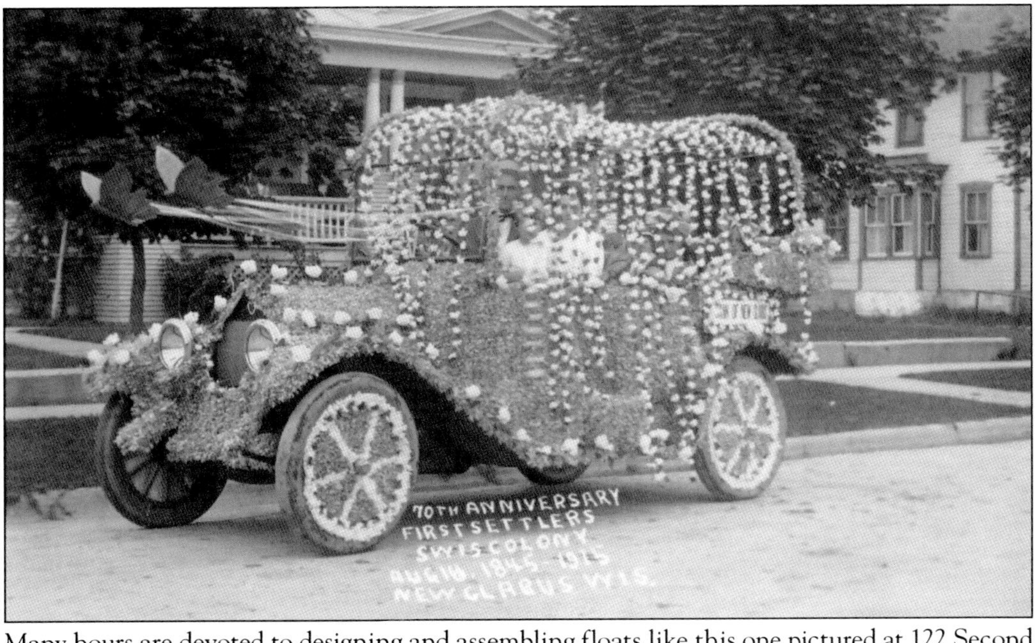

Many hours are devoted to designing and assembling floats like this one pictured at 122 Second Street. In the background is the Dr. McQuillin home. Dr. McQuillin served the New Glarus area for many years as a medical doctor. He also owned a farm north of New Glarus.

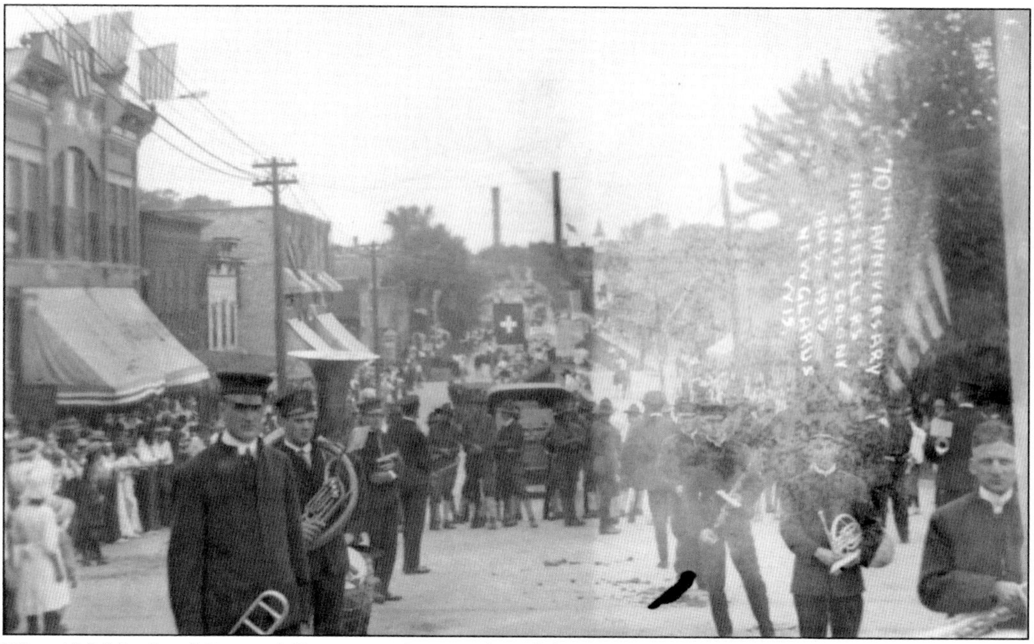

The 400 block of Second Street is alive with celebrants in town for the 70th anniversary of the founding of New Glarus. Buildings on the left are Stricklers Market, the blacksmith shop, Stuessy's Grocery Store, and New Glarus Hardware. The two tall chimneys in the background are part of the Pet Milk factory.

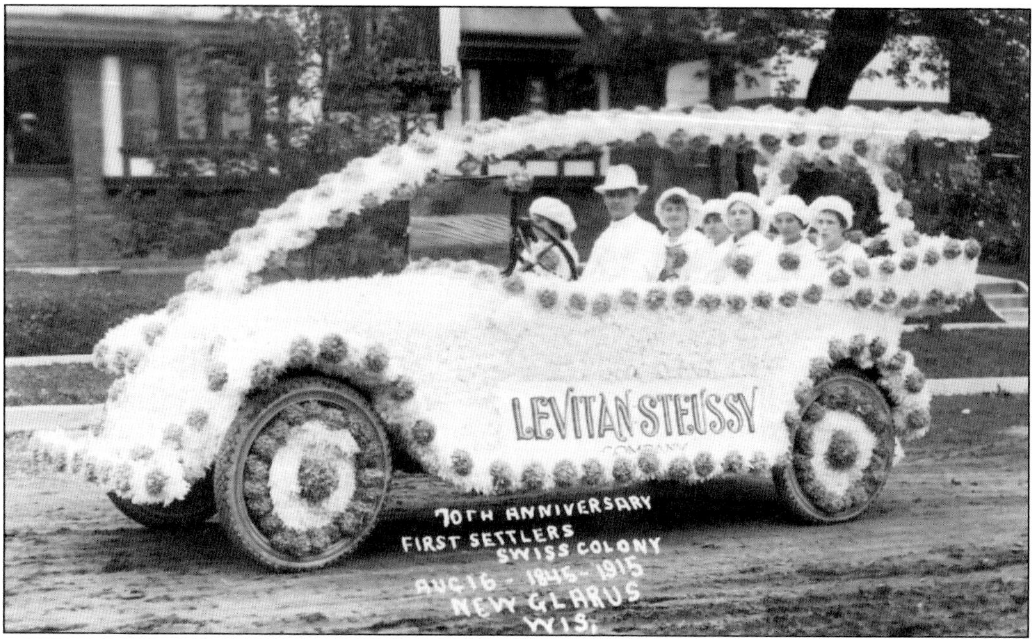

This Levitan Steussy float is parked in front of the Dr. McQuillin home on Second Street. Levitan and Steussy was a general merchandise store located at 523 First Street. The building later housed the J. Fred Uffelman variety store, Roy's Market, and a second-floor bowling alley that burned on January 18, 1959. It was rebuilt and is today known as Anderson Mall.

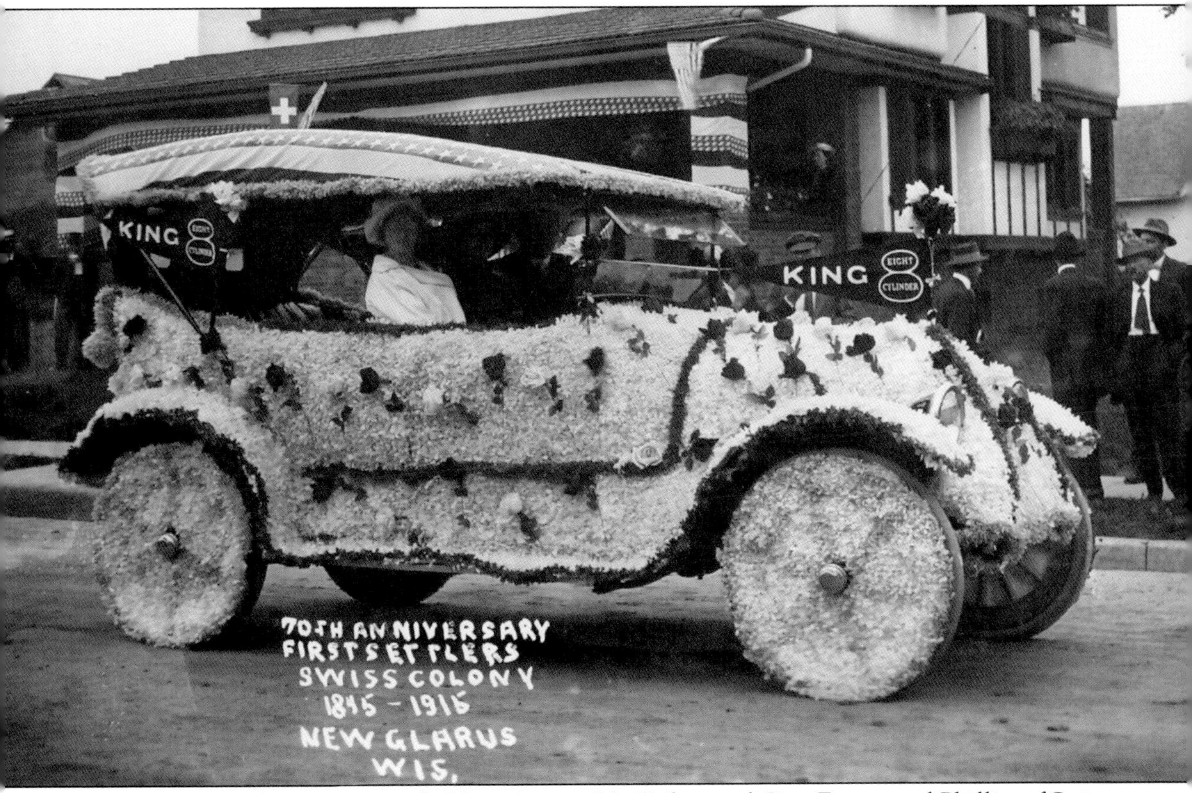

New Glarus's 70th anniversary, held on August 16–17, featured Gov. Emmanuel Phillip, of Swiss ancestry, as the guest speaker. The Luchsinger Monument Works of Monroe, Wisconsin, erected the pioneer statue made of 10 pieces of Barre, Vermont, and Montello, Wisconsin, granite.

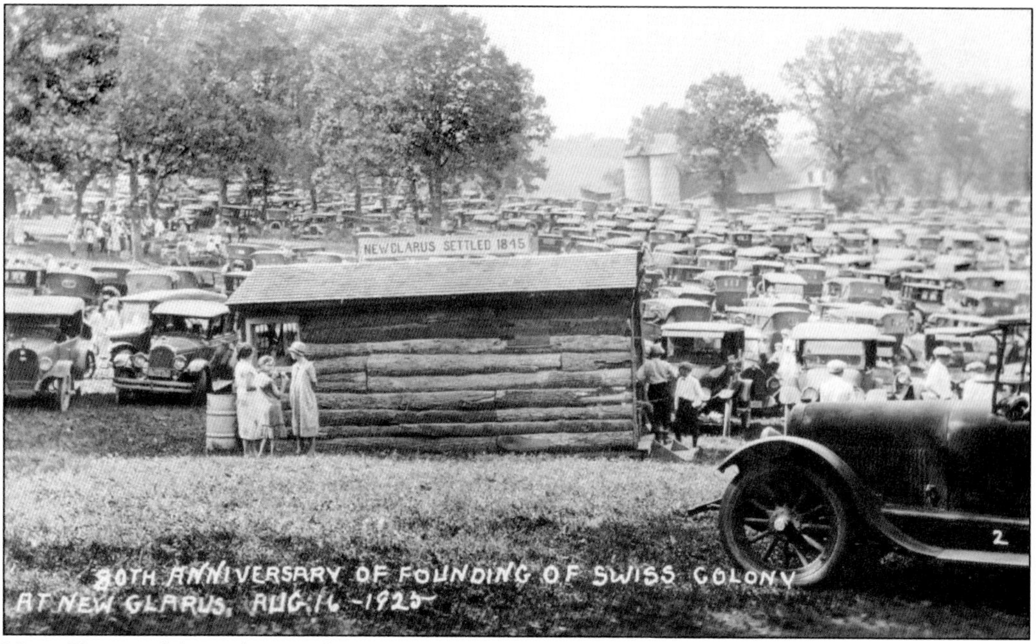

New Glarus celebrated its 80th anniversary on August 16, 1925, at the Shooting Park, located at the north edge of New Glarus. The log cabin was built as somewhat of a replica of the earliest log homes in New Glarus. Several still survive, and one in its original condition is on display at the Swiss Historical Village, which is open to the public daily May through mid-October.

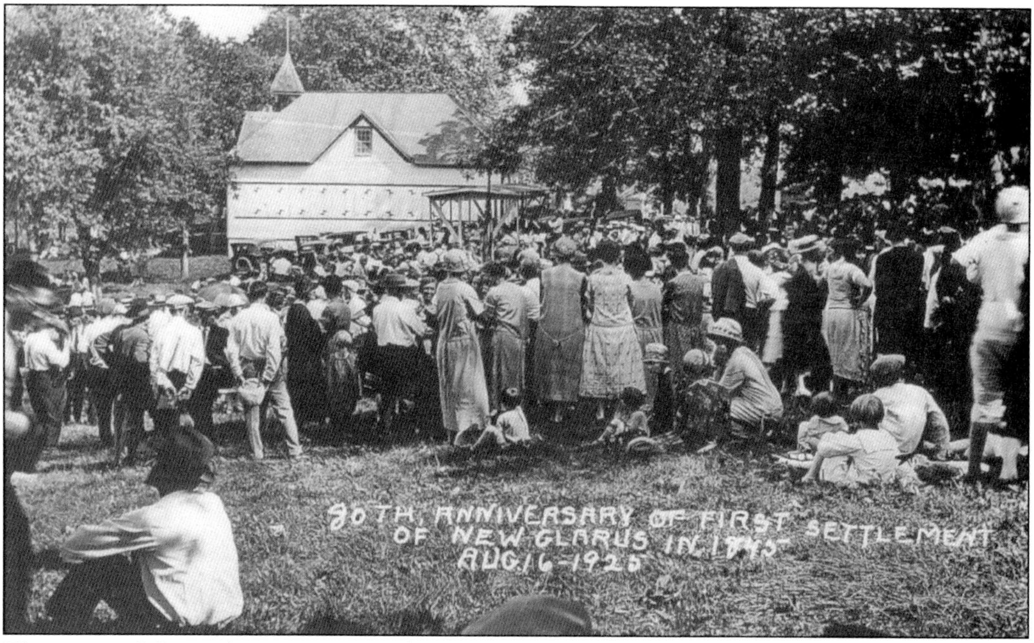

This view of the 80th anniversary of New Glarus is looking south toward the Shooting Park Barn. The doors on the building were opened, and competitive shooters shot out of these doors to targets that were behind the crowd shown here. The Shooting Park is the site of the annual New Glarus Volksfest held on the first Sunday in August. The barn was renovated several years ago and hosts several events each summer.

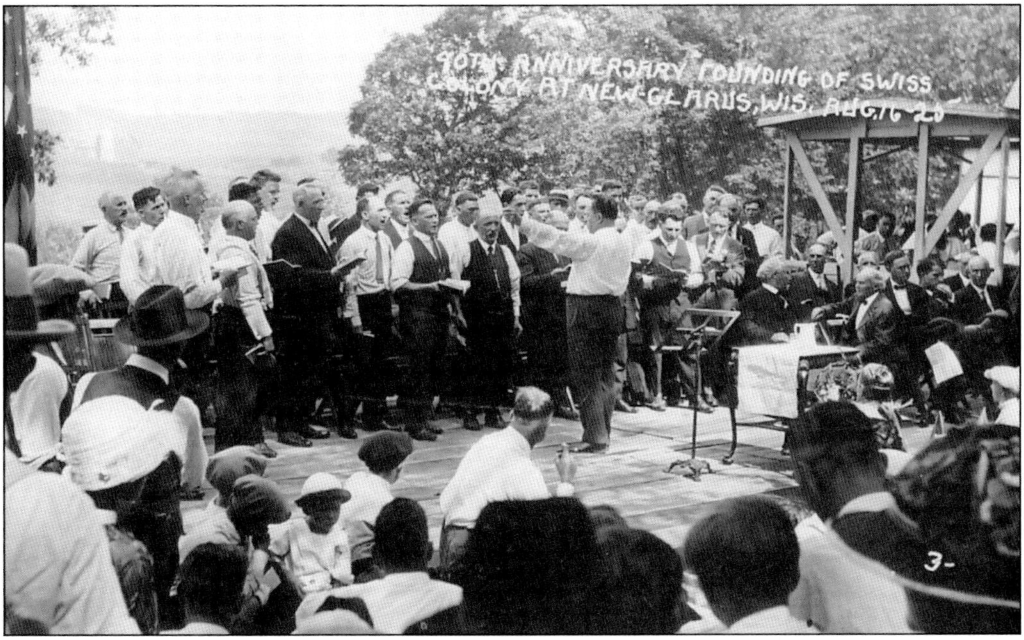

The New Glarus 90th anniversary was also held at the Shooting Park. Shown singing is one of the men's choirs and is probably the New Glarus Maennerchor. The group is still active and serves as the sponsor of the annual New Glarus Volksfest. The man sitting at the table on the left appears to be Sol Levitan, who became Wisconsin state treasurer.

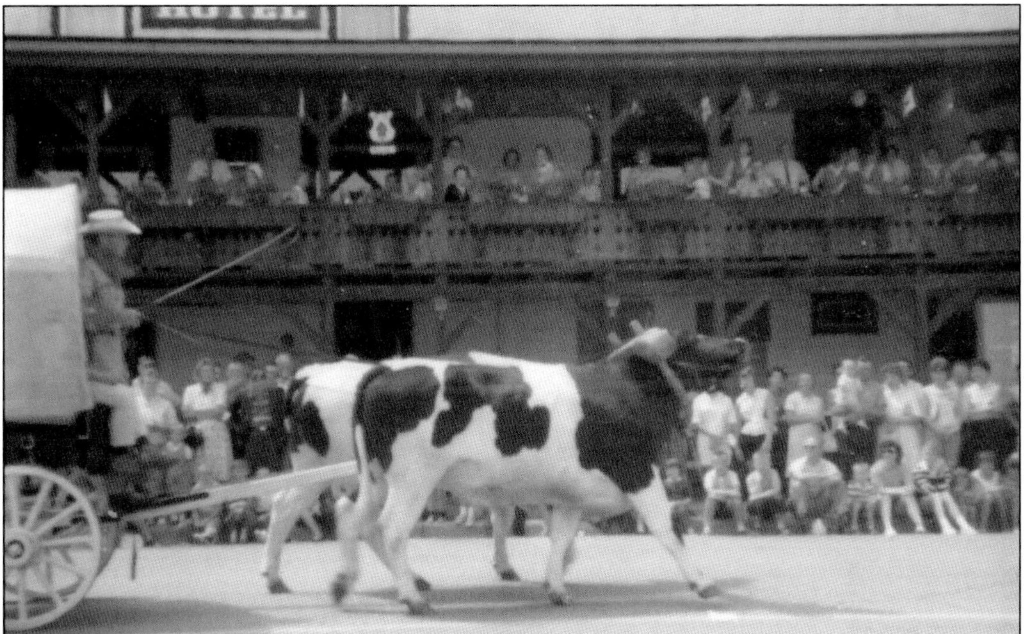

The 120th anniversary of New Glarus took place in 1965, which brought with it many events. This photograph shows a covered wagon being pulled by a pair of specially trained Holstein cows. The *Heidi* drama was performed in New Glarus for the first time, and, because of its success it has become its own festival and will mark its 50th anniversary in June 2015. (Russ Bethke collection.)

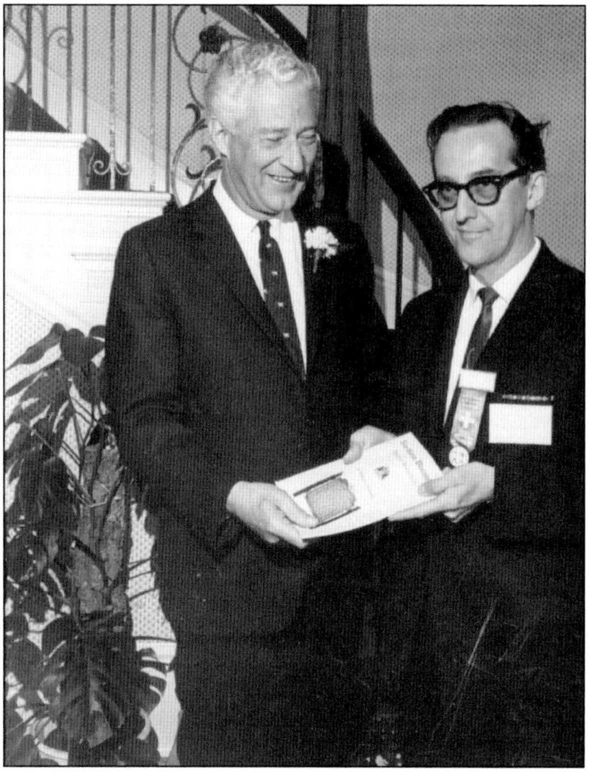

The year 1965 brought New Glarus's 120th anniversary. A multitude of events were held, including a Hall of History in the village hall. Shown here is Gov. Warren Knowles (left) accepting a copy of the book *New Glarus, Wisconsin, Mirror of Switzerland* from 120th anniversary chairman Millard Tschudy.

Wisconsin governor Warren Knowles was present for a number of the activities, as well as the social events, included with New Glarus 120th anniversary in 1965. Governor Knowles is shown here with Olive Leuders and Virginia Tschudy.

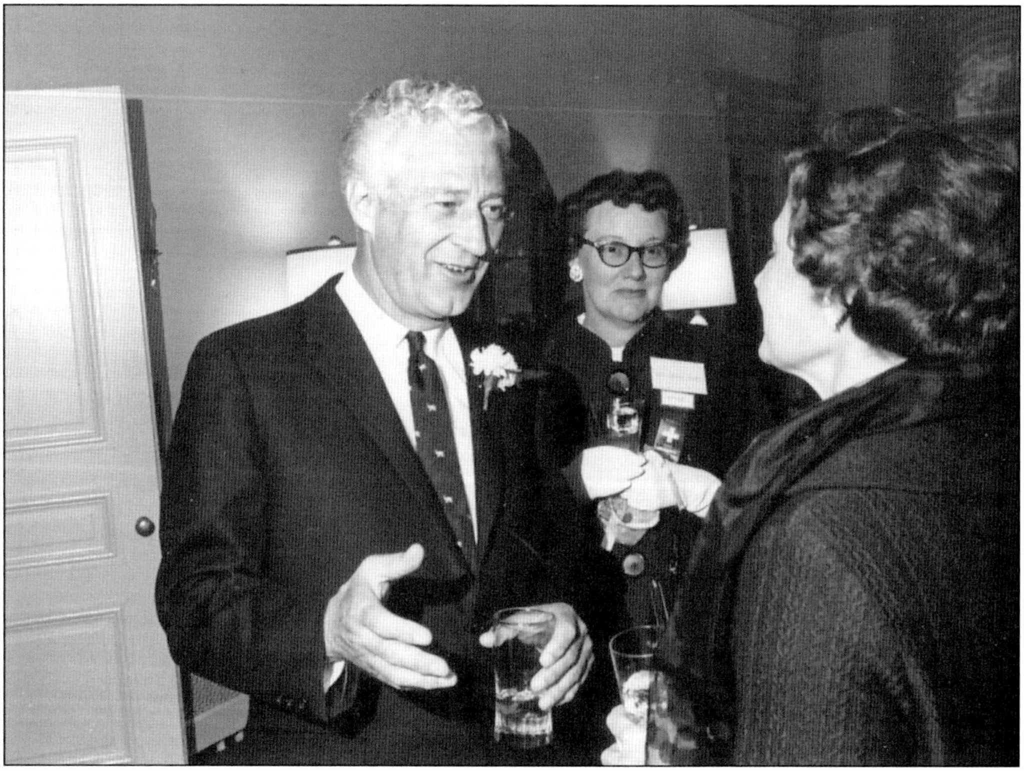

New Glarus's 150th anniversary was celebrated in August 1995. Shown here with the official sesquicentennial cake are Christoph Stuessi, the governor of Glarus, Switzerland, and a diplomat from the Swiss Embassy in Washington, DC. The event played itself out over 13 days of various displays, programs, concerts, and a large parade. (Schiesser collection.)

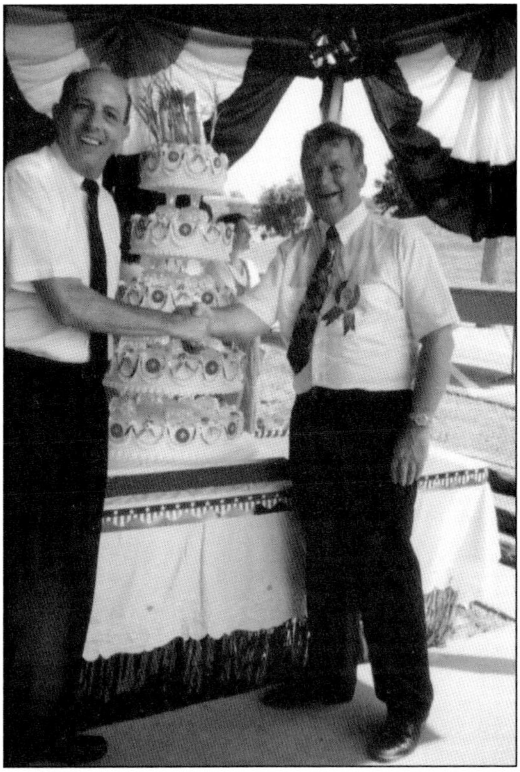

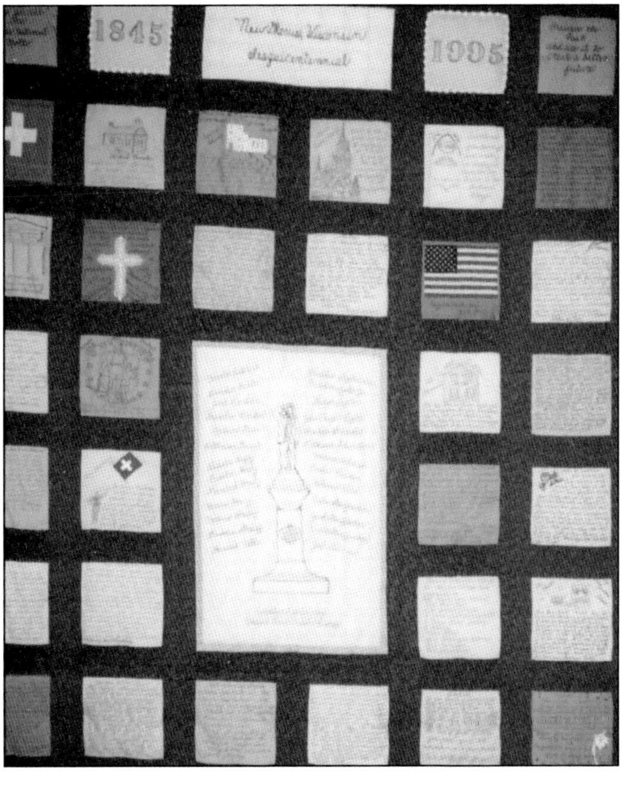

This New Glarus sesquicentennial quilt tells the story of New Glarus in stitches. The large quilt block in the middle depicts the First Settler's Monument and the names of the first families to settle New Glarus in 1845. The Settler's Monument is located on the churchyard in downtown New Glarus. (Schiesser collection.)

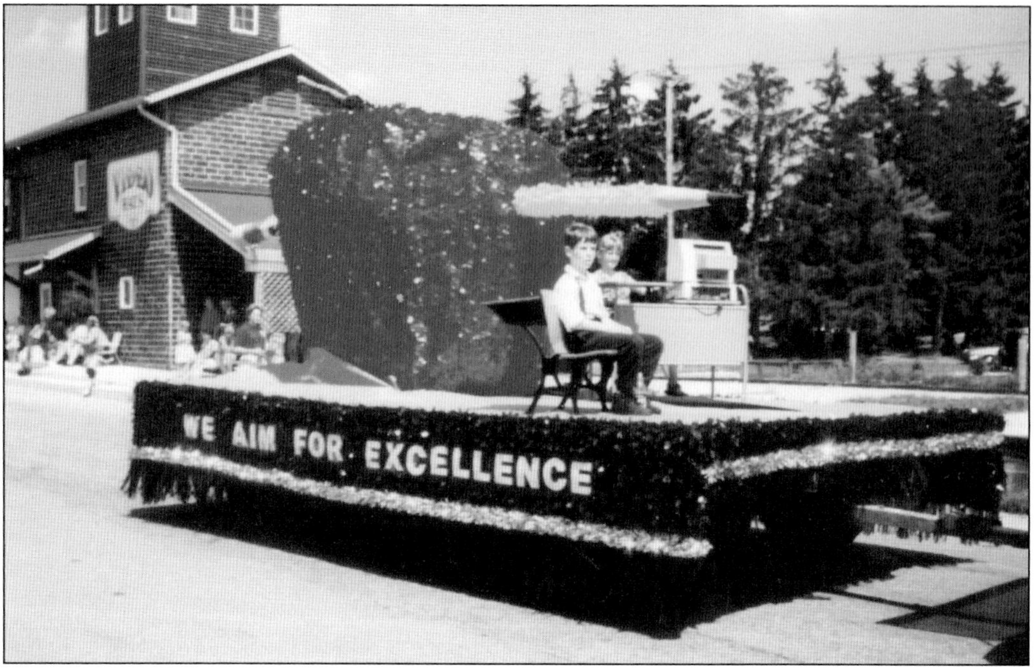

The New Glarus School District float depicts the value of education and a bit of earlier tradition with an apple for the teacher. On the desk is one of those new-fangled things called a computer. By today's standards, the computer shown would now be considered folk art of the computer age. (Schiesser collection.)

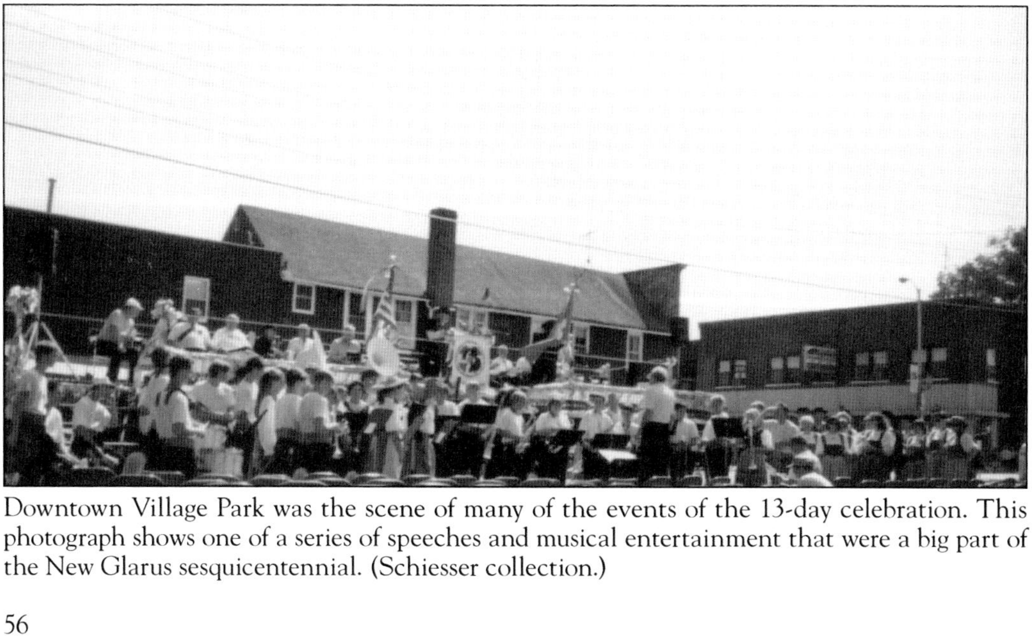
Downtown Village Park was the scene of many of the events of the 13-day celebration. This photograph shows one of a series of speeches and musical entertainment that were a big part of the New Glarus sesquicentennial. (Schiesser collection.)

This float tells the story of the strong ties between New Glarus and Switzerland. These ties have been as solid as the Matterhorn Mountain in Switzerland for the past 170 years. The two women on the float depict Lady Liberty and Switzerland's equal, Helvetia. (Schiesser collection.)

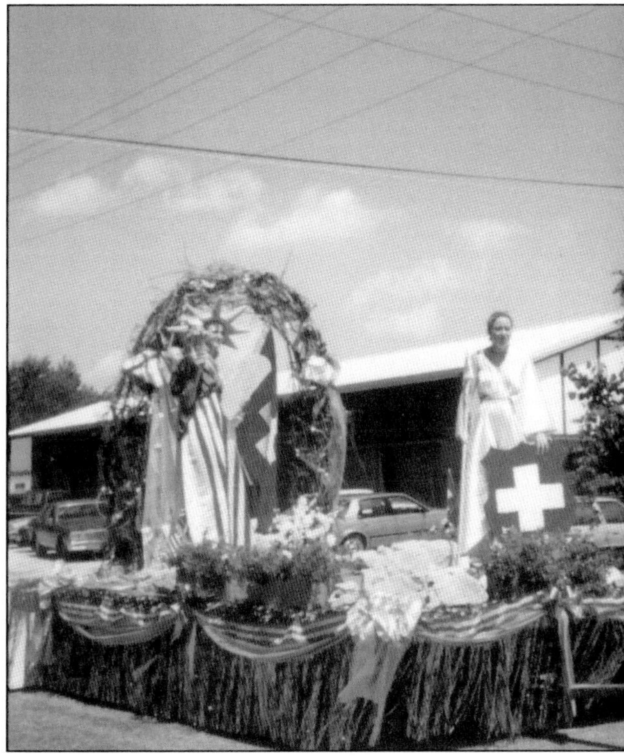

The New Glarus American Legion Post has been very active since shortly after World War I. The post has served in many civic endeavors, all of which have greatly benefited the community. At the present time, the group is working on completion of a New Glarus Veterans Memorial located near the entrance to Veterans Park. (Schiesser collection.)

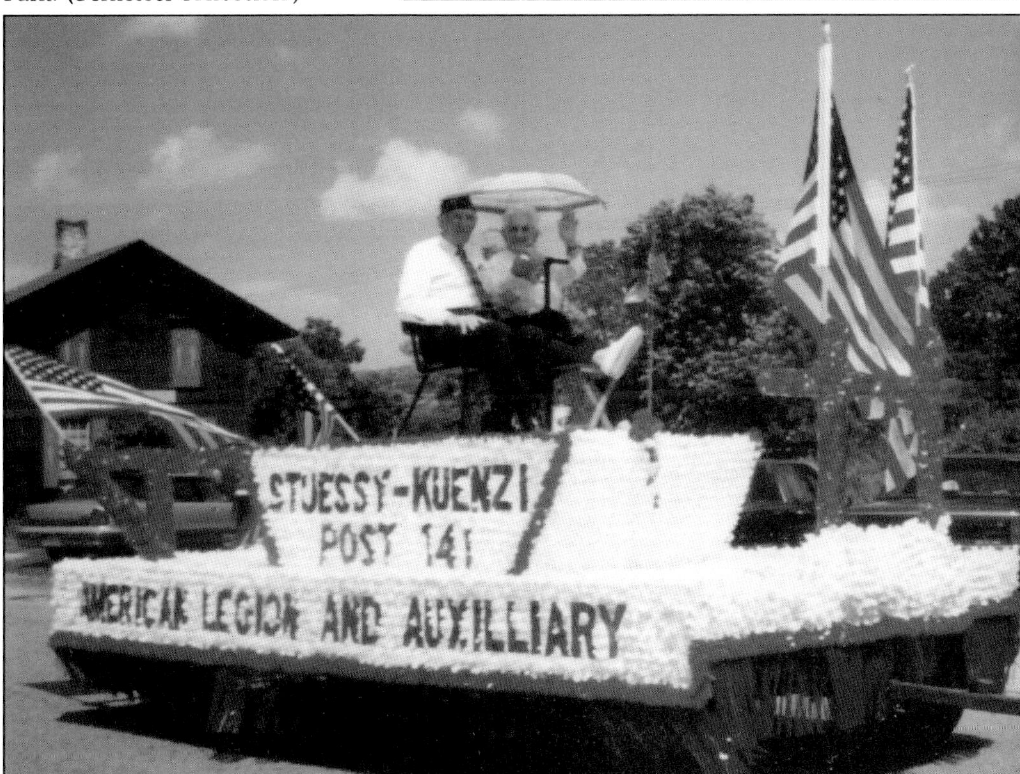

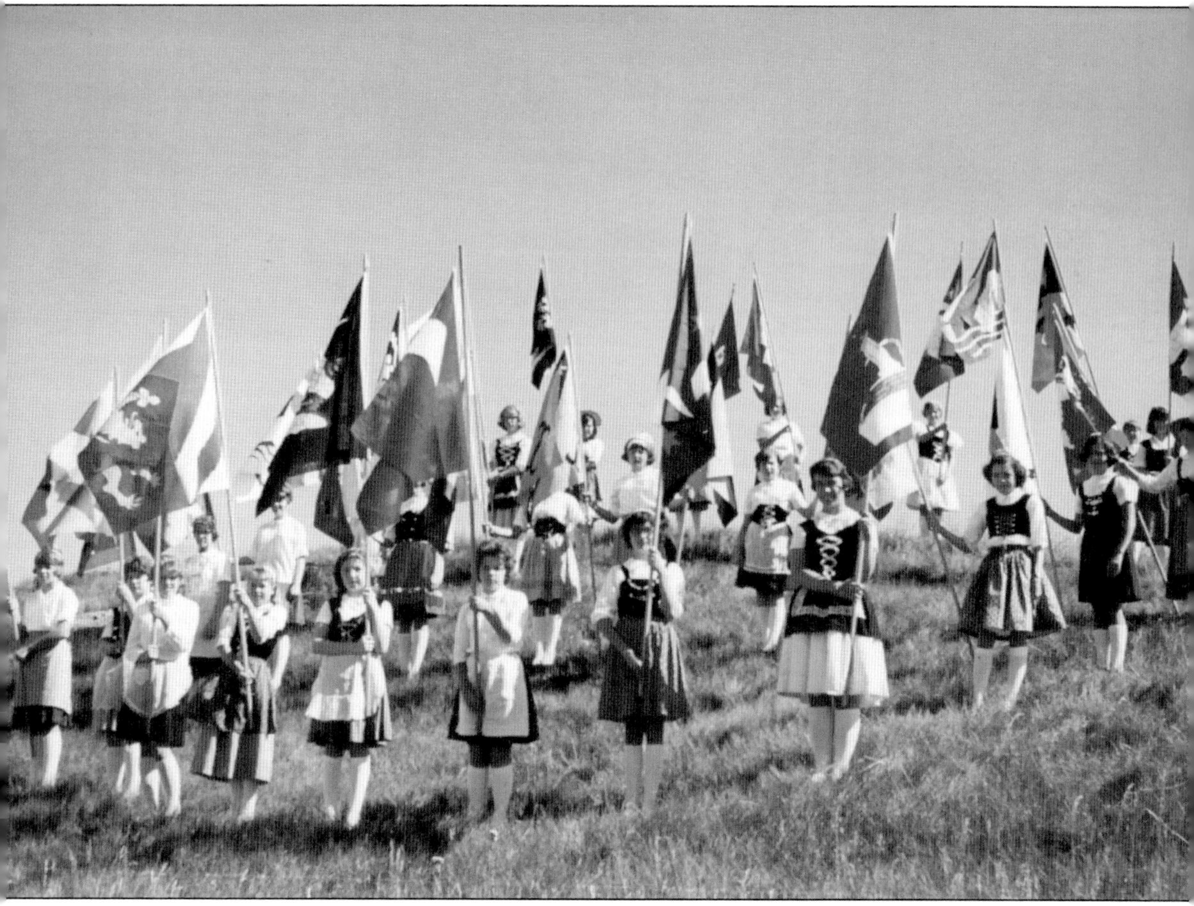

These young girls are showing off the new flags of the villages in the canton of Glarus, Switzerland. The flags were purchased for New Glarus's 120th anniversary in 1965. For many years, they were on display at the Swiss Historical Village in New Glarus.

Five

Annual Celebrations

New Glarus's history is in many ways coupled with the history of Switzerland. Because New Glarus was for so many years a very insular community, those early ties to Switzerland were kept strong through the flavor of the many annual celebrations. While the Swiss in New Glarus readily celebrated American holidays, these events often took on a Swiss theme with the music played, songs sang, and patriotic speeches made. Colorful Swiss costumes and dances added a touch and reminder of their roots in Switzerland.

Winter was a time for concerts at the Wilhelm Tell Hall, as the hall hosted all sorts of events. Over-wintering cheese makers hosted several Swiss wrestling tournaments, the New Glarus Maennerchor would present its annual winter concert, and assorted other groups would perform, helping make the winters pass a bit more quickly. Traveling shows would often make a stop in New Glarus for one or two performances. These events were a time to catch up with neighbors and relatives.

Edwin Barlow, a world traveler who resided in New Glarus, proposed to have the community stage the Wilhelm Tell Pageant he witnessed in Altdorf, Switzerland. With rented costumes, borrowed cattle, horses, and goats, Barlow and a few other local volunteers convinced the townsfolk of the value of this endeavor. Some thought the Tell Pageant would be a failure. In 2012, the Tell Pageant staged its 75th-year performance.

The Swiss Volksfest, the longest-running annual event in New Glarus, celebrating Switzerland's founding, is performed annually on the first Sunday in August at the beautifully wooded Tell's Shooting Park. Each year, the Volksfest features Swiss musical groups, as well as others, including the Monroe Swiss Singers, Madison Maennerchor, New Glarus Maennerchor, New Glarus Yodel Club, Kinderchor, Swiss Flag Throwing, and unexpected musical groups from Switzerland.

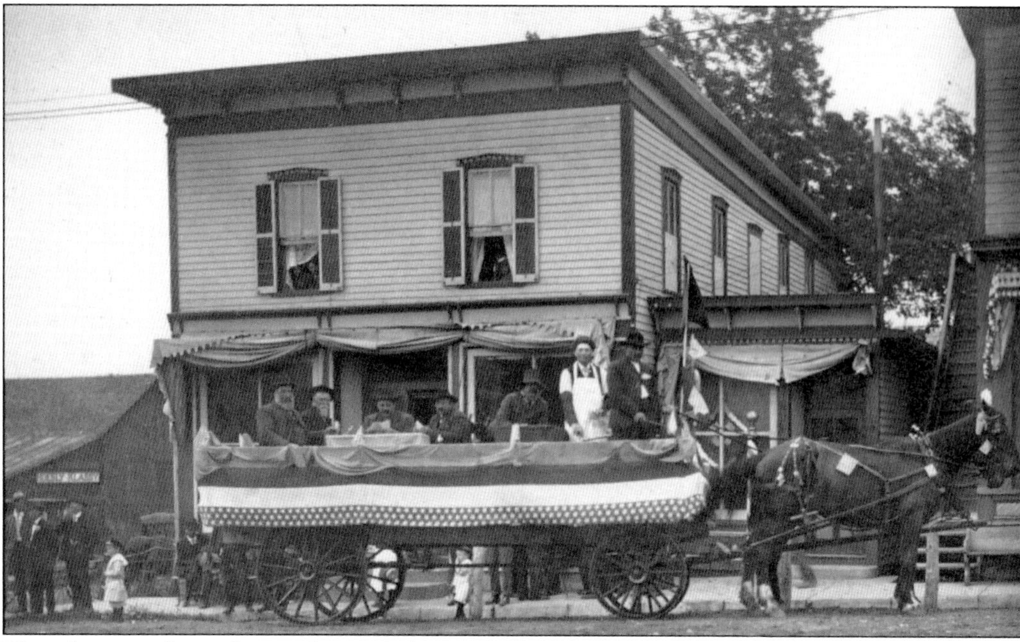

This photograph is taken in front of what is now Primrose Winery located at the corner of Fifth Avenue and First Street. The event being celebrated appears to be a Fourth of July parade. Over the years, this building served as restaurants that were operated by the Glaeden, Schuetz, Hoffman, and Arn families and Fred and Margaret Ryser.

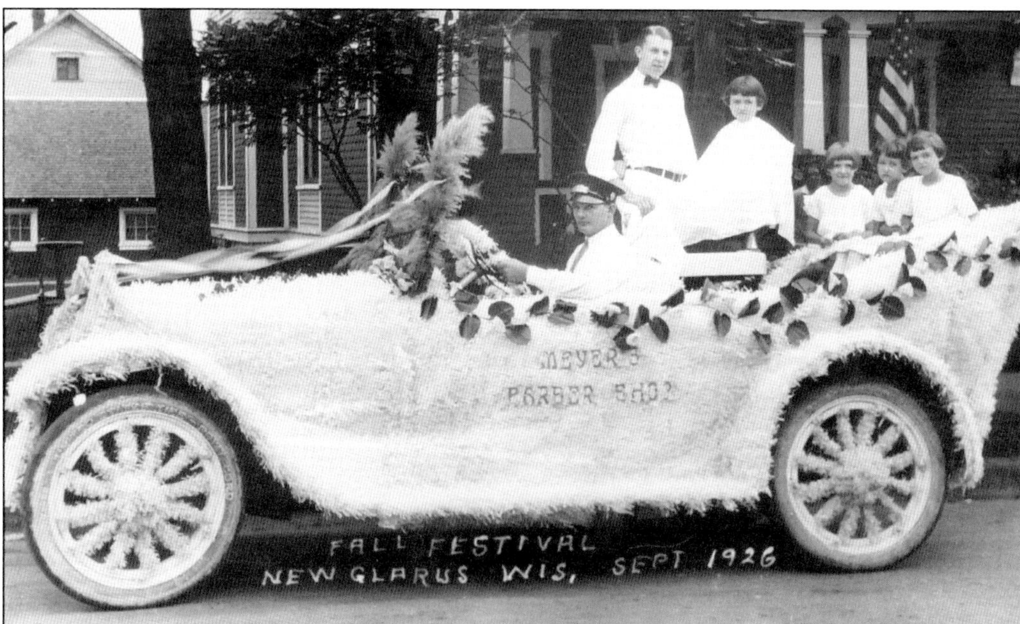

The New Glarus Fall Festival was held for a couple of years in the mid-1920s during the middle of the week instead of on the weekend, as is now the practice. The Meyers Barber Shop parade entry is shown in front of 200 Second Street.

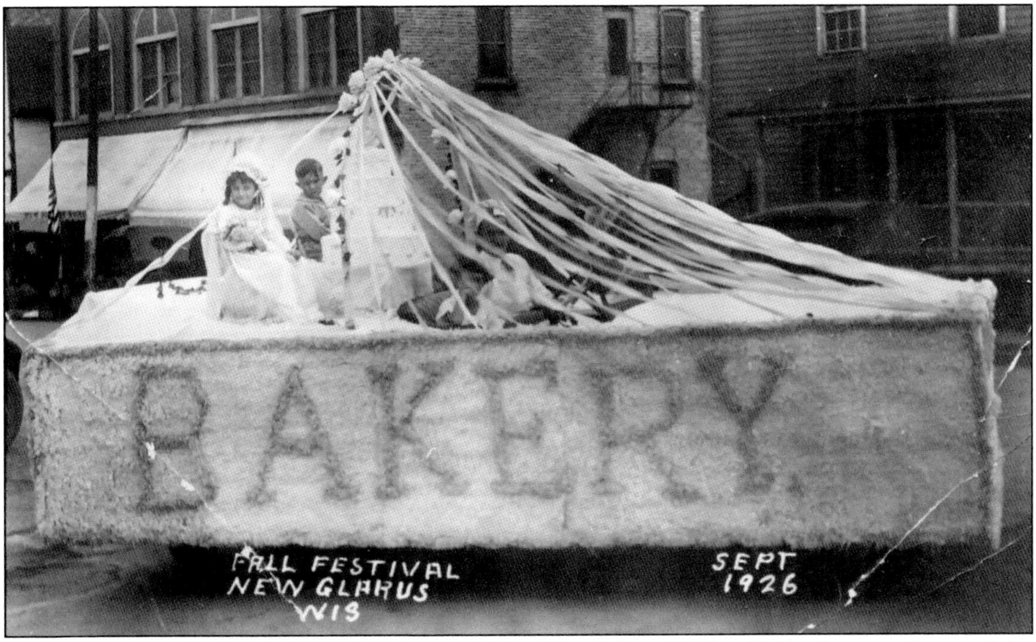

The New Glarus Bakery Fall Festival float from September 1926 is shown here in front of the New Glarus Bakery and the Farmer's Meat Market at 534 First Street. The bakery was located in the left side of the building in the background.

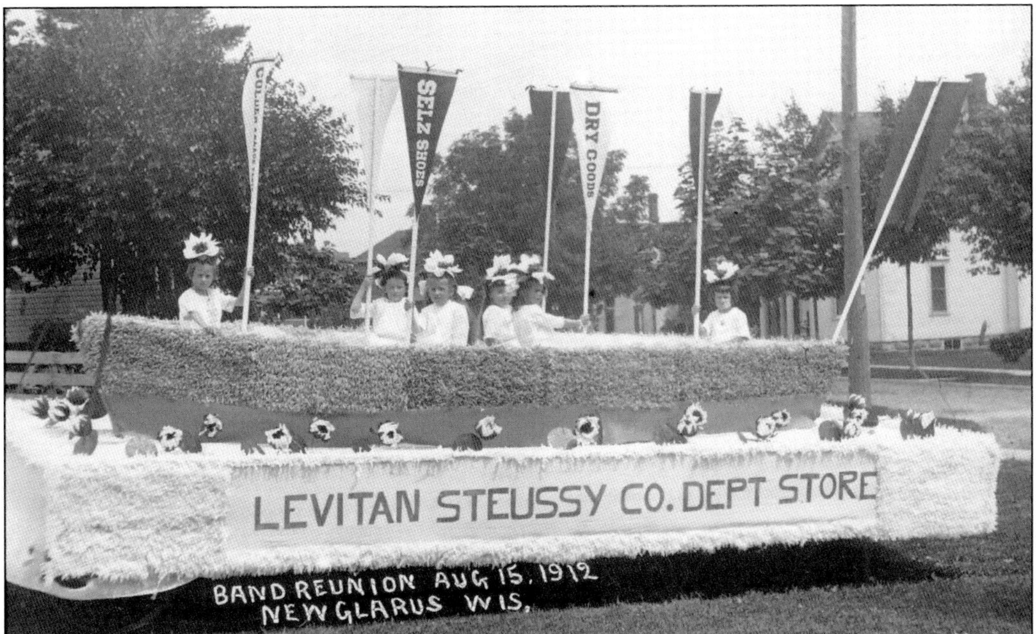

This photograph of the Levitan and Steussy store float was taken on August 15, 1912, at the corner of Eleventh Avenue and Second Street. Music and local bands were a large part of the social-cultural fabric of New Glarus, and any chance to have a band reunion was embraced.

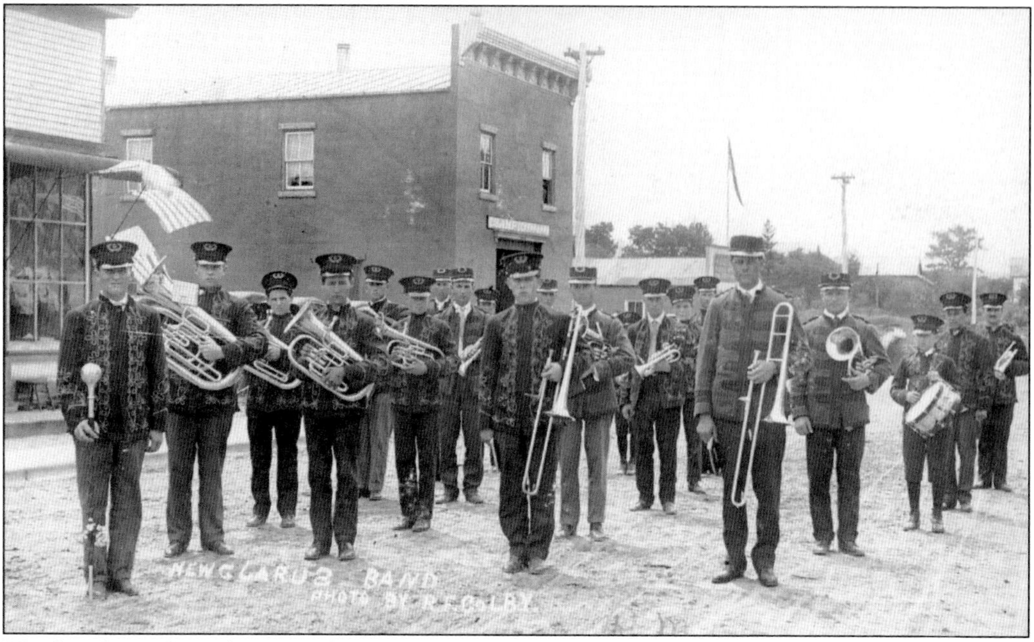

The band may have been small in number, but with all the brass instruments shown, the New Glarus Community Band no doubt was heard from far away as they approached downtown. The musician on the far right (background) appears to be J.J. Figy.

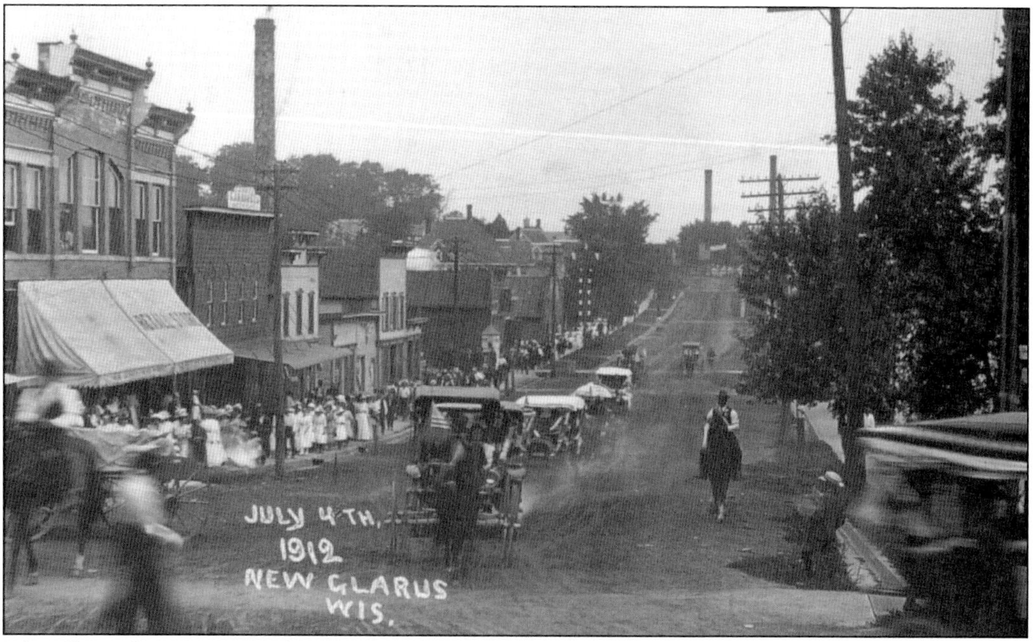

Like all good Americans, the Swiss of New Glarus celebrated the Fourth of July each year with a parade through Main Street. Following the parade, a number of other activities filled the day. In her reflections on growing up in (Irish) Lynn Valley, southeast of New Glarus, Elisabeth Moore Wallace reflected, "We went to New Glarus for the July Fourth celebration. We didn't understand Swiss, but we enjoyed our time in New Glarus."

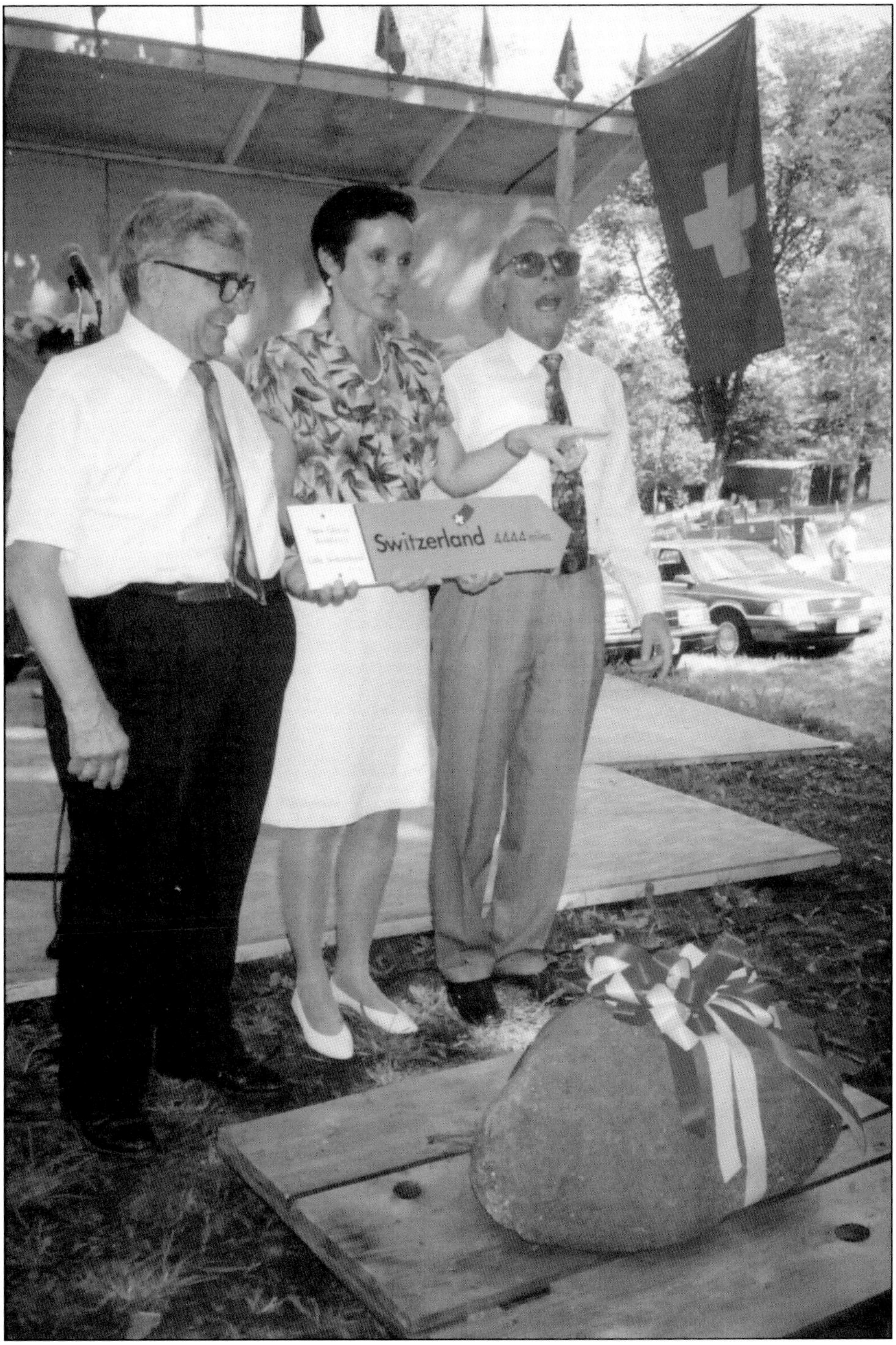

In 1991, Switzerland celebrated its 700th anniversary. The Swiss government requested that all cities and towns around the world that had roots in Switzerland pick out a local rock to be shipped by Swissair to Berne, Switzerland, for a sculpture in front of the parliament building. Shown here from left to right are Hubert Elmer, New Glarus village president; Monica Knoetfel, Midwest director for the Swiss National Tourism Office; and Frederich Vogel, Swiss consul general.

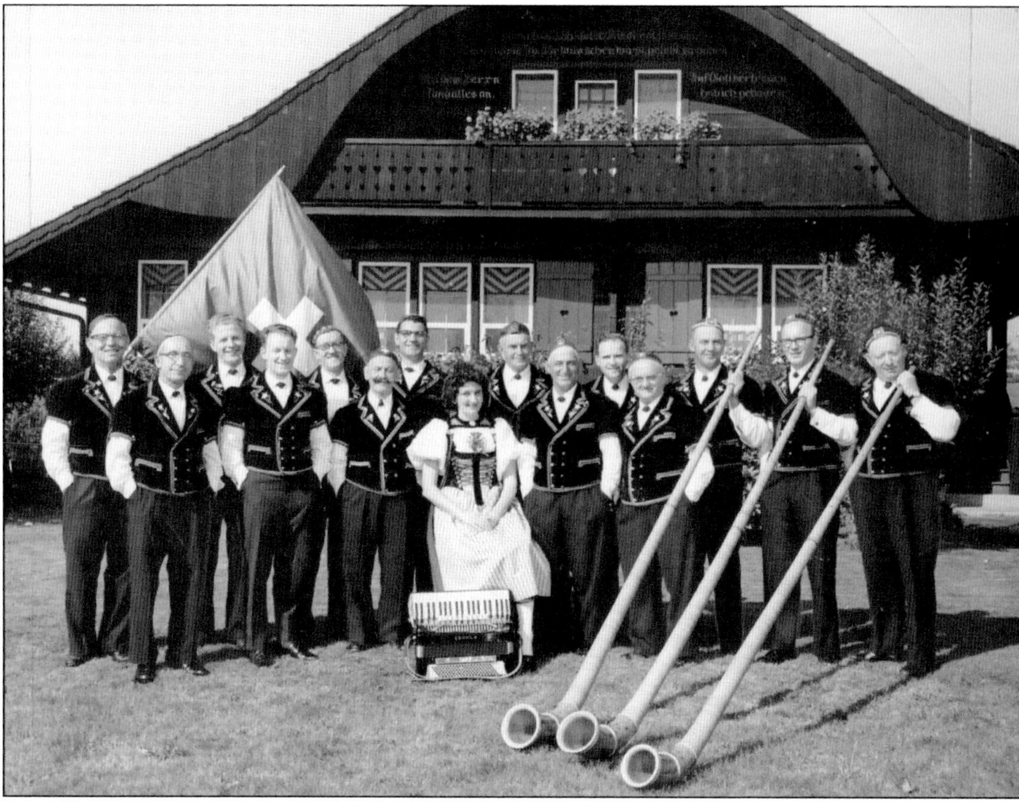

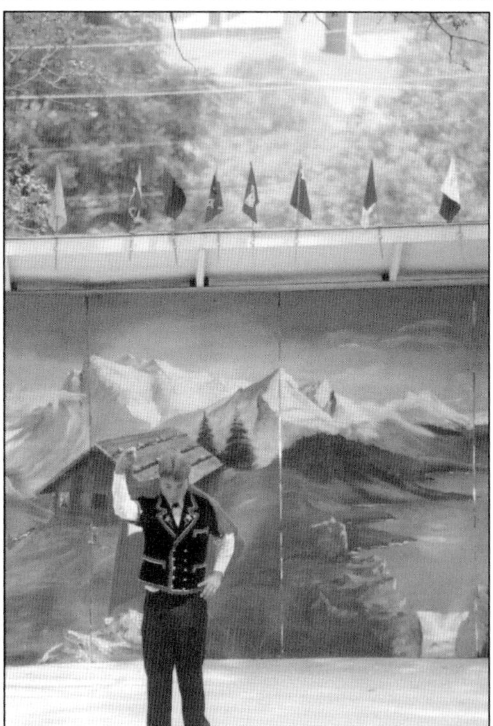

Various Swiss singing groups entertained at the annual Volksfest. This August 29, 1965, photograph of the New Glarus Yodeler Club posing for a formal picture in front of Ernest Thiestein's Chalet was used in a *Chicago Sun-Times* article about the annual Wilhelm Tell Pageant. Shown with the Yodelers is their accordion player and yodeler Betty Vetterli.

Volksfest offers young Swiss entertainers a chance to perform before a large audience. Michael Arn was in late grade school when this photograph was taken. Michael followed in his father Richard Arn's footsteps. Richard still performs flag throwing each year at a number of area Swiss events.

Theodore Wyrsch, age 24 at the time of this photograph and a native of Switzerland, was visiting friends in New Glarus in 1959. Wyrsch was thrown out of the Swiss Union of Flag Throwers for one year for throwing more than one flag at a time and also for wearing a red uniform instead of the approved blue uniform.

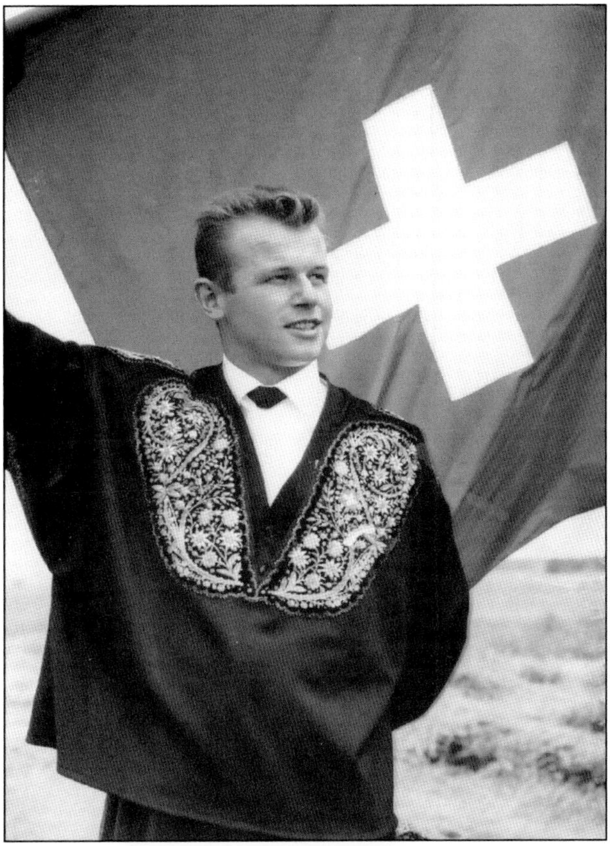

Ernie and Teresa Jaggi, both natives of Switzerland, immigrated to the United States in the 1950s. Ernie worked for many years as a cheese maker in an area cheese factory. He and Teresa have become celebrities across the country as well as having appeared on several national television programs. Ernie and Teresa are renowned yodelers.

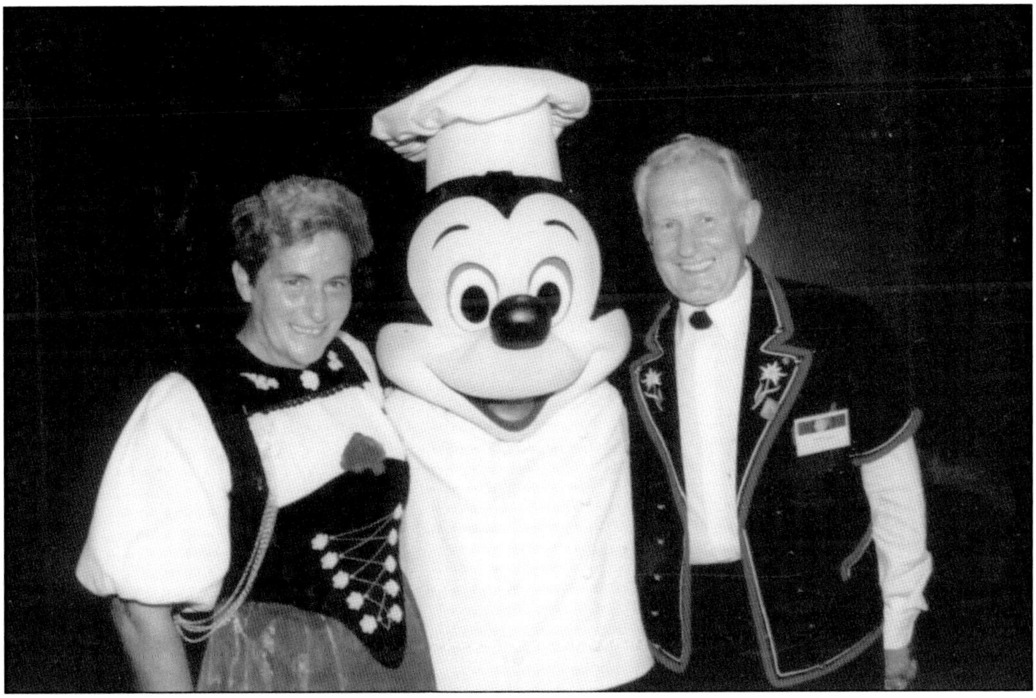

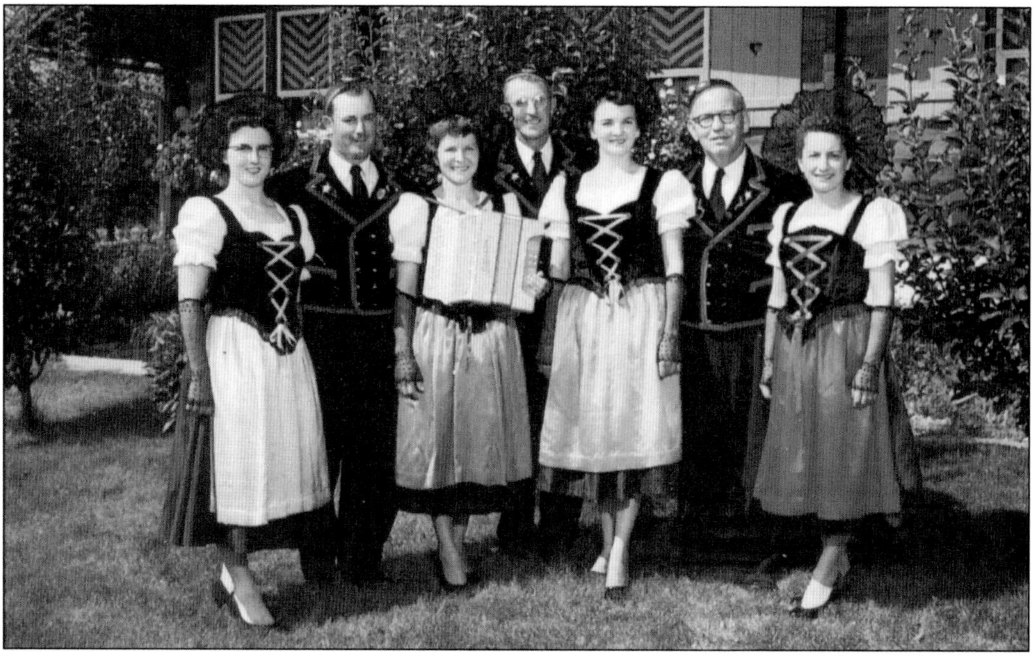

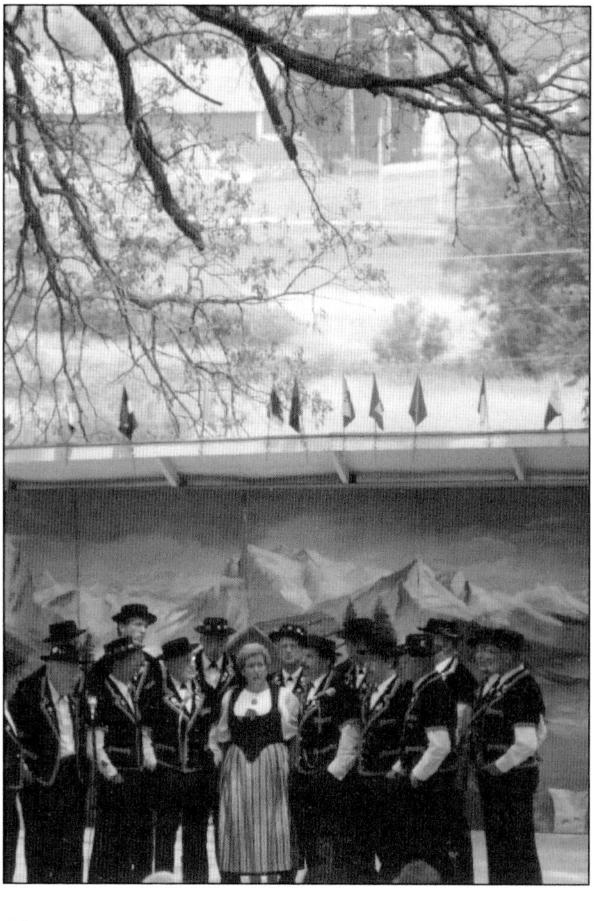

The Edelweiss Stars performed at numerous Swiss and folk music events across the United States. They performed in a several-part Disney series, *Adventures in Dairyland*, filmed at nearby Verona, Wisconsin. From left to right are Marion Streiff, Clayton Streiff, Dorthea Ingwell, Red Zentner, Katie Ingwell, Paul Grossenbacher, and Margaret Wild. Clayton and Red also played parts in the Disney series.

Each year, on the first Sunday in August, the Shooting Park comes alive with the beautiful sounds of Swiss folk music from a number of various musical groups from the New Glarus and Monroe area celebrating Volksfest, the Swiss Independence Day, which is August 1. The New Glarus Yodel Club performs here each year. In the background is the Dean and Doris Streiff farm. Several members of the Streiff family are performers at Volksfest.

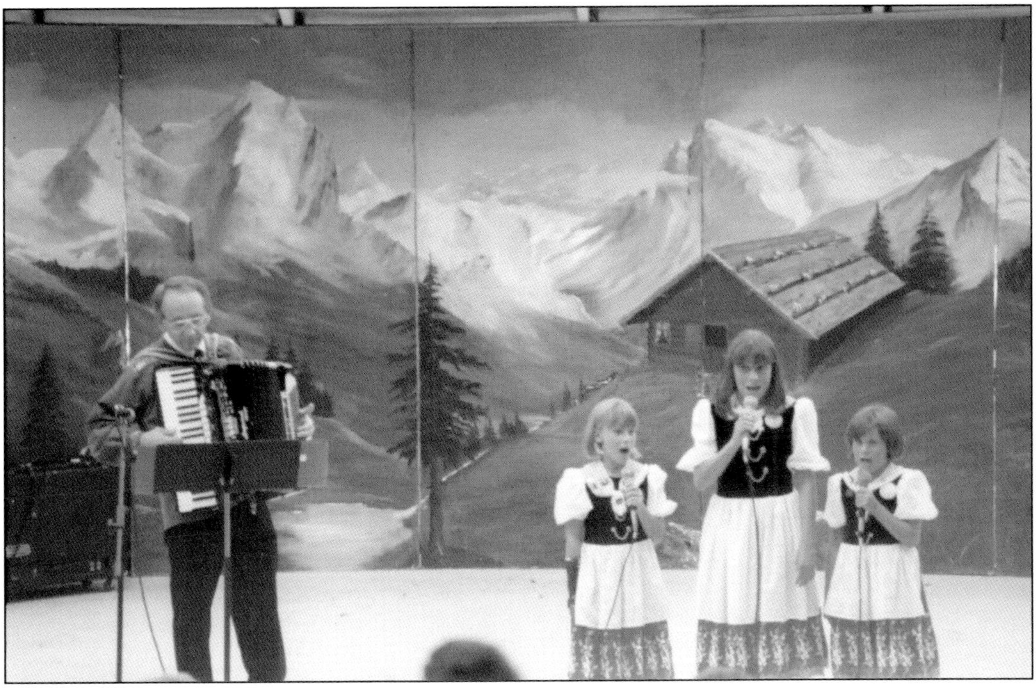

This Volksfest photograph dates to the early 1990s when the Moser Sisters (from left to right, Danielle, Kristina, and Brianna) of Monroe were regular performers at the celebration. Accompanying them on the accordion is Mike Campbell, also of Monroe.

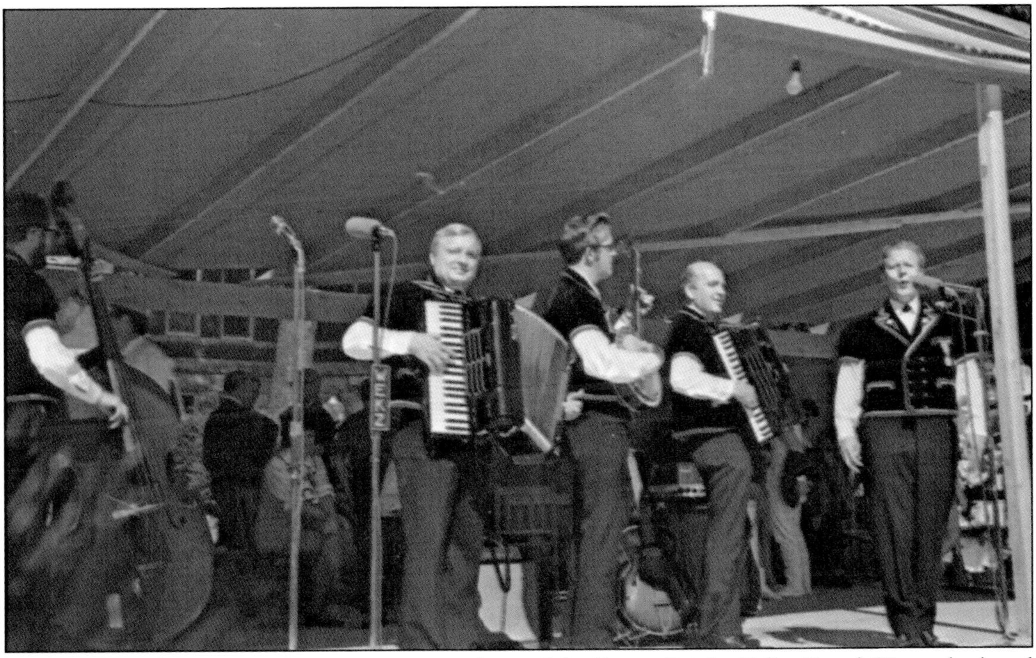

Among the other past performers were members of the Roger Bright Polka Band. Here, the band is shown playing at Cheese Days in Monroe, an event celebrated in mid-September on even-numbered years. From left to right are Karl Gmur, Bobby Lorenz, Roger Pulver, Roger Bright, and Robbi Schneider.

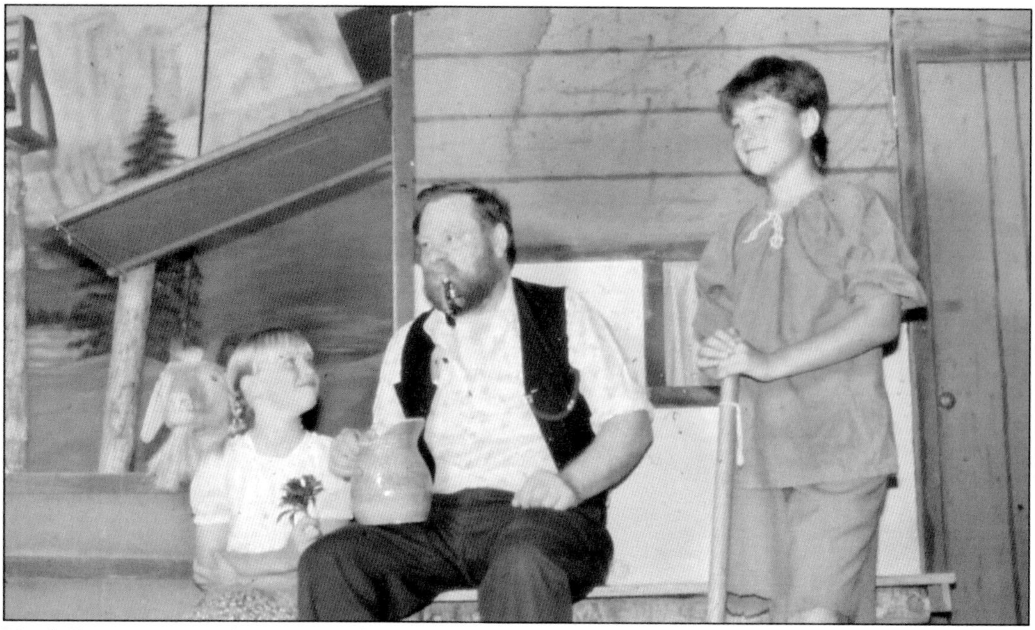

Heidi Fest was started as a part of New Glarus's 120th anniversary in 1965. It was thought that the event needed something special for children to partake in. Because of the success of the *Heidi* performance, the following year Heidi Fest was formed as an independent group. Shown here are Heidi, Heidi's gruff mountain grandfather (played by Willy Ruef), and Peter the playful mountain boy.

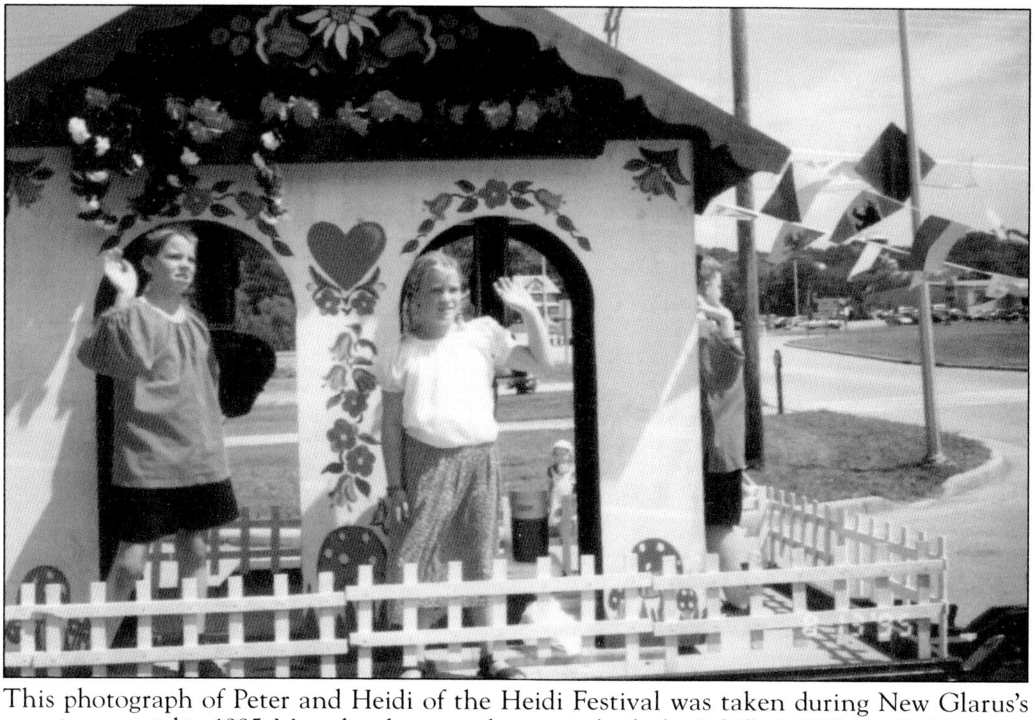

This photograph of Peter and Heidi of the Heidi Festival was taken during New Glarus's sesquicentennial in 1995. Many local actors take part in both the Schiller's Wilhelm Tell Pageant and the *Heidi* drama. (Schiesser collection.)

The year 1988 saw Dave Johnson play the part of Mr. Sesemann, Kari Marean playing the part of Clara, and Barbara Marty playing the part of Mrs. Sesemann. (Ruef family collection.)

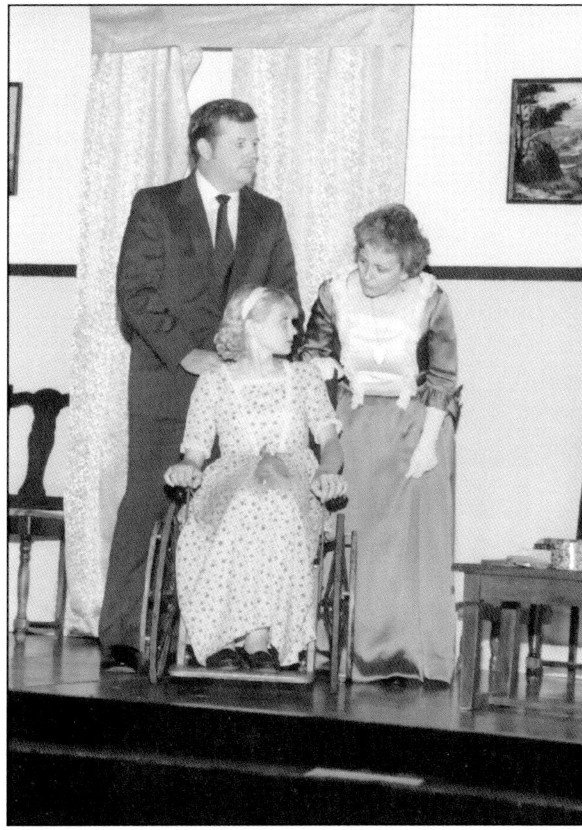

The *Heidi* cast in 1977 included, from left to right, Nancy Reuter as Dete, Mary Ott as Heidi, Ernest Lufi as the minister, Marie Vetterli as Brigetta, Frieda Mauer as the blind grandmother, Kevin Lueschow as Peter, and Willi Ruef as Grandfather. In 2014, Marie Vetterli played the role of Brigetta for her 50th year. (Ruef family collection.)

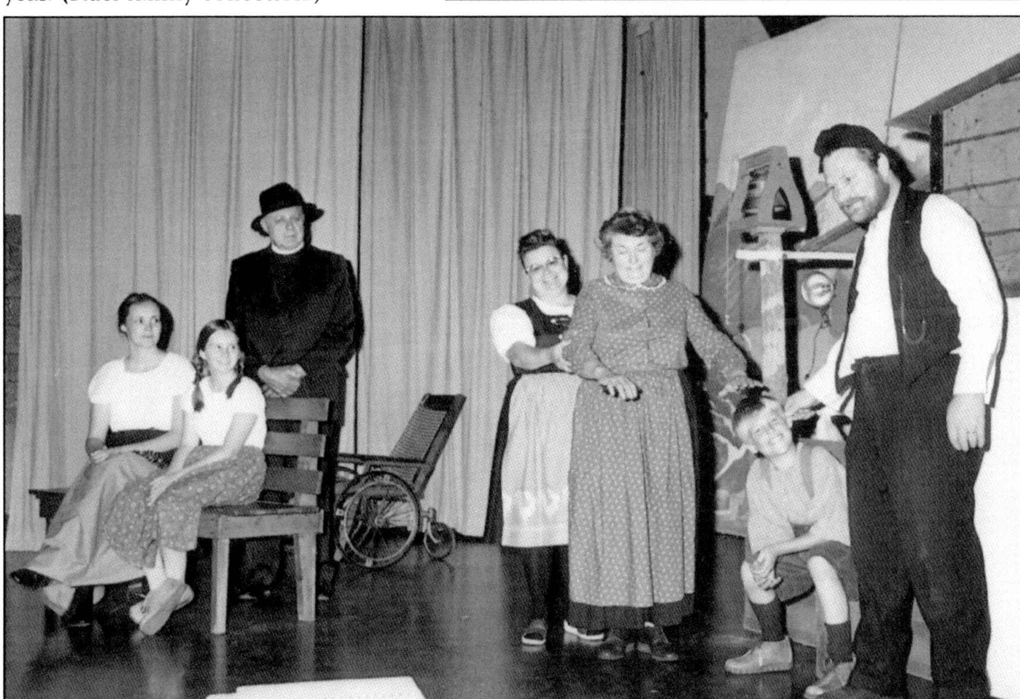

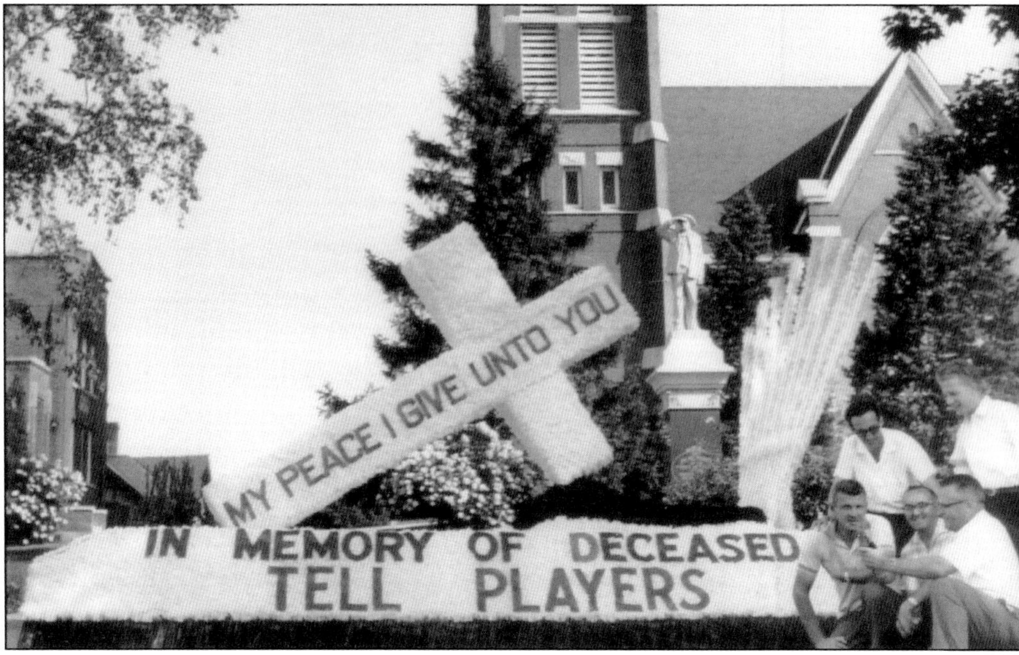

In 1957, to commemorate the 20th anniversary of the Wilhelm Tell Pageant, many special activities were planned, including a large parade. This beautifully done float paid homage to deceased Wilhelm Tell Pageant players. One of the highlights of the weekend was a Queen for a Day winner taking part in the New Glarus festivities. Shown here are, from left to right, Waldo Freitag, Millard Tschudy, Gerald Disch (WIBA Radio reporter), and Robbi Schneider.

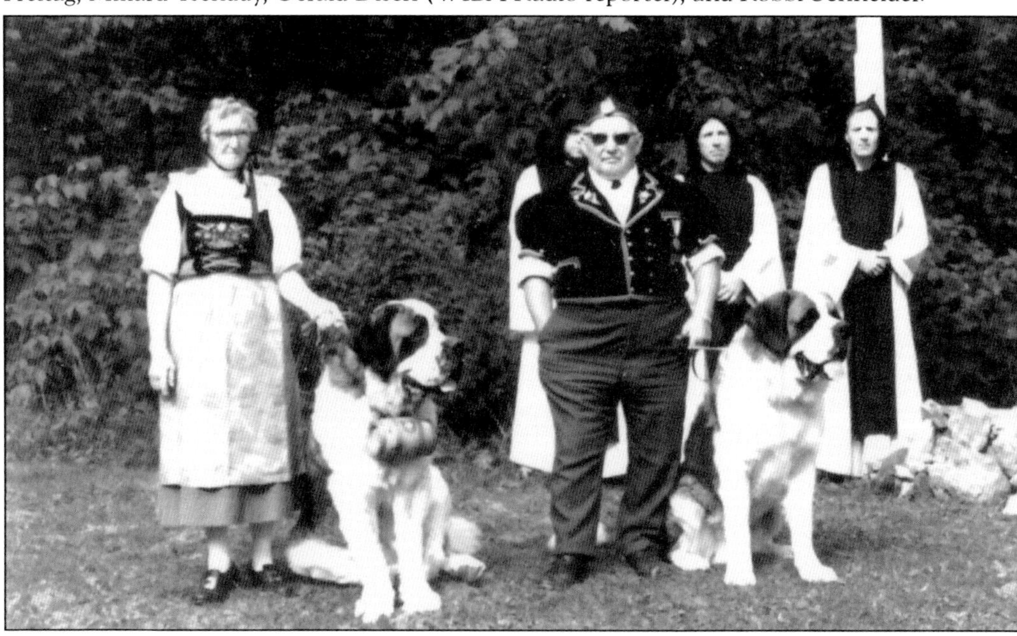

Mr. and Mrs. Shorty Meier of Monroe, Wisconsin, were always a big hit with their two St. Bernards. The Meiers brought the St. Bernards to all three performances of the Wilhelm Tell Pageant each year. Their dogs and the play's monks are shown here in the background. (New Glarus Historical Society.)

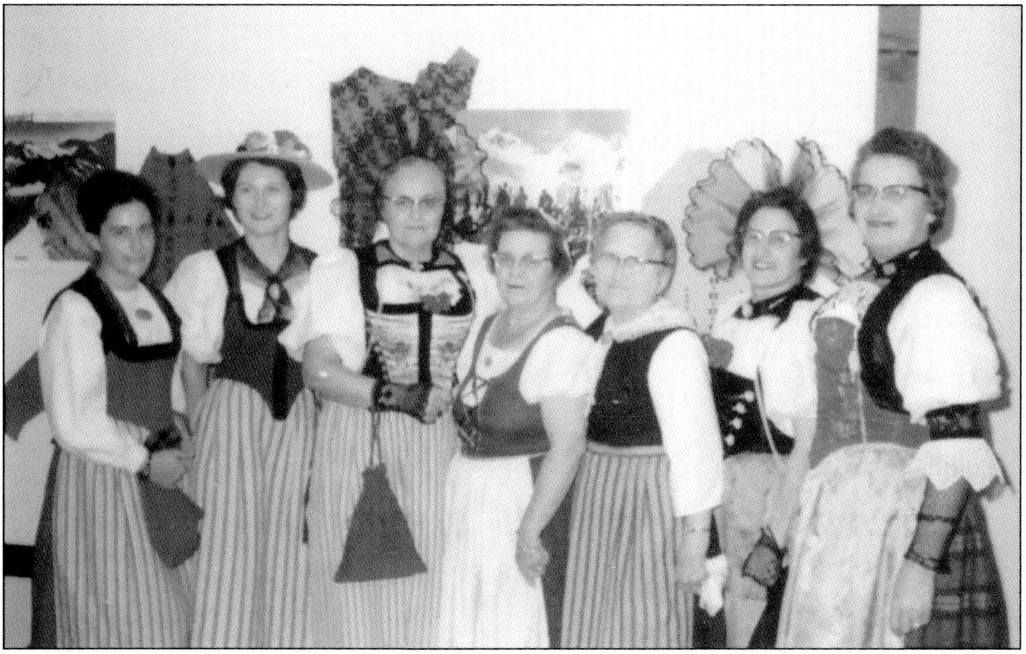

A big part of the success of the annual Tell Pageant was the colorful promotions used to draw thousands of people to the New Glarus area each Labor Day weekend. Shown here in the costumes of the various Swiss cantons are, from left to right, Teresa Jaggi, Pauline Boss, Elmira Grossenbacher, Dora Ott, Ella Schiesser, Ellen Weiland, and Elda Schiesser. (Schiesser collection.)

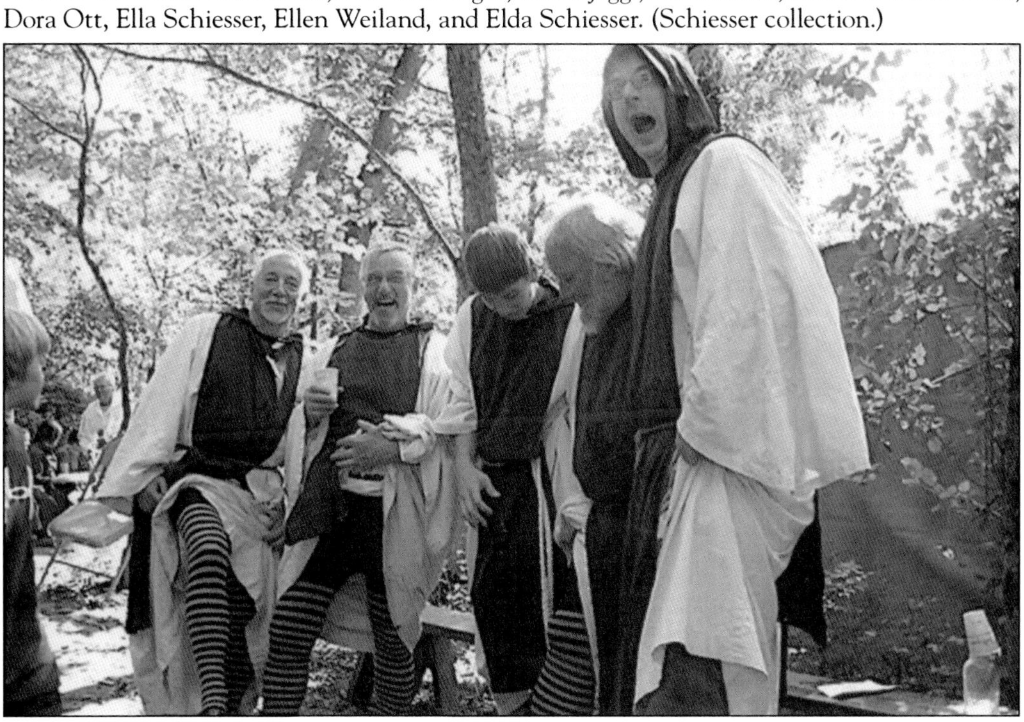

This group of Wilhelm Tell Pageant monks is getting into a bit of monkey business as they show off a bit of leg before going on stage in a few minutes. The two monks on the left are Peter Herdig (far left) and Heinz Mattmann. (Wilhelm Tell Guild.)

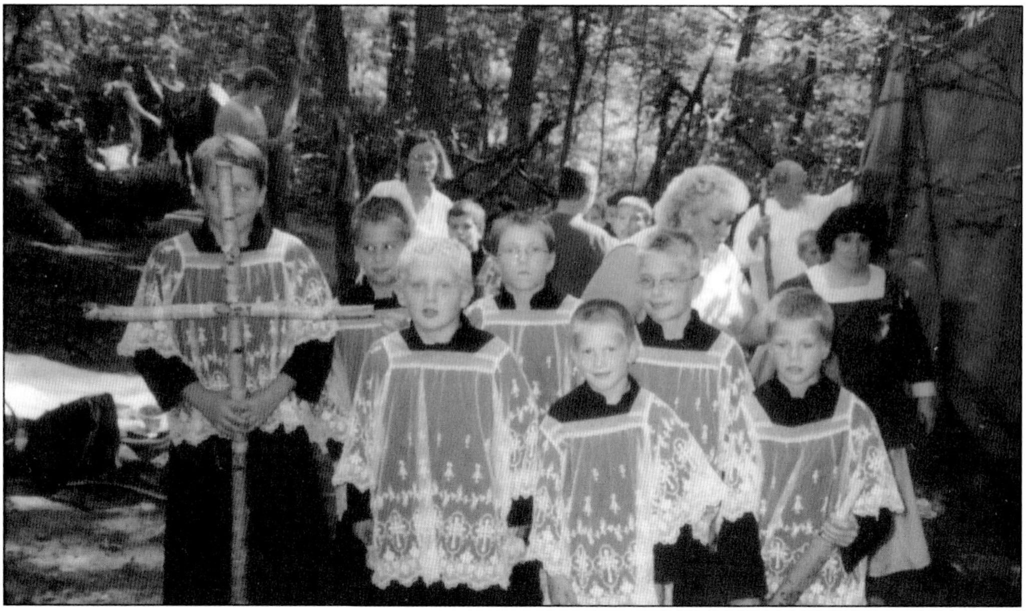

This behind-the-scenes photograph shows the choir boys preparing for their entrance on stage to lead the funeral procession of Baron von Attinghausen, who has just passed away. Many young boys in New Glarus begin their Wilhelm Tell Pageant acting career as goat boys, graduating to the role of choirboys. (Wilhelm Tell Guild.)

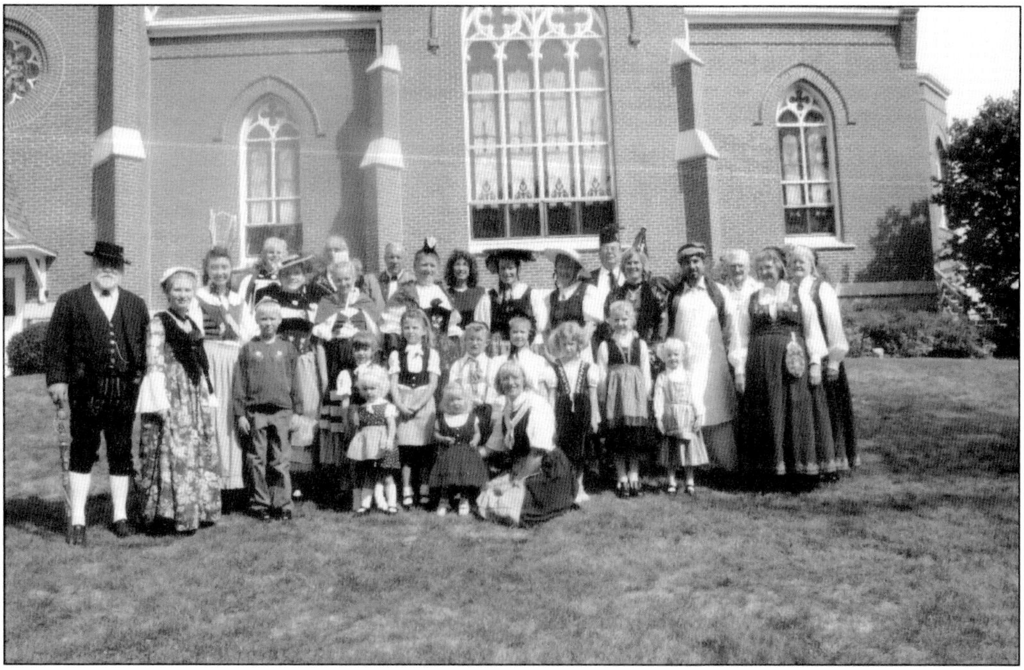

Each year, an additional event held in conjunction with Labor Day weekend Wilhelm Tell Pageant, an ethnic fashion show, is presented in downtown New Glarus. This September 2005 photograph shows models displaying their ethnic costumes. The models, standing on the front yard of the Swiss United Church of Christ, are wearing their German, Swiss, and Norwegian costumes. (Wilhelm Tell Guild.)

Six

Military History

New Glarus has a long and proud military history, dating back to the Civil War, which drew approximately 120 men from New Glarus into the Union Army. Some of these men had arrived just months earlier in New Glarus from Switzerland before they were inducted into the army. Many could not speak a word of English, but they understood their obligation as Americans.

These veterans served in numerous regiments. The Wisconsin 9th German Regiment was home to many New Glarus soldiers. A number of them ended up in the Wisconsin Iron Brigade, the toughest regiment in the Union Army. Some marched across Georgia with General Sherman and later in the Grand Review, barefoot and in tattered uniforms, just as they had marched through Georgia. Several men stood at attention saluting as a broken man, General Lee, quietly rode away from his surrender at Appomattox Courthouse.

World War I saw approximately 75 area men go off to war in Europe to what was to be "the war to end all wars." Some years after this war, these same men gathered at the New Glarus Woods State Park on a beautiful Memorial Day weekend to dedicate a marker commemorating an earlier group of veterans, Col. Henry Dodge's militia, who passed through here during the Black Hawk War of 1832.

By the time World War II had come to an end, well over 200 New Glarus men and women wore the uniforms of the US military. They served in every battle in every theater of the war. New Glarus has the distinction of having sent to off to war five men who would rise to the rank of colonel: Gilbert Strickler, Ray Kundert, Richard Streiff, Harold Zweifel, and Kenneth Fjelstad. Another local man, Walter Schindler, rose to the rank of Navy admiral. World War II saw three men become POWs: Robert Gmur, George Hartman, and Walt Wenger. Each man made it home alive.

The Korean and Vietnam Wars both drew significant numbers of residents, who once again served their country. In these two wars, all came home alive; however, Agent Orange claimed the life of Steve Alderman a number of years after his return from Vietnam.

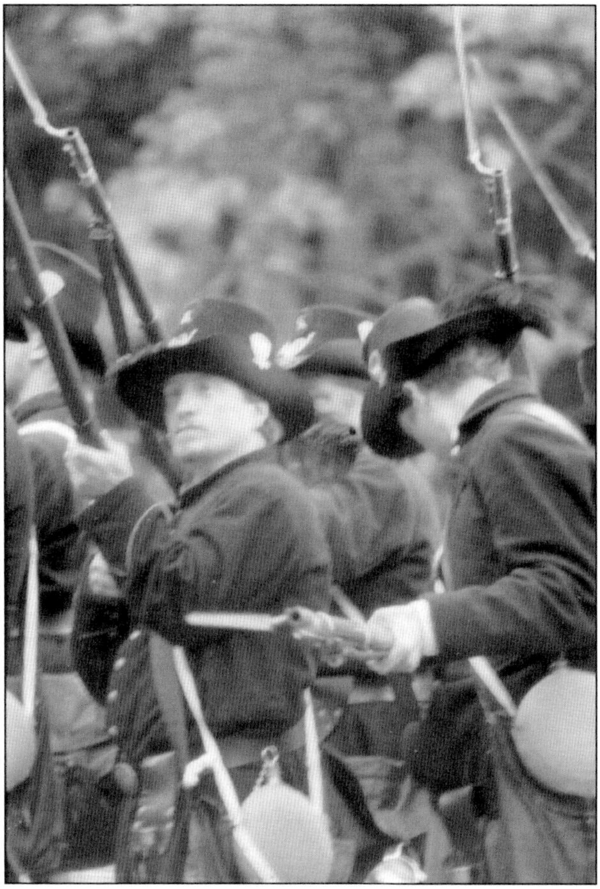

Fridolin Streiff arrived in New Glarus in April 1861. By early October, he enlisted in the Union Army, serving in the famed Iron Brigade. Streiff was given the nickname "The Iron Dutchman" for his bravery in battle. Shown here is Streiff's great-great-grandson Peter Ott portraying Fridolin Streiff in the 1995 New Glarus Sesquicentennial Civil War Encampment.

Fridolin Streiff is shown on the left in this photograph many years after the Civil War. Streiff and John Ulrich Kundert, on the right, were given the honor of lighting off the Parrott deck gun for one of New Glarus's celebrations. It appears these two Civil War veterans put a bit too much powder in the barrel.

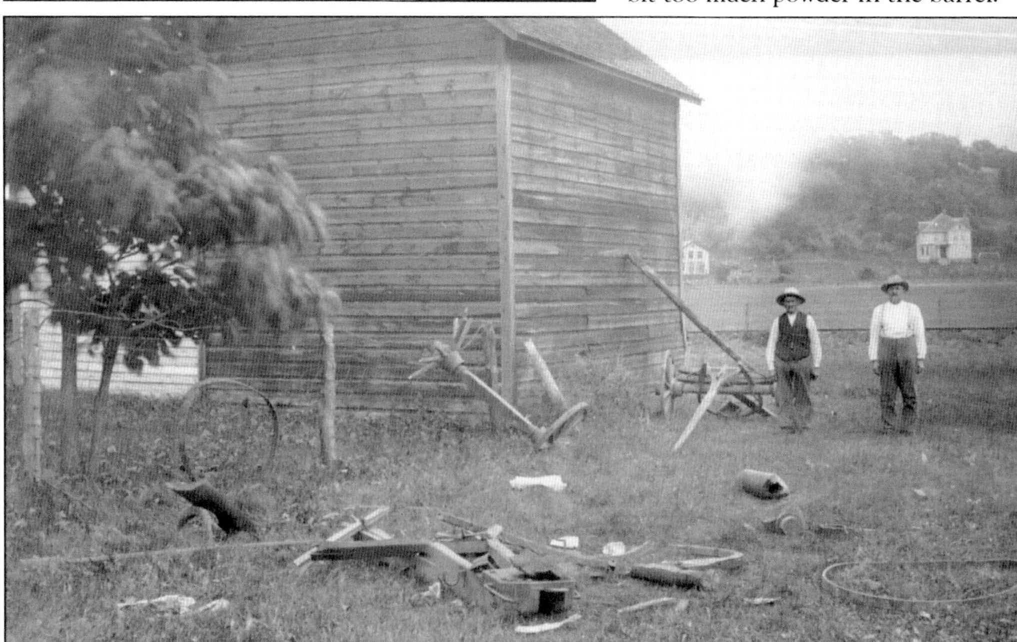

This cannon and another similar one were given to the Village of New Glarus by the US War Department. It stood in front of the New Glarus Public School for many years, and because of it the school newspaper was named *The Old Guard*.

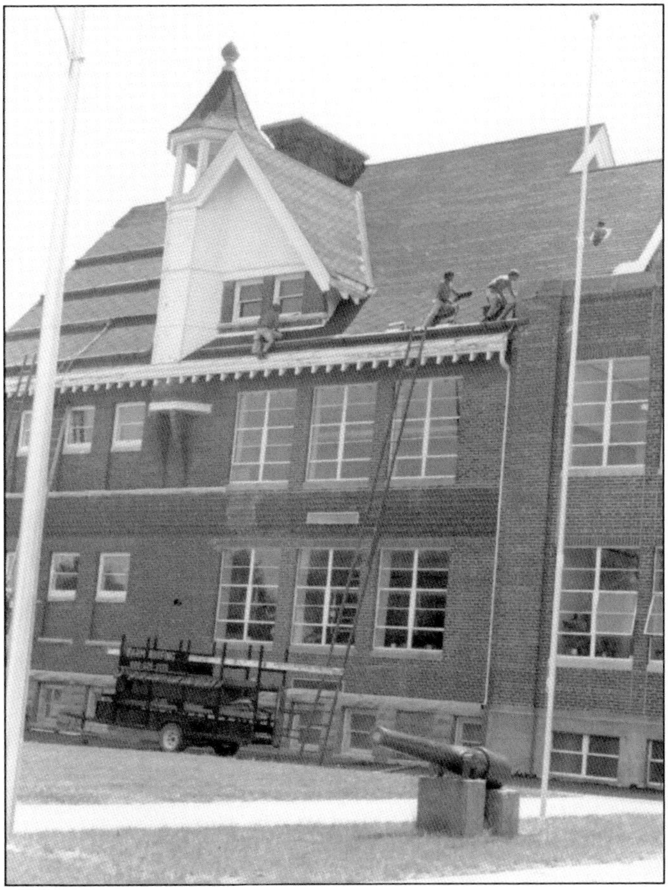

This 20-pound Parrott cannon is the same cannon as is in the previous photograph. It was rebuilt to working condition and is being shown off at the New Glarus sesquicentennial in 1995. The Civil War reenactors kneeling represent each of the men from New Glarus who served in the Civil War. This cannon was in the epic film *Gettysburg*.

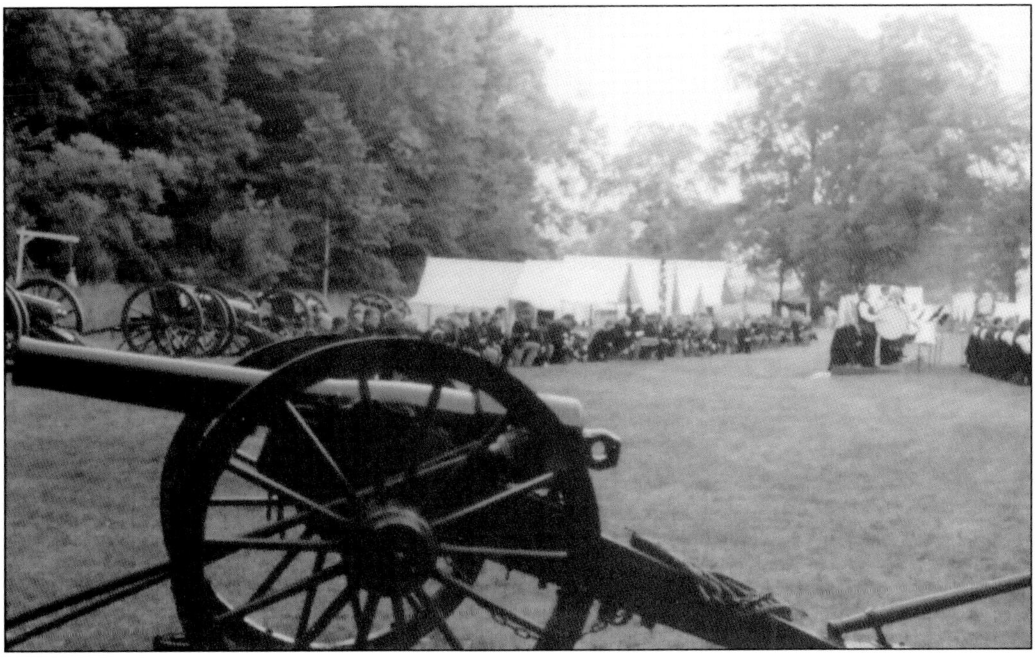

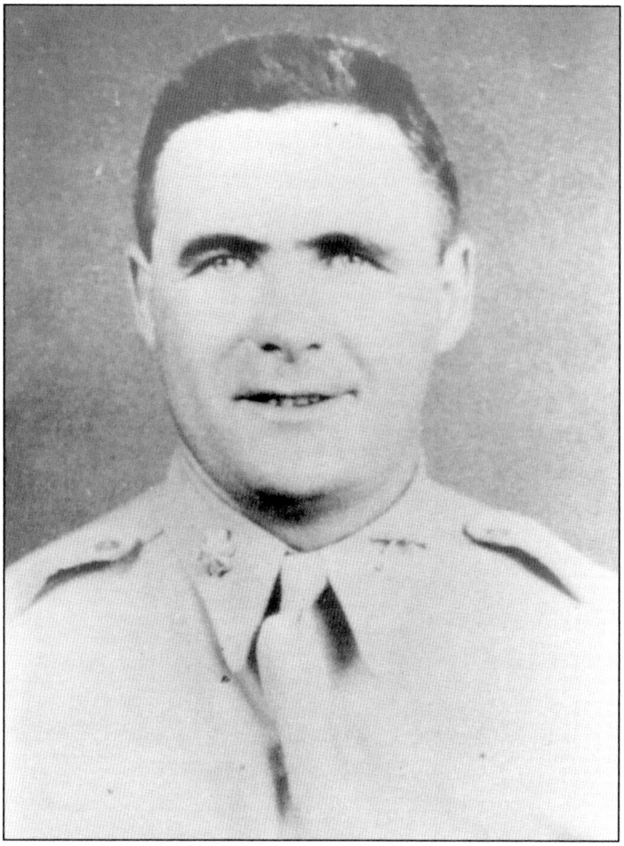

Col. Gilbert Strickler, a New Glarus native, joined the military for the World War II effort like many of his peers and retired from the Army. Colonel Strickler served in three wars: World War II, Korea, and Vietnam.

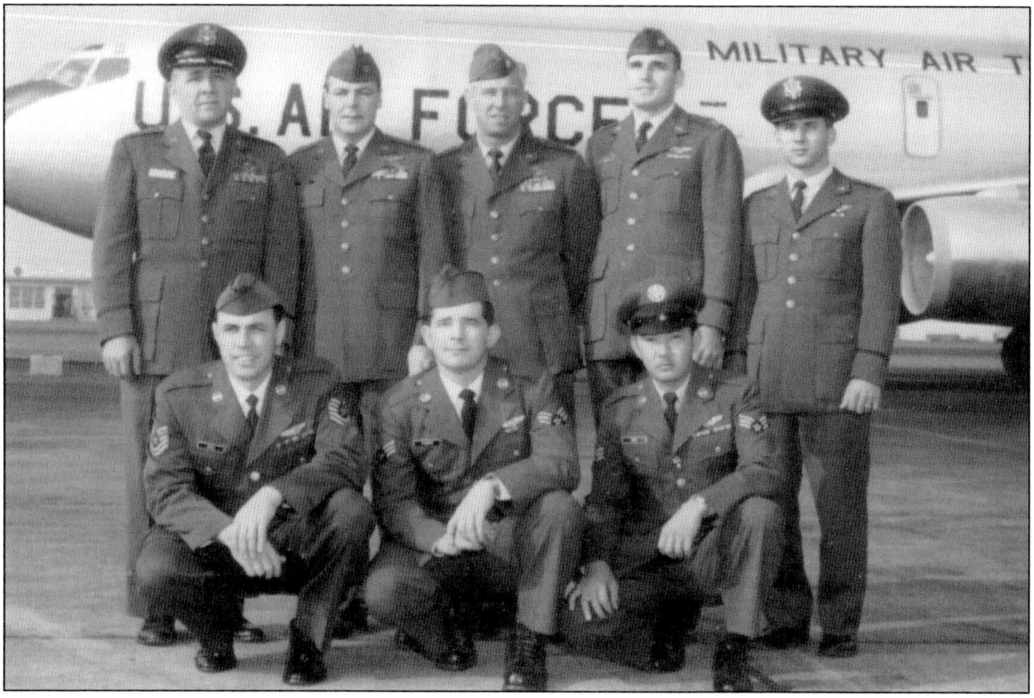

Col. Harold "Dutch" Zweifel (back row, far left) was a New Glarus farm boy who wanted to fly, not farm. His long military career spanned World War II, Korea, and Vietnam. He was awarded four Distinguished Flying Crosses and six Air Medals. Zweifel, an outstanding soldier, was said to, "command both fear and respect."

Army colonel Dave Zweifel was raised on a dairy farm just outside New Glarus. He went to the University of Wisconsin—Madison, where he received his journalism degree and began working for the *Madison Capital Times*, rising to the position of editor. His journalism career started in high school when he established the *Star Banner*, an alternative newspaper for New Glarus.

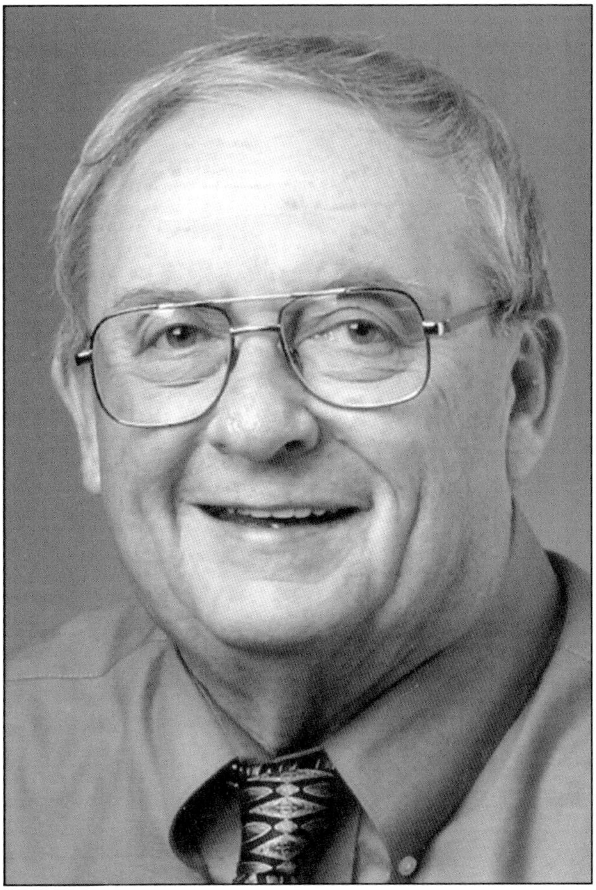

Col. John Jacobson was in the Air Force for 29 years. He served as an intelligence mission pilot in the U-2 spy plane. During Operation Desert Storm, he flew 95 combat hours in a U-2R. Throughout his military career, he logged over 3,800 flight hours flying F-111, T-37, T-38, TR-1, U2S, and U2ST planes. He was also a U-2 instructor pilot. (Jacobson family.)

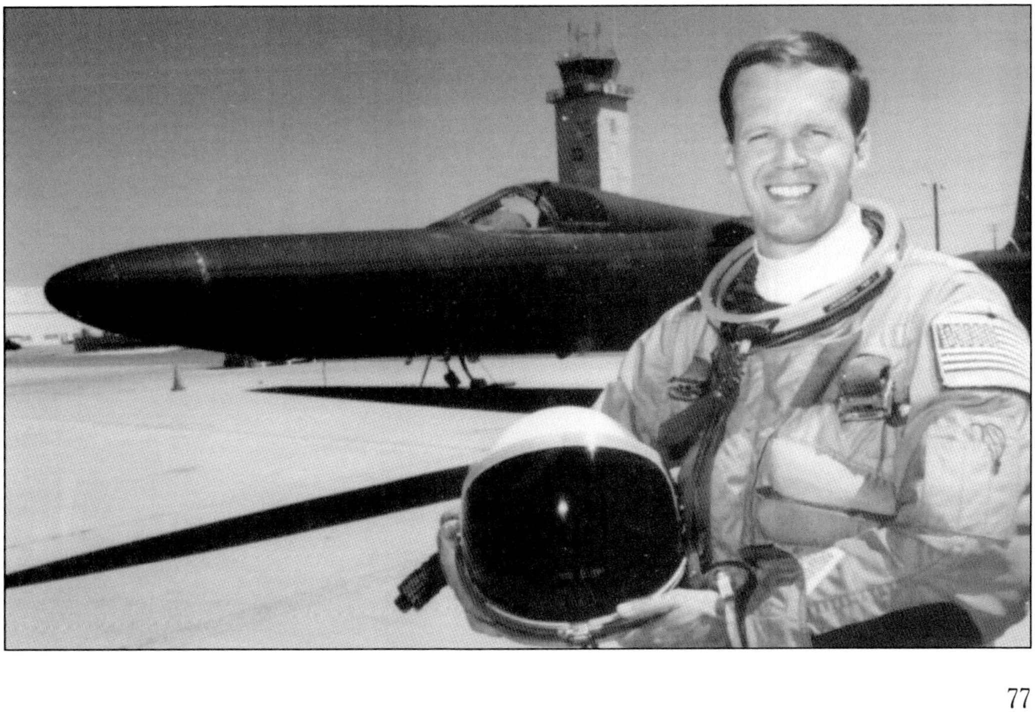

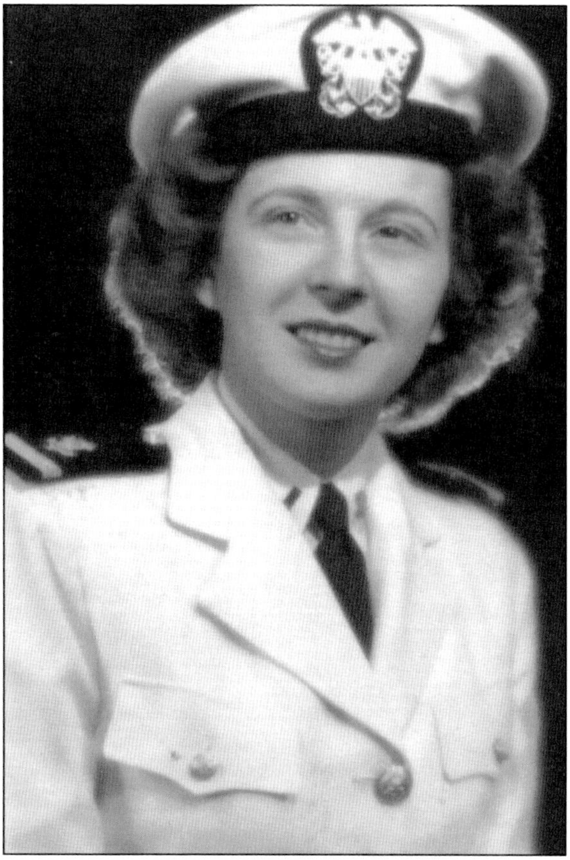

Jocelyn Saether Elmer was one of New Glarus's female veterans who served in numerous areas during World War II. Jocelyn's husband, Art Elmer, was also a World War II veteran. (Bob Elmer.)

In the 1980s, the Wisconsin Vietnam Veterans Chapter 3 of New Glarus sponsored a number of events during Winterfest. Anne Fischer of Madison is speaking about her brother Richard Fischer, a missing-in-action Marine. His body was found and returned to Madison, Wisconsin. Behind Fischer is Julie Iverson, a Vietnam veteran social worker for the Red Cross.

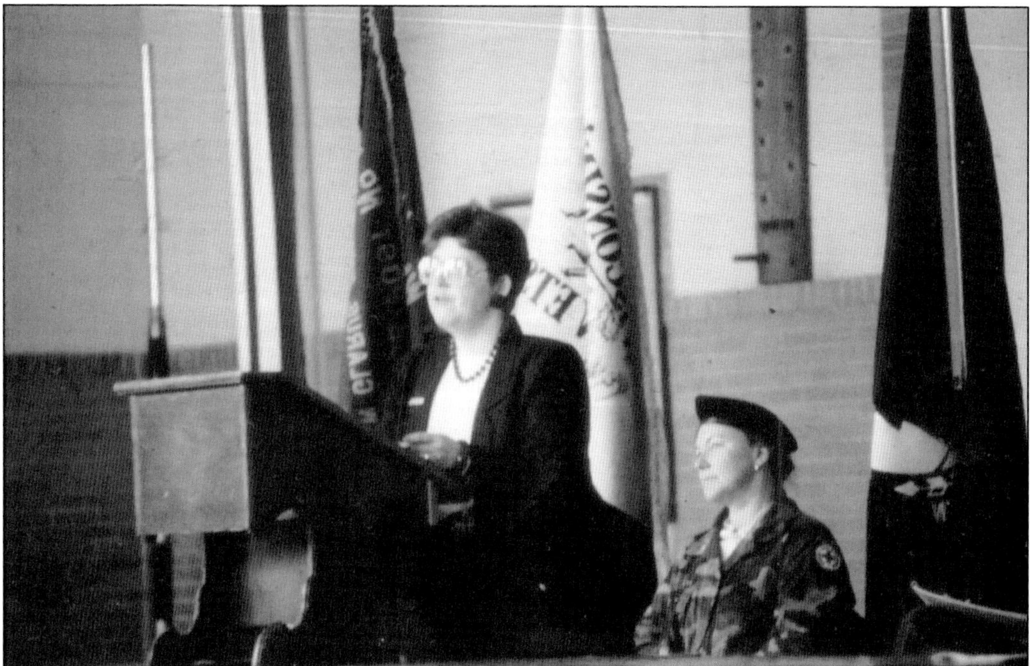

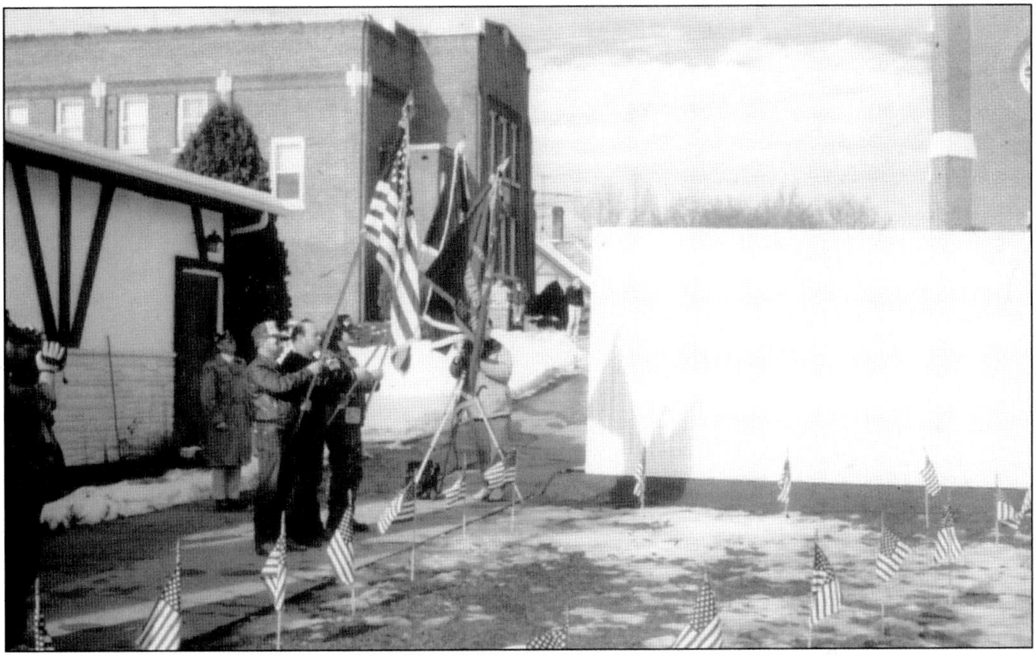

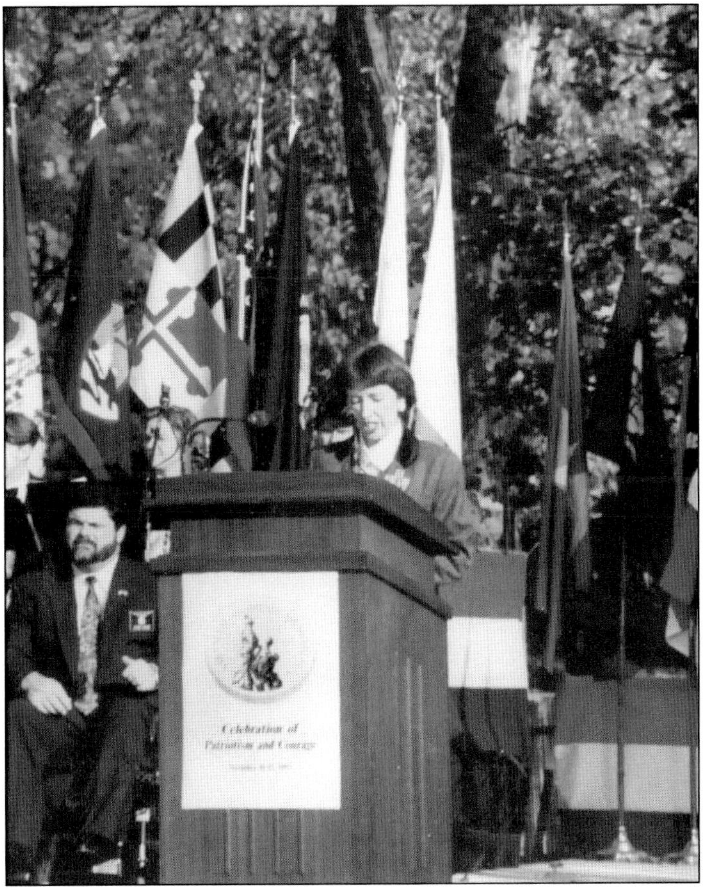

This photograph shows Iowa Vietnam veterans who traveled to Memorial Wall, containing the names of the 58,000 American veterans who died in Vietnam. This reverse of the National Vietnam Veterans Wall, done with white lettering on a black stone, is shown during a short ceremony on the Swiss Church of Christ lawn at the annual Winterfest event.

Diane Evans, a Vietnam nurse from Wisconsin and the founder of the Women's Vietnam Memorial, is delivering the dedication speech in Washington, DC. In a few minutes, the cover will be removed from the long overdue women's memorial. Evans was a regular guest speaker at the annual New Glarus Winterfest Vietnam Veterans Reunion.

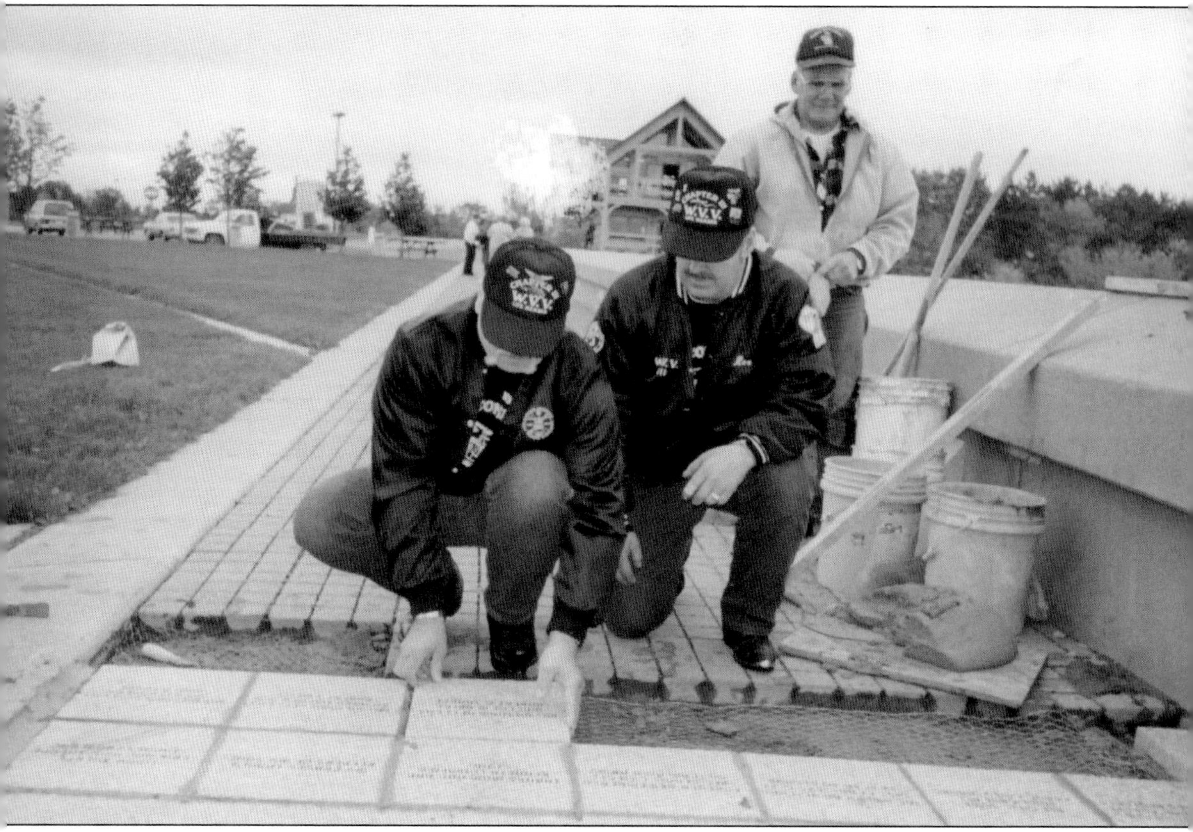

Wisconsin Vietnam Veterans Chapter 3 members Dick Goth (left) and Ron Lewis are shown placing a commemorate brick at The Highground, the Wisconsin Vietnam Veterans Memorial at Neillsville, Wisconsin.

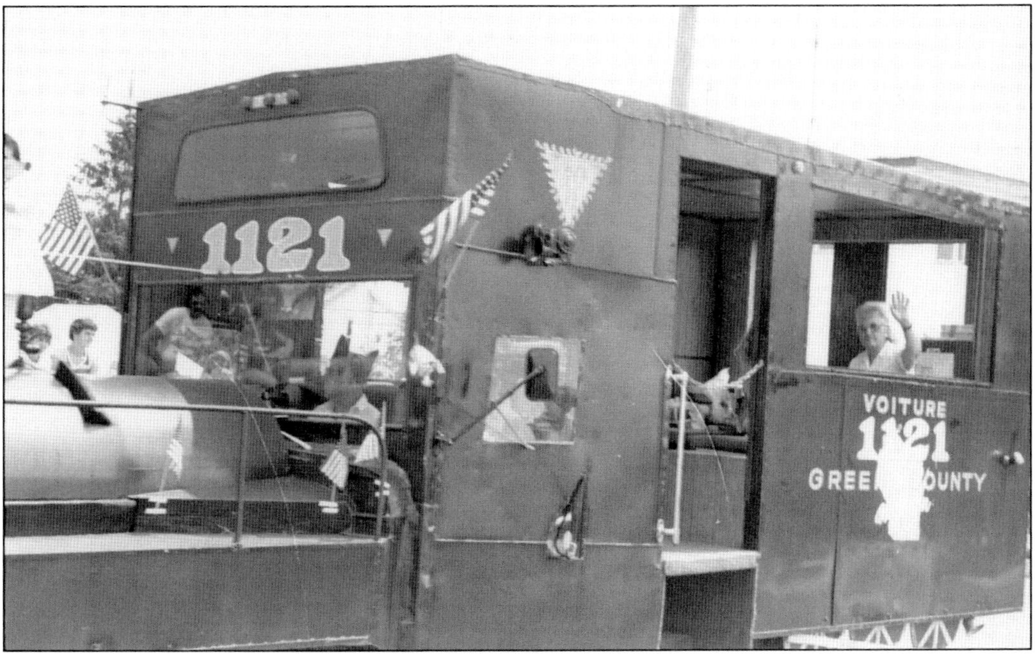

For many years, Green County 40 & 8 Post Voiture 1121 had its train in the New Glarus Memorial Day Parade. The 40 & 8 is a military group for World War I veterans, all of whom have passed on. The train is driven by Orion Paulson, and his wife, Henrietta Paulson, is in the back waving to parade watchers.

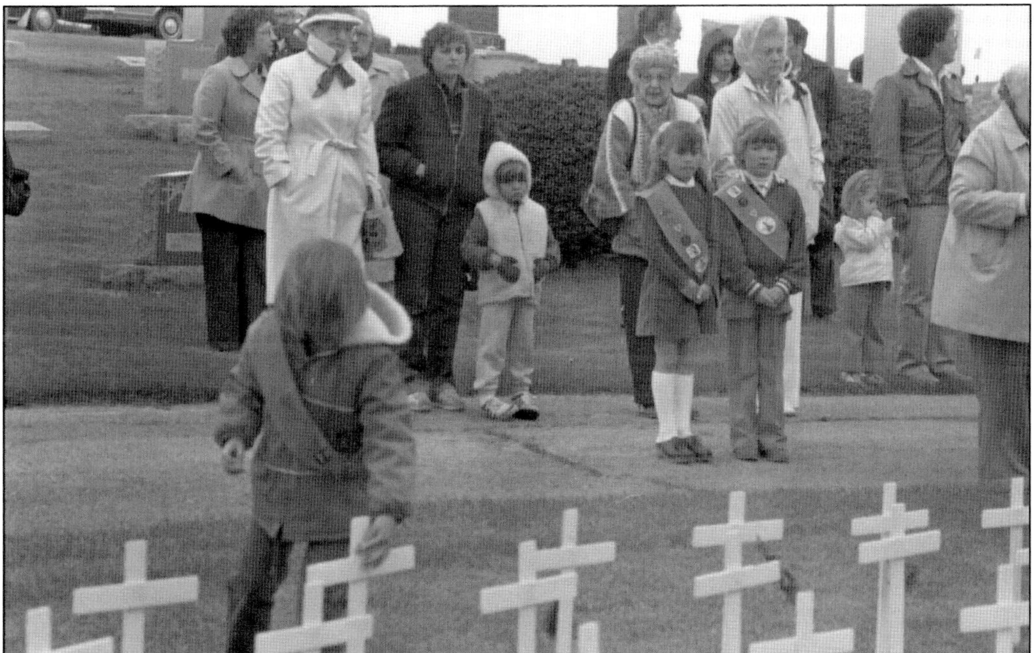

Each Memorial Day, the New Glarus Brownie and Girl Scouts place a poppy on each cross as yet another deceased veteran's name is read from the roll call, dating to the Civil War. The list has grown so long that only the names of the veterans who died in the past year are read.

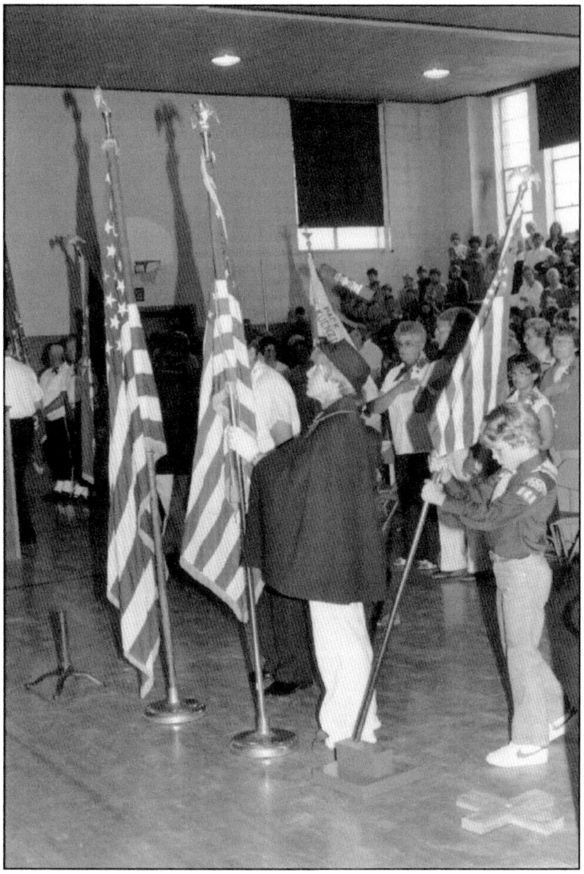

Each Memorial Day, a parade and program are held in memory of local veterans. Local service organizations present flags, several speeches are made, and Memorial Day poster winner names are announced. When the program closes, the crowd walks to the cemetery for the final memorial of the day.

Village president Richard Schmied (right), a Vietnam veteran, and Ken Nyland, a Navy retiree, are shaking hands to reflect the name change from Southside Park to Veteran's Memorial Park.

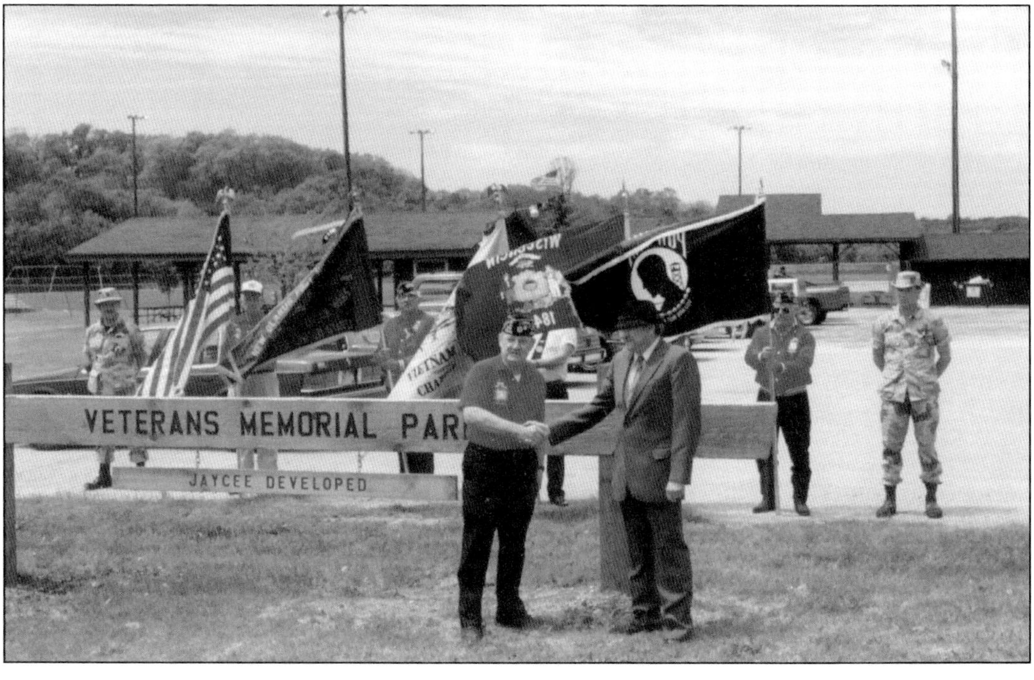

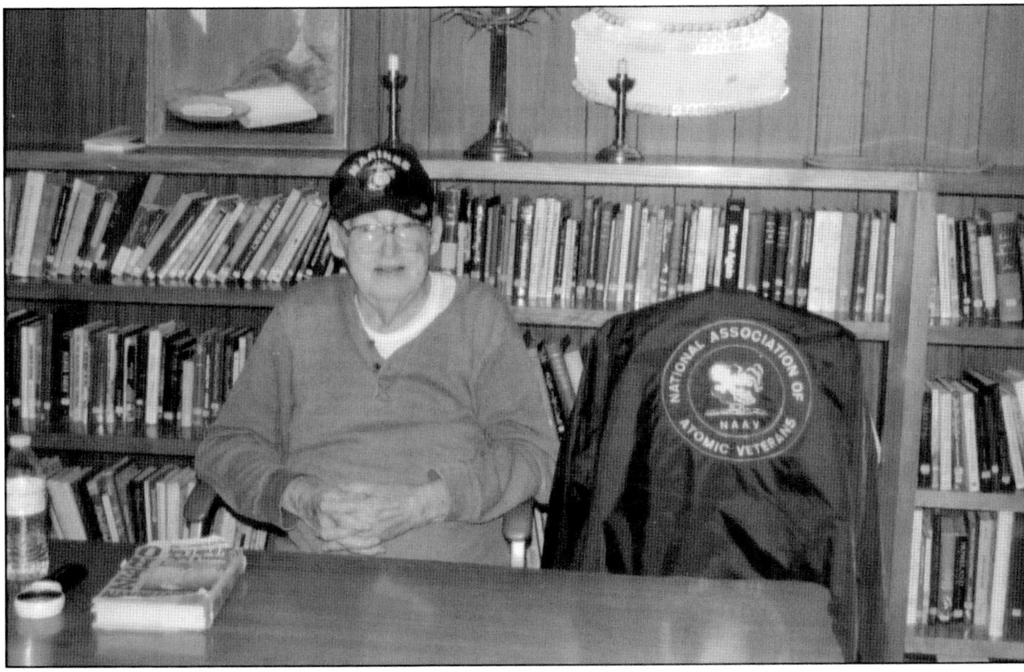

Francis Beers spent his first years in the Marine Corps. During his time in the Marines, he was one of the thousands of American servicemen used as live tests for nuclear bombs. Beers has given numerous speeches about his experiences during that time. He also served for many years in the Army Reserve.

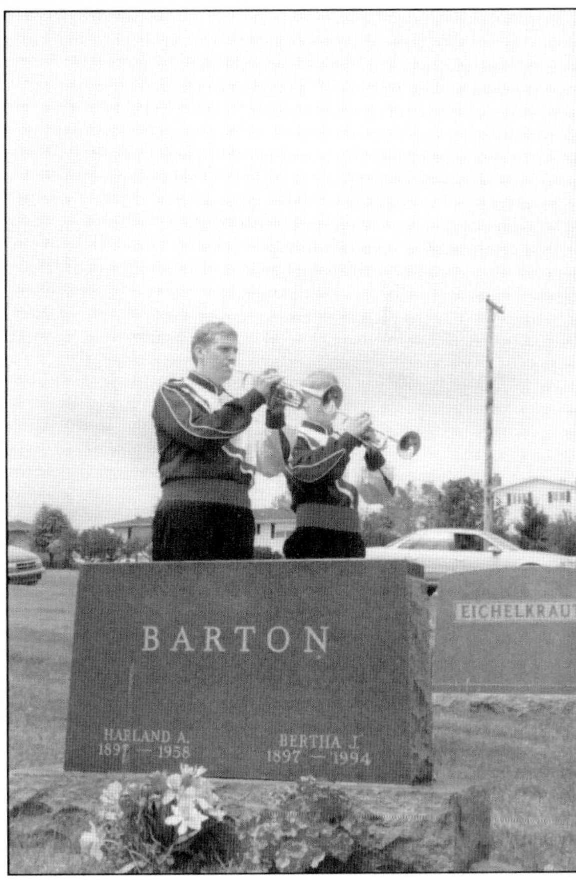

New Glarus High School trumpeters Tom Schenkel (left) and Al Zweifel played "Taps" for a number of Memorial Day commemorations, as well as funerals of local area veterans, which for many families was the most emotional time during the funeral for their family's fallen veteran.

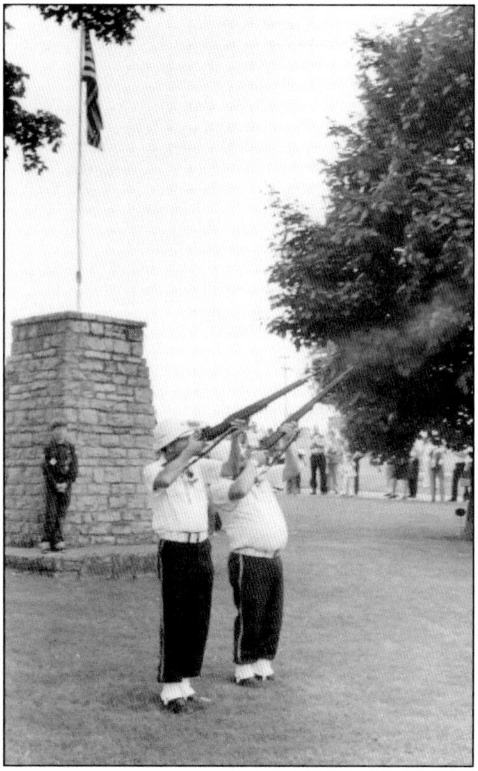

The order is given by the American Legion commander, "Load . . . aim . . . fire!" Three volleys of shots ring out honoring those veterans who have died. In the background, standing next to the flagpole, is a Cub Scout taking part in the Memorial Day commemoration.

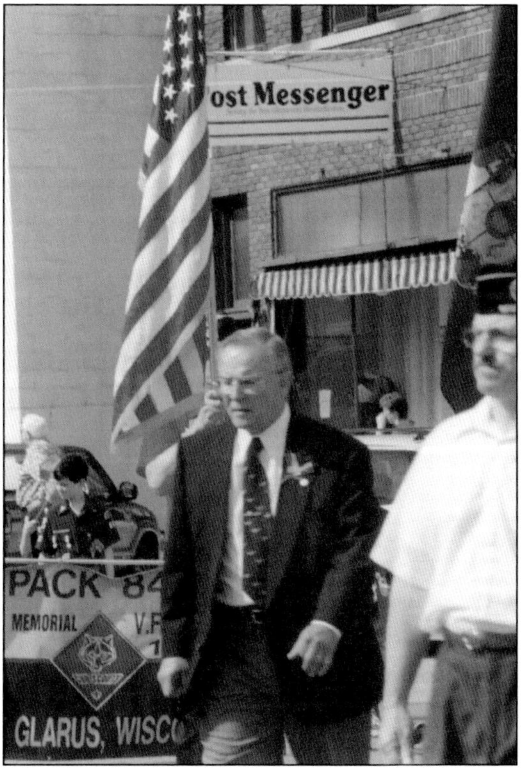

Capt. Gary Beck (center, in the suit), former captain of the USS *Eisenhower*, was the guest speaker at the Memorial Day program. Captain Beck is a Vietnam veteran who did several tours of duty. More than half of his more than 700 aircraft carrier landings were made at night. Upon retirement from the Navy, Beck was certified on 37 different military aircraft. Shown with Captain Beck is Heinz Mattmann, also a Vietnam veteran.

Co-pilot George Hartman was on his first bombing mission in a B-24 Liberator over Germany when his plane got shot down. The crew was close to the German/Swiss border and decided to land in neutral Switzerland. His group was captured and sent to prisoner-of-war camps in Switzerland. (Hartman collection.)

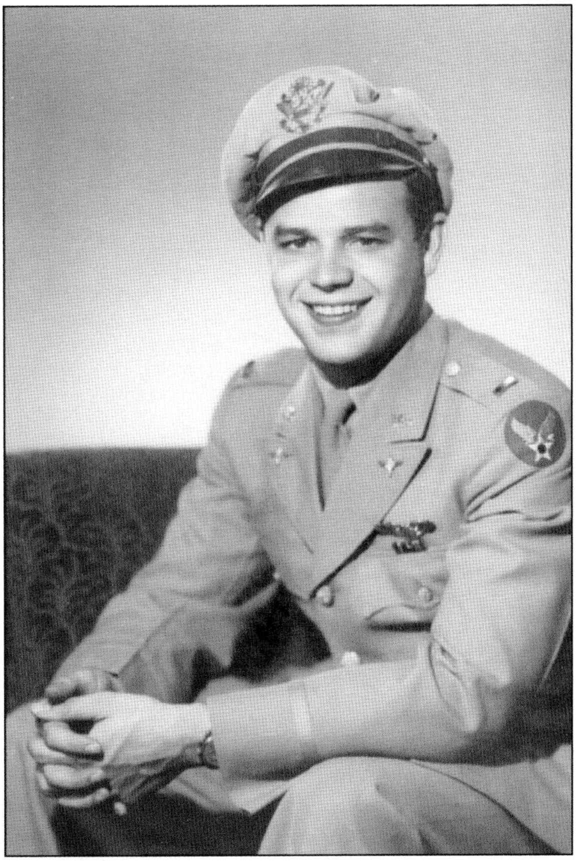

George Hartman's daughters April, Peggy, Mary, and Barb are shown holding George's Prisoner of War Medal, which was finally awarded on April 30, 2014. He escaped and was locked up in Switzerland's Wauwilermoos POW camp, run by a sadistic Nazi. His treatment was as bad or worse than American soldiers in German POW camps in Germany. (Hartman collection.)

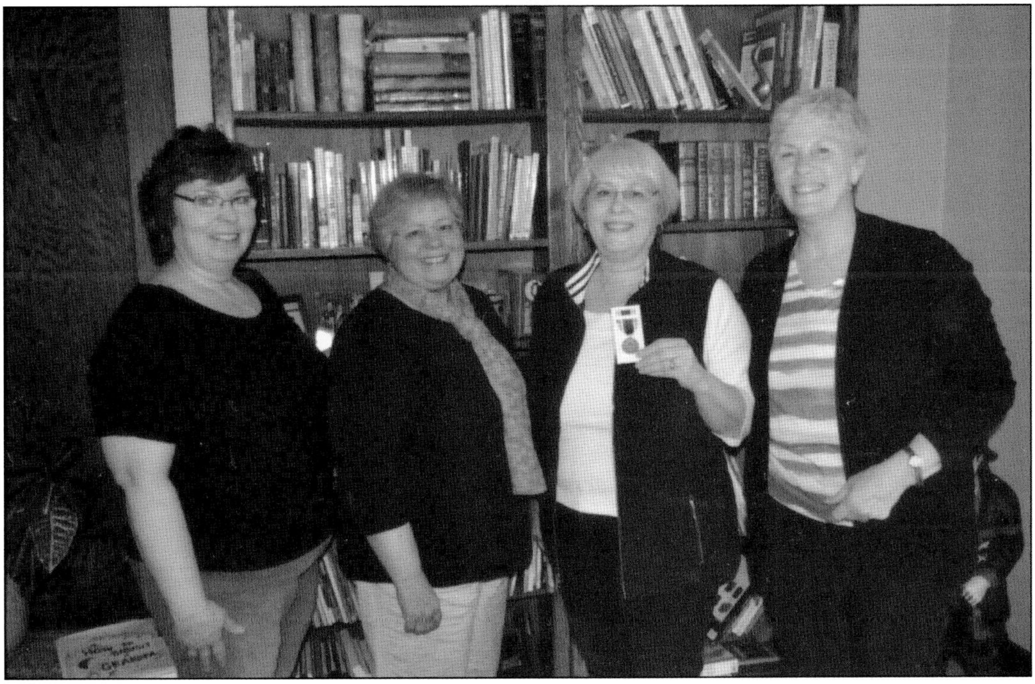

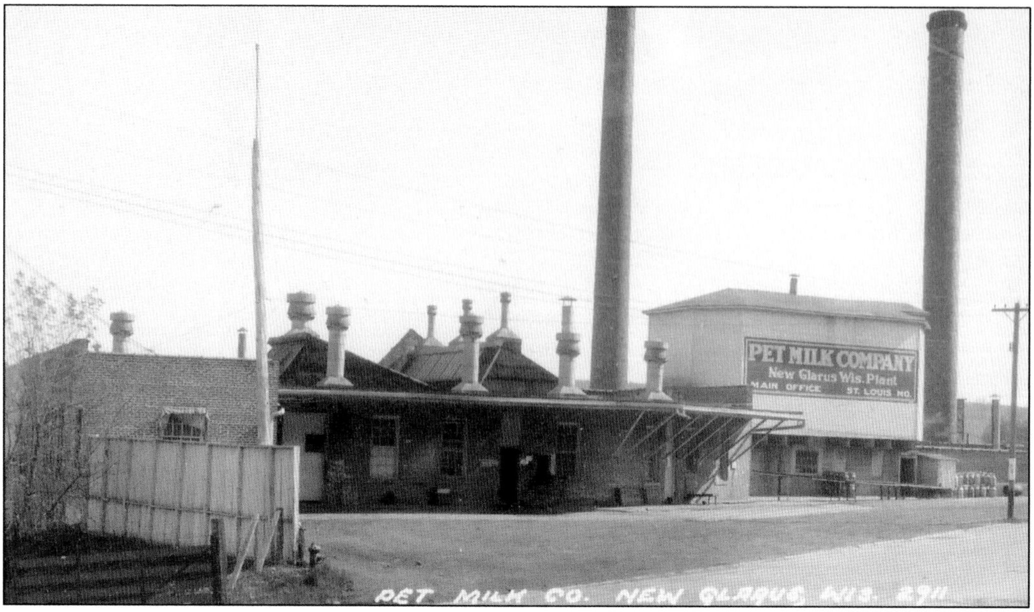

For local World War II soldiers serving in the Pacific or Atlantic campaigns, a can of Pet Condensed Milk was one of the greatest gifts from home they could hope to receive. Many packages sent from relatives to family members contained that can of Pet milk. During the war, Pet milk in New Glarus shipped out several boxcars of condensed milk each day.

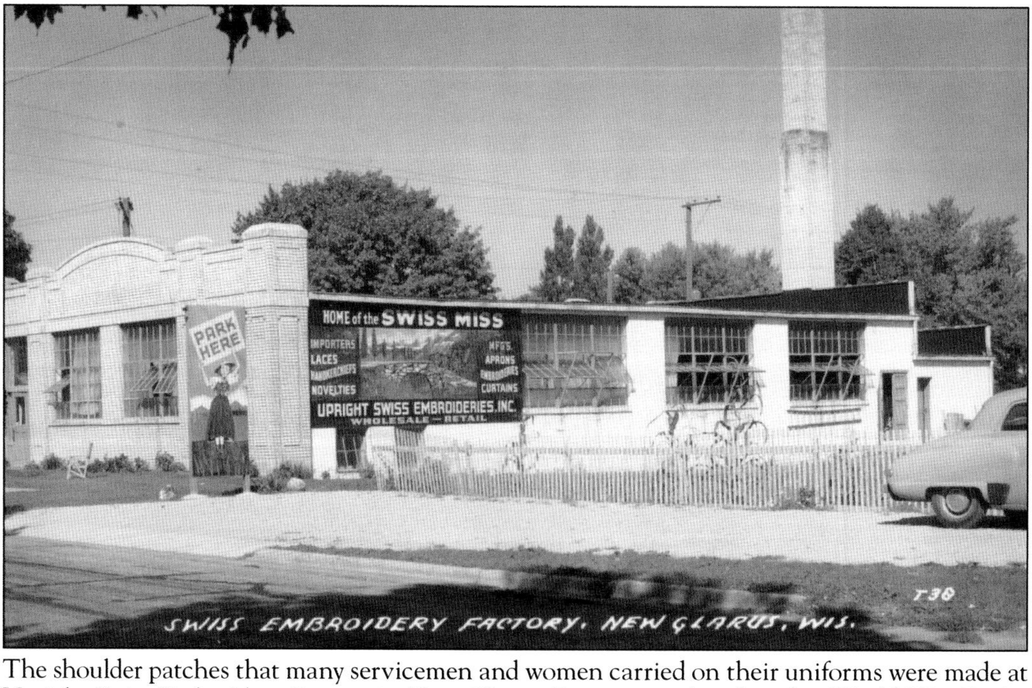

The shoulder patches that many servicemen and women carried on their uniforms were made at Upright Swiss Embroidery Factory in New Glarus. Even many decades after World War II, the shoulder patches show up from time to time at area garage sales.

Seven

The Amish Years, Yoder v. Wisconsin

The first five Amish families arrived in early 1964. By the end of the year, the Amish population had reached 70 people. Concern was expressed within the business community that the Amish would not patronize local businesses. A meeting of the members of the New Glarus Businessmen's Association was held to confront what they saw as a potential problem. New Glarus realtor Fred Lienhardt, who sold most of the farms to the Amish, was summonsed to this meeting to answer the group's questions.

A controversy in Iowa over the compulsory education law mandating students to remain in school until age 16 was on the mind of New Glarus school superintendent Roy Habeck, who stated, "I do not foresee any points of controversy. We have agreed to try and fully cooperate." Habeck took a job with another school district. Ken Glewen took over Habeck's position.

In August 1968, the Amish opened Pleasant View Parochial School. Within days of the school opening, Glewen sent a letter to the Amish parents, warning them that they may be in violation of Wisconsin school laws. Glewen sent a second letter to Amish parents, issuing another warning to the Amish of their possible violation of the Wisconsin truancy law. On October 23, 1968, Glewen filed truancy charges against Jonas Yoder, Wallace Miller, and Adin Yutzy.

The New Glarus School District tried to come to a resolution. Glewen spoke with three Amish fathers, Jonas Yoder, Wallace Miller, and Adin Yutzy, to offer a deal to end the issue. If the Amish were to agree to keep their children in the public school until after the third Friday of September, Glewen would drop the case.

The third Friday of September is the day when the annual school census is taken. The census determines the amount of state aid schools receive. The Amish saw through this, telling Glewen they did not want to be part of his scheme to get more school aid.

The court battle was on. Nobody expected this case (Yoder v. Wisconsin) of three Amish parents in New Glarus refusing to send their children to the New Glarus public school to be resolved by the US Supreme Court. The court's 7-0 decision in favor of the Amish still stands as the landmark case of religious freedom in the United States.

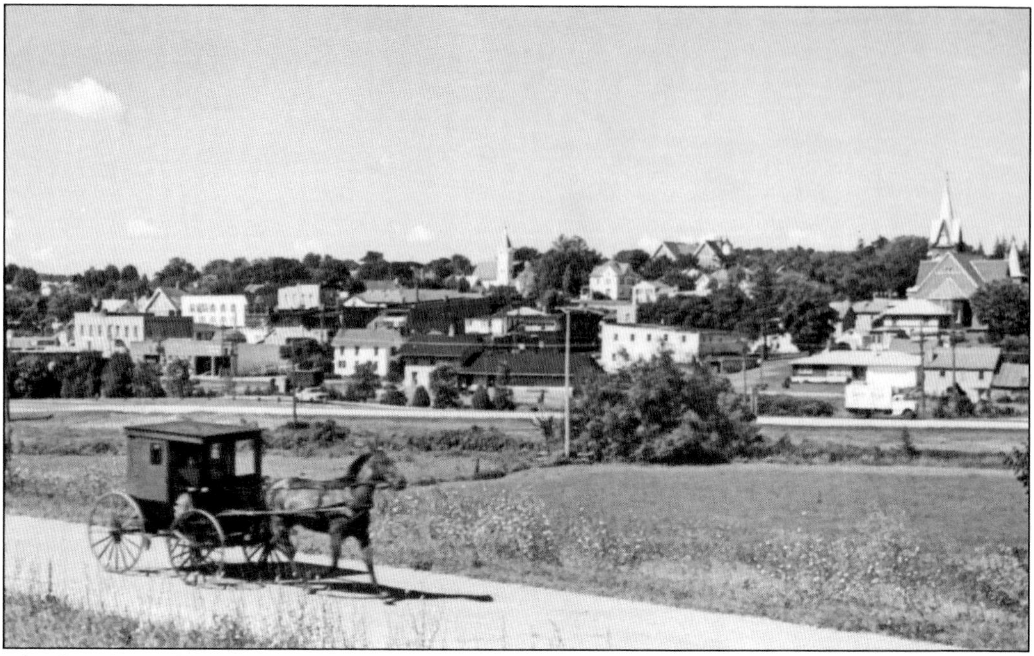

The first five Old Order Amish families arrived in New Glarus in 1964. They purchased five farms north of New Glarus that belonged to retiring or soon-to-retire farmers. Slowly, more Amish families moved into the area, with a large number of them settling east of New Glarus. This Amish family is headed home from New Glarus to their farm just a couple of miles to the east.

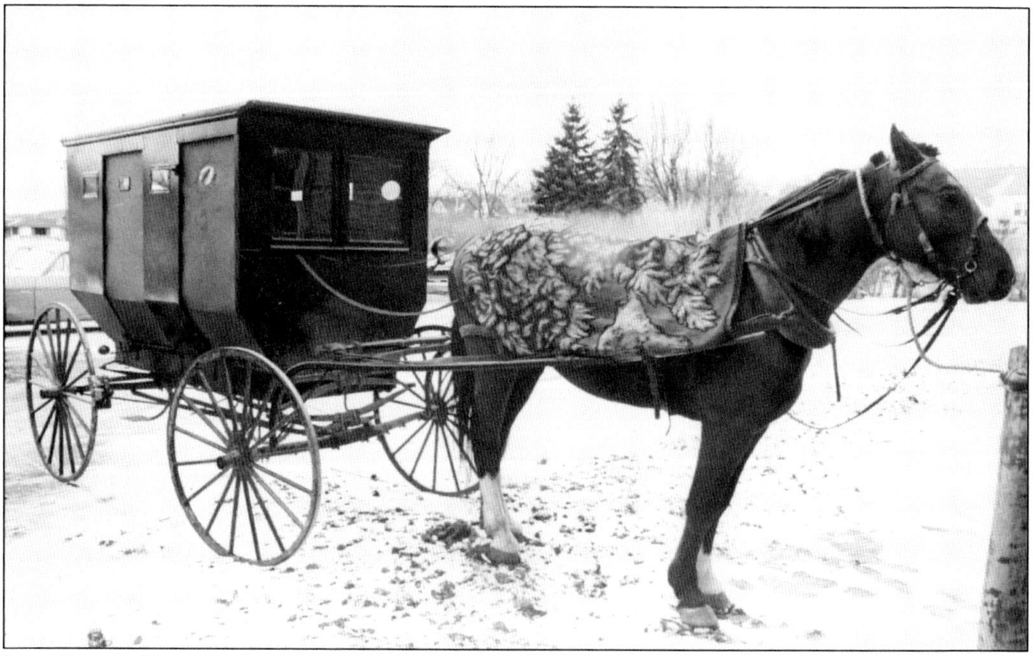

Initially, residents were not sure what to expect, but the Amish neighbors quickly became both friends with the local people and good customers in their stores and shops. In the beginning, some businesses were sure the Amish would not purchase anything in town. The Village of New Glarus wisely installed a couple of hitching posts behind the village hall.

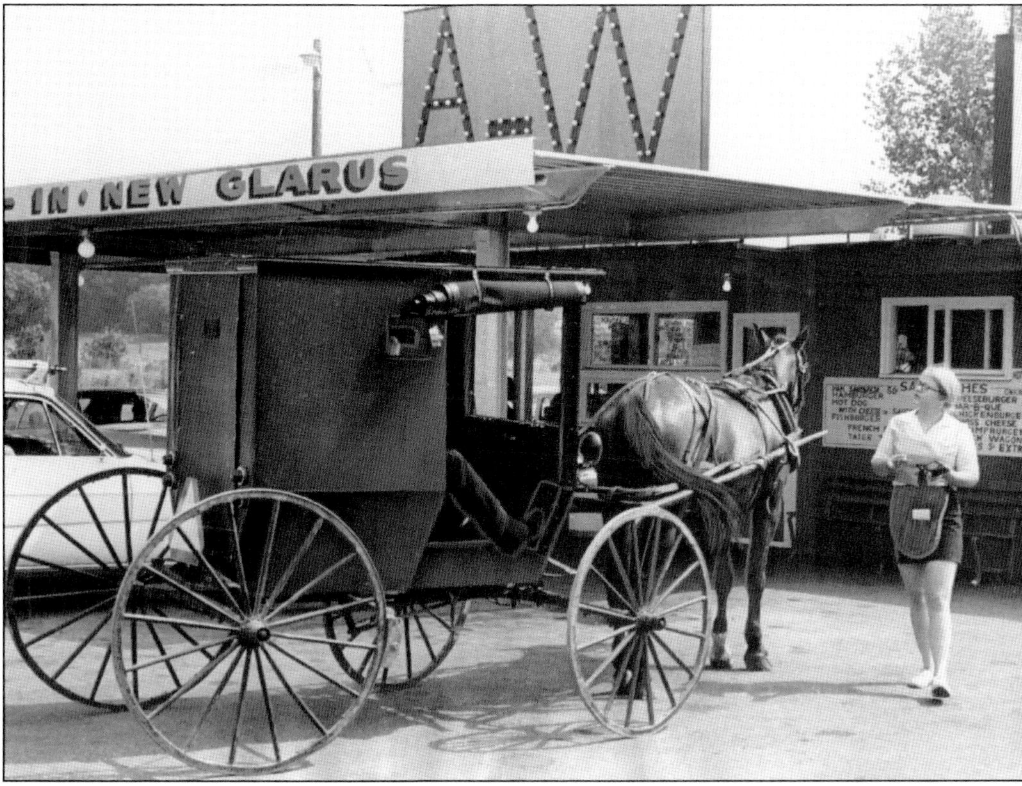

This September 21, 1970, photograph shows an interesting mix of cultures at Gilbert and Hilda Duerst's A&W Root Beer Stand on Highway 69. Beth Alderman is delivering a pair of large cold mugs of A&W root beer to a young Amish couple.

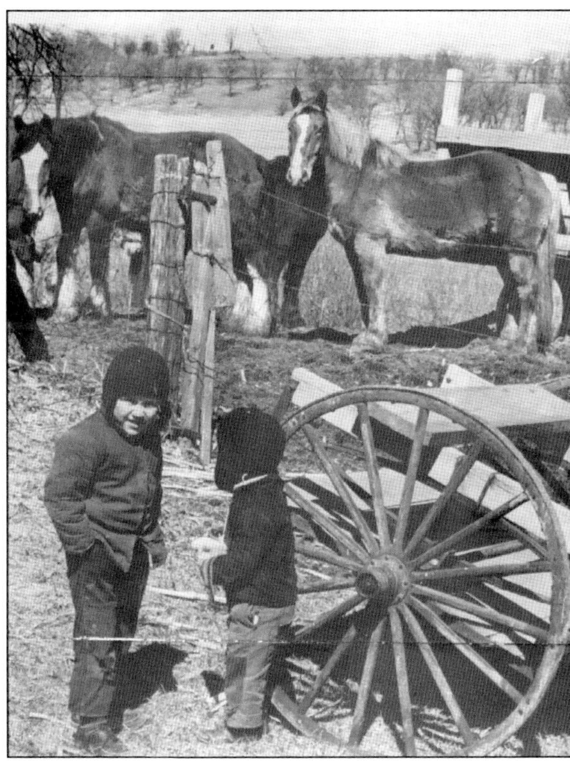

Harry Miller's sons Harry and Samuel are spending some time outside on a rather cold April day. Miller had a small blacksmith and handyman shop on the family farm on Pioneer Road.

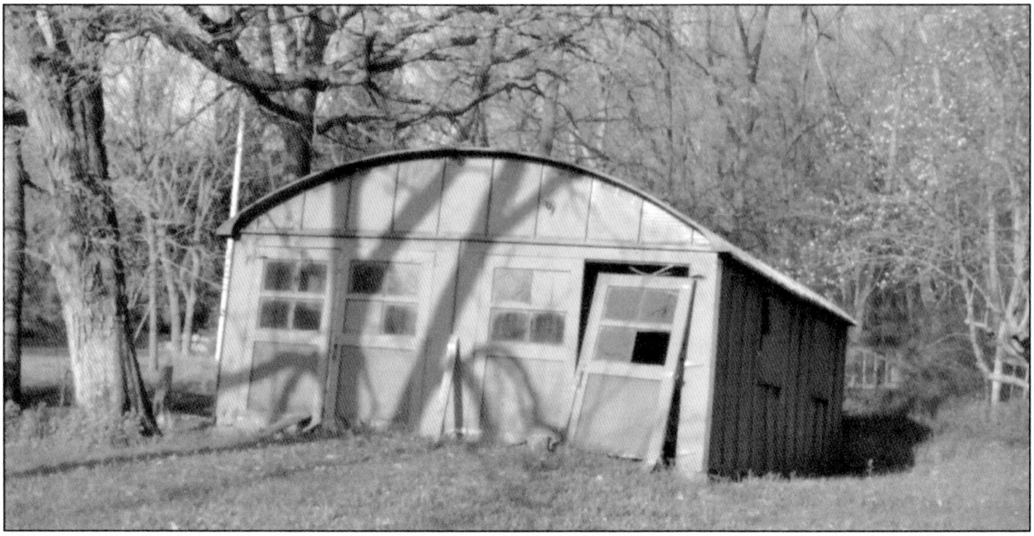

This building started its life as the Fred Haldiman Blacksmith Shop on Fourth Avenue. It was moved to Pioneer Road, where Henry Miller started a blacksmith shop. Both Harry and Henry Miller attracted not only Amish patrons but also people from nearby New Glarus.

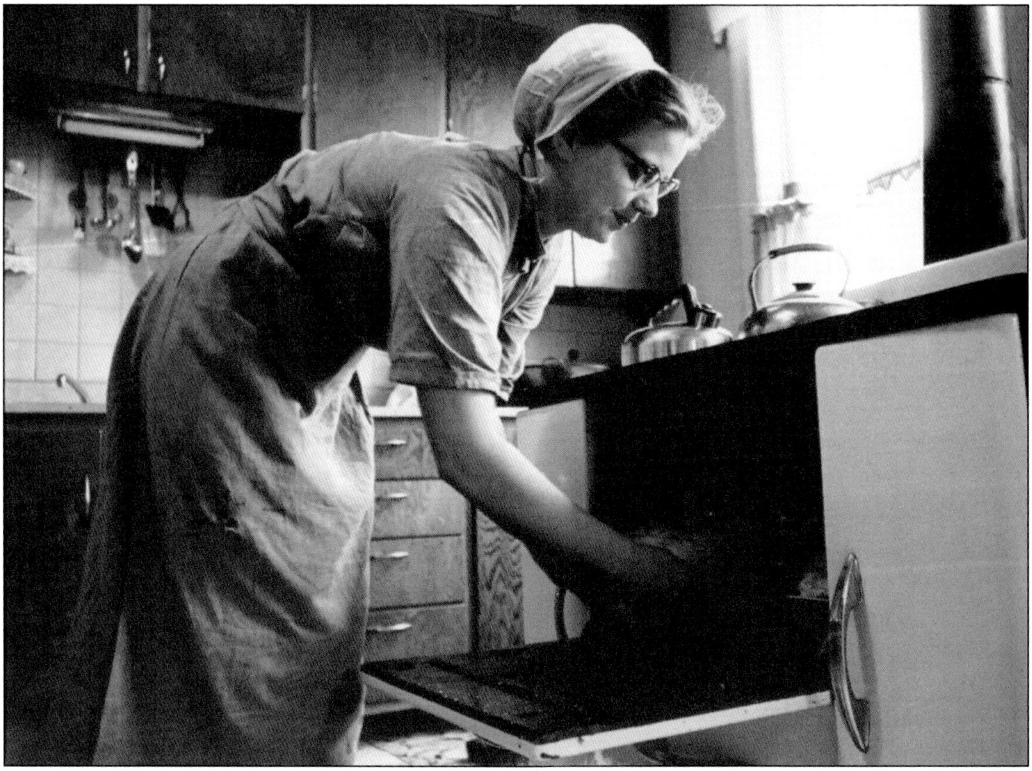

Elizabeth Hershberger operated a bakery in an addition to the family home on Pioneer Road. It was not too long after she opened her bakery that the Wisconsin Department of Agriculture attempted to shutter her business because it was "an unlicensed bakery." She kept on baking and summed up the charges against her, "If I believed it were a sin, I would quit." That statement quickly made her bakery a tourist attraction.

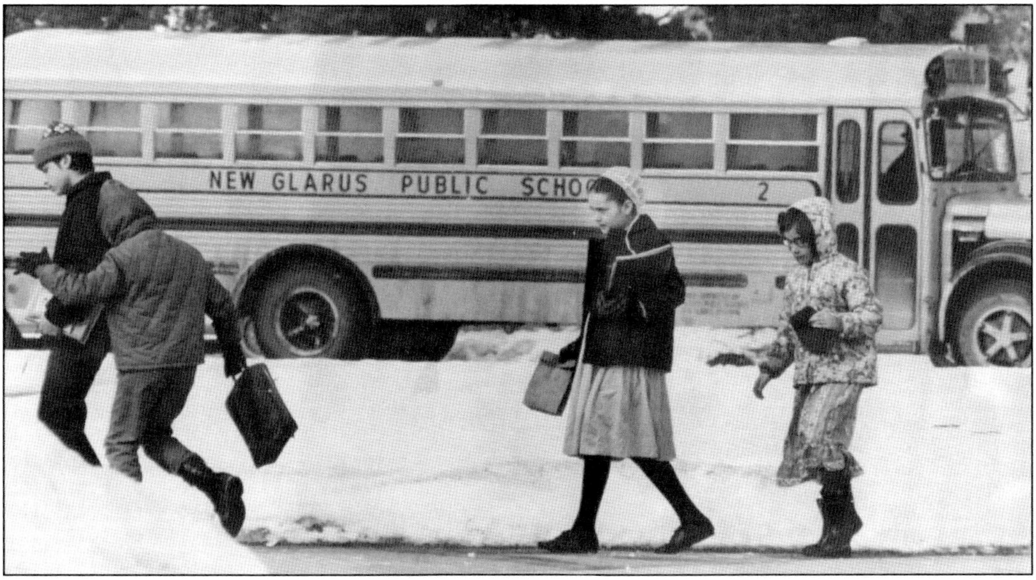

When they first arrived in New Glarus in 1964, the Amish sent their children to the public school system. Several problems arose between the New Glarus School Board and the Amish community, which ultimately led to building their own school. The Kraemer family chose to send their children to the public school.

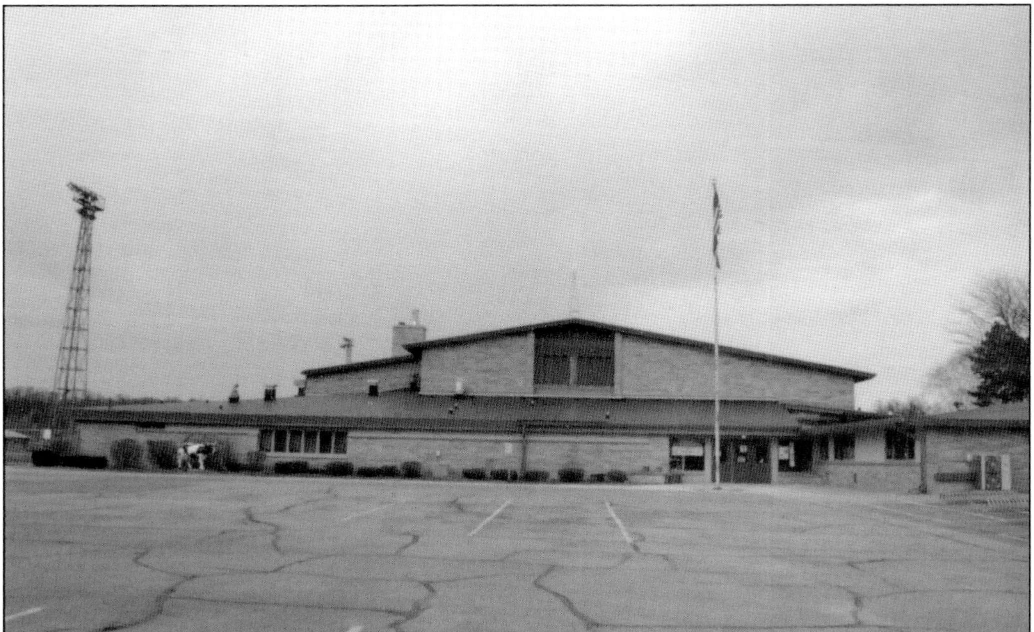

Little did anyone think when New Glarus High School was opened in 1958 that within 10 years it would be the center of what was to become a landmark US Supreme Court case. The case took four years to wind itself through the courts to a final decision.

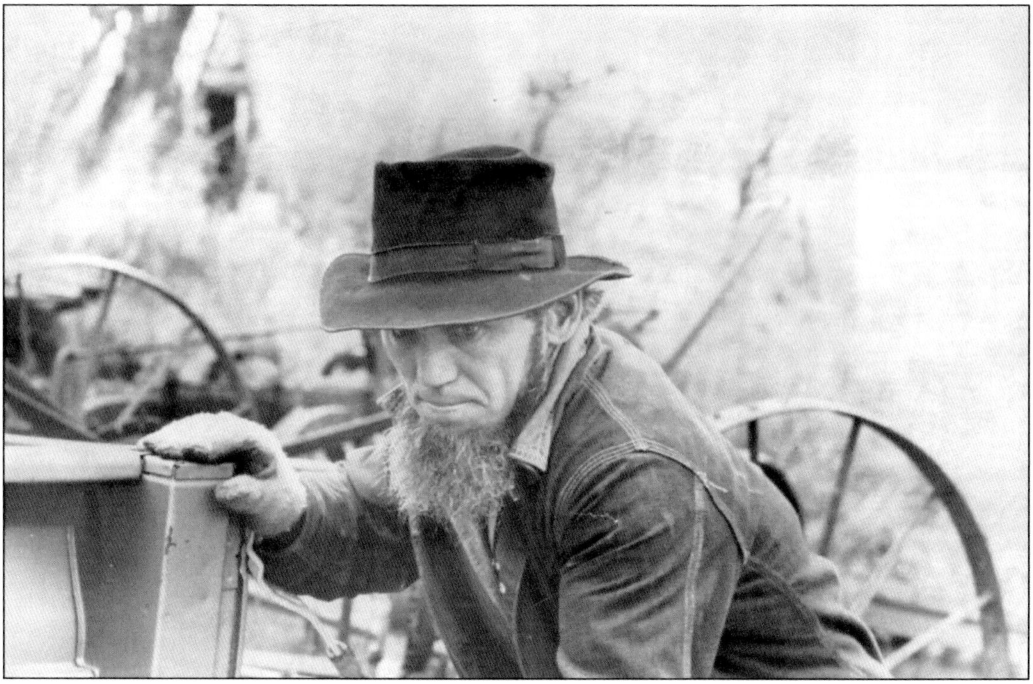

Jonas Yoder is the Amish farmer after whom the landmark US Supreme Court decision Yoder v. Wisconsin is named. Jonas, like most of the Amish, pulled his children out of the public school system once the Amish established their own school.

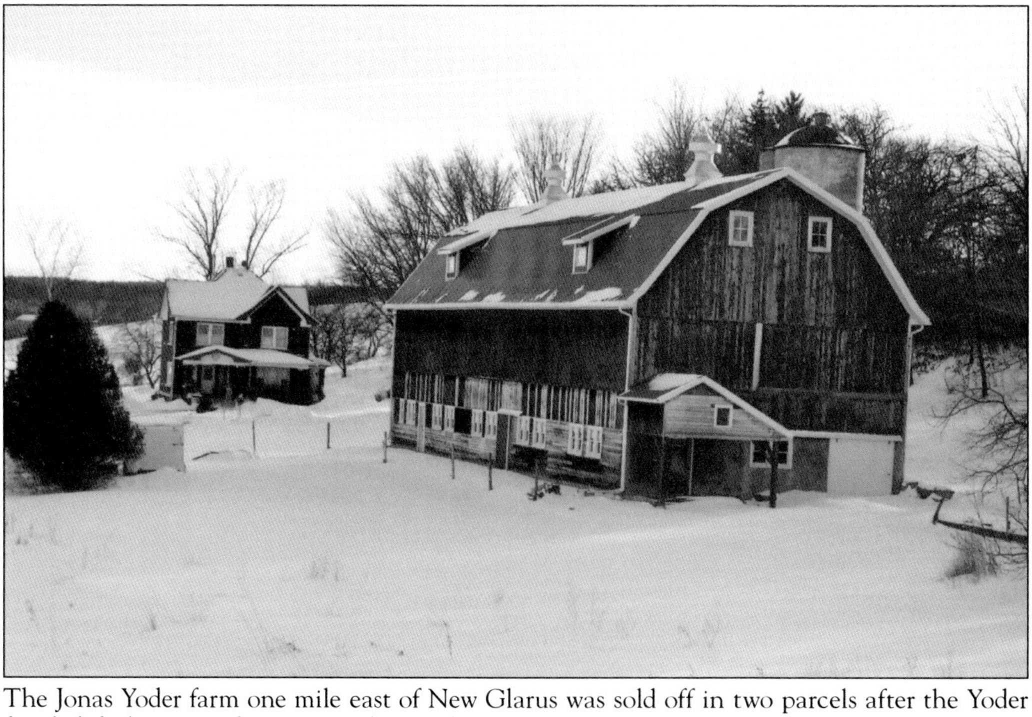

The Jonas Yoder farm one mile east of New Glarus was sold off in two parcels after the Yoder family left the New Glarus area. The cropland was sold off separately from the buildings several years ago.

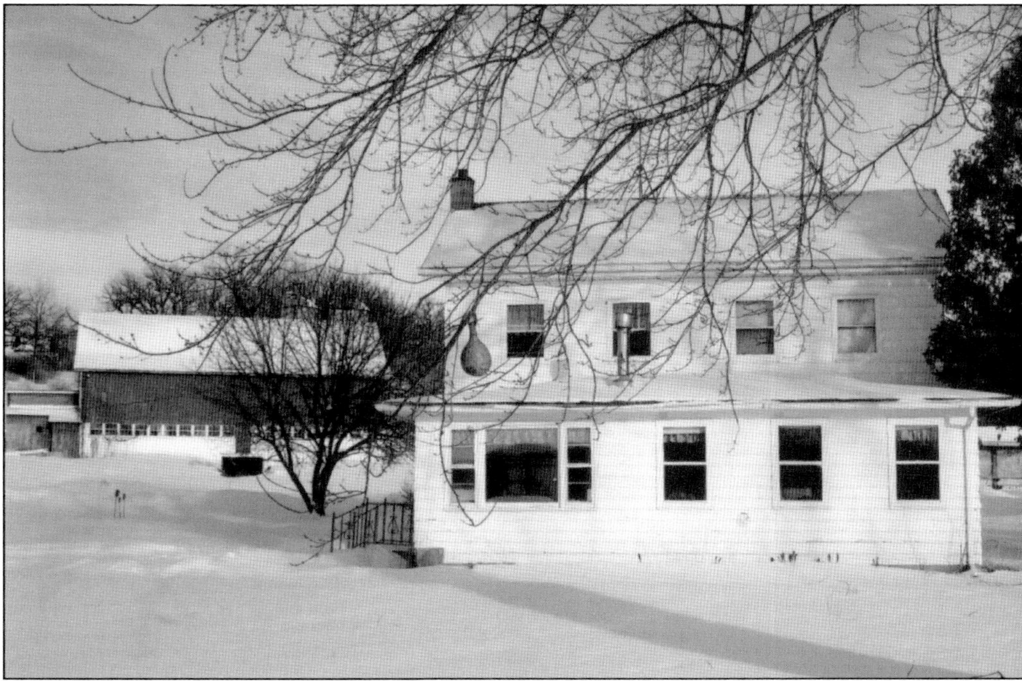

Wallace Miller was one of the three defendants in the Yoder v. Wisconsin Supreme Court case. The Miller family owned and operated this dairy farm. The Miller children said that their parents never talked about the case once it was settled.

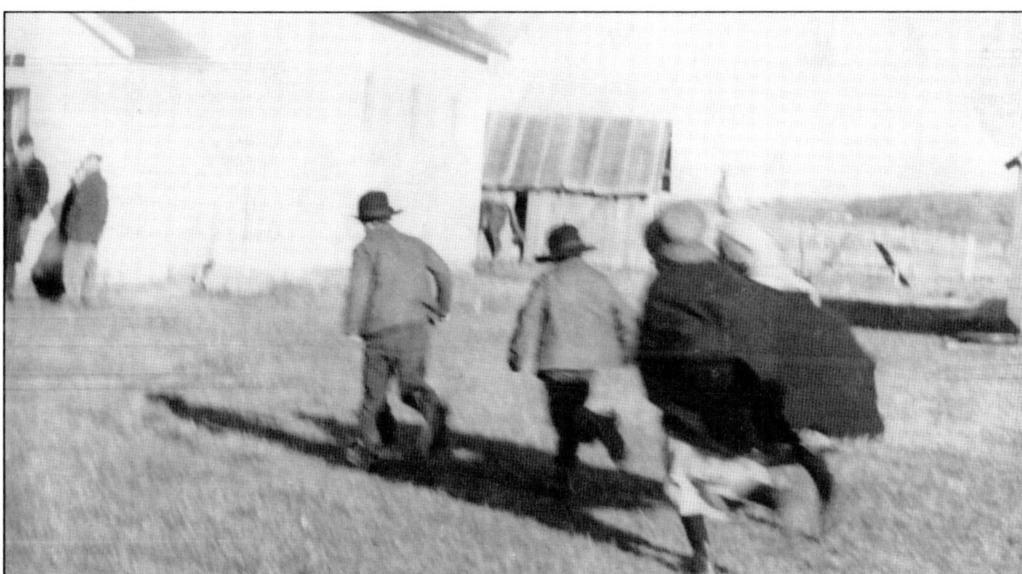

Adin Yutzy was from Buchannan County, Iowa, where he had experienced problems with the compulsory school attendance law before moving to New Glarus. This November 22, 1965, photograph shows an Amish mother and her children dashing toward the Amish schoolhouse after Iowa authorities tried to force the Amish children onto a public school bus. Yutzy's children were students at this school until they moved to New Glarus in hopes of avoiding further school problems with local and state authorities.

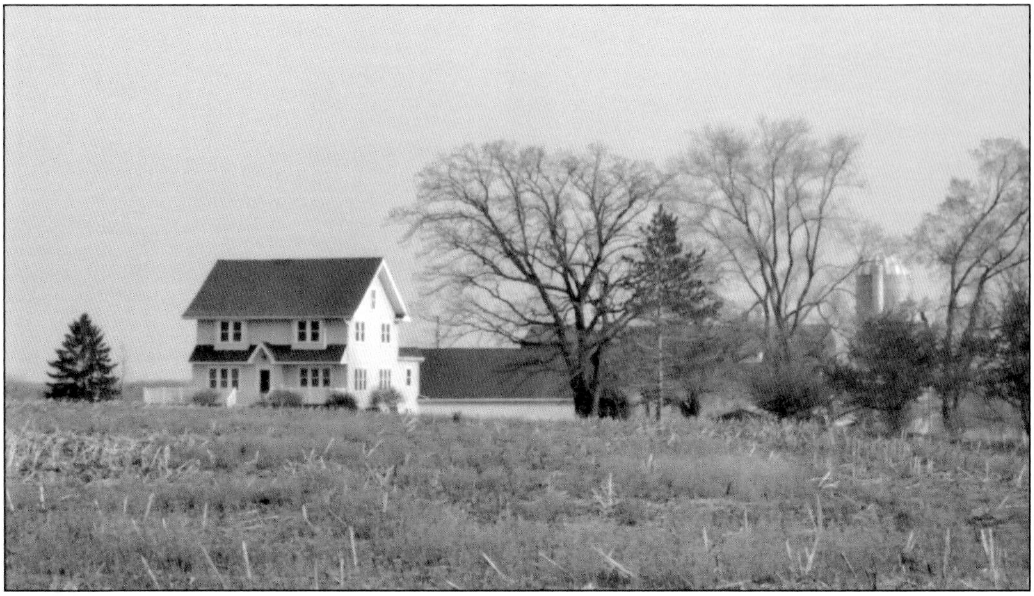

The Adin Yutzy farm was just west of New Glarus. Yutzy was the third defendant in the Yoder v. Wisconsin Supreme Court case. When asked in court if he was Amish, Yutzy shocked everyone, answering that he was not Amish but Mennonite and did not belong to the local Amish church.

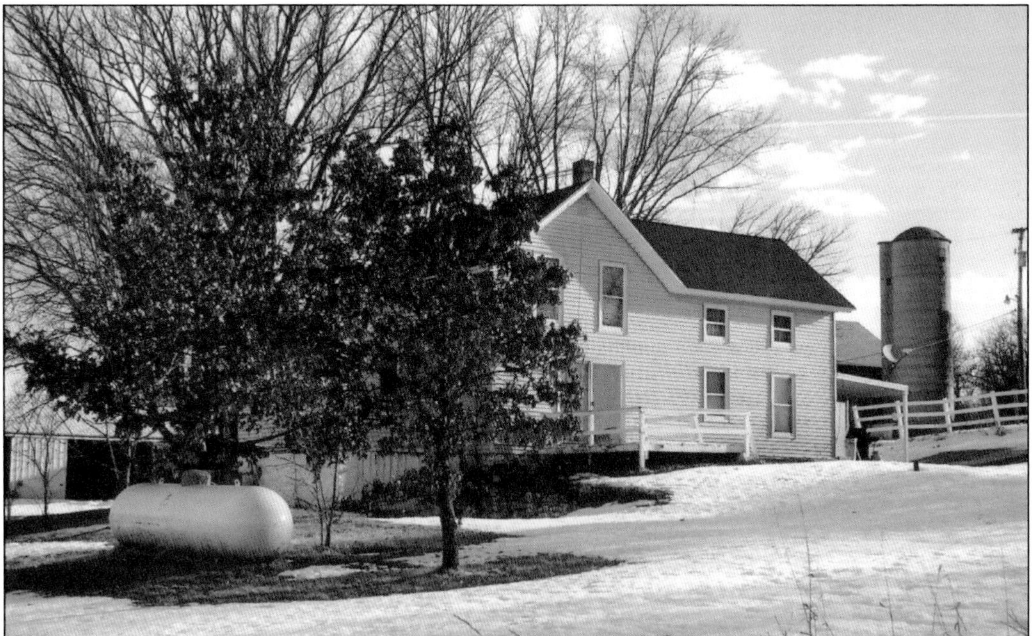

Eli Hershberger (this farm) and his next-door neighbor Willis Miller were the fourth and fifth Amish, initially, to be charged in court, but in the end they were never formally charged. Both families lived just over the county line in Dane County. Ken Glewen, the New Glarus School administrator, went to the Dane County district attorney James Boll to press formal charges. Boll refused to charge Hershberger, contending that the Amish have a 370-year history, and he was not going to be bothering them.

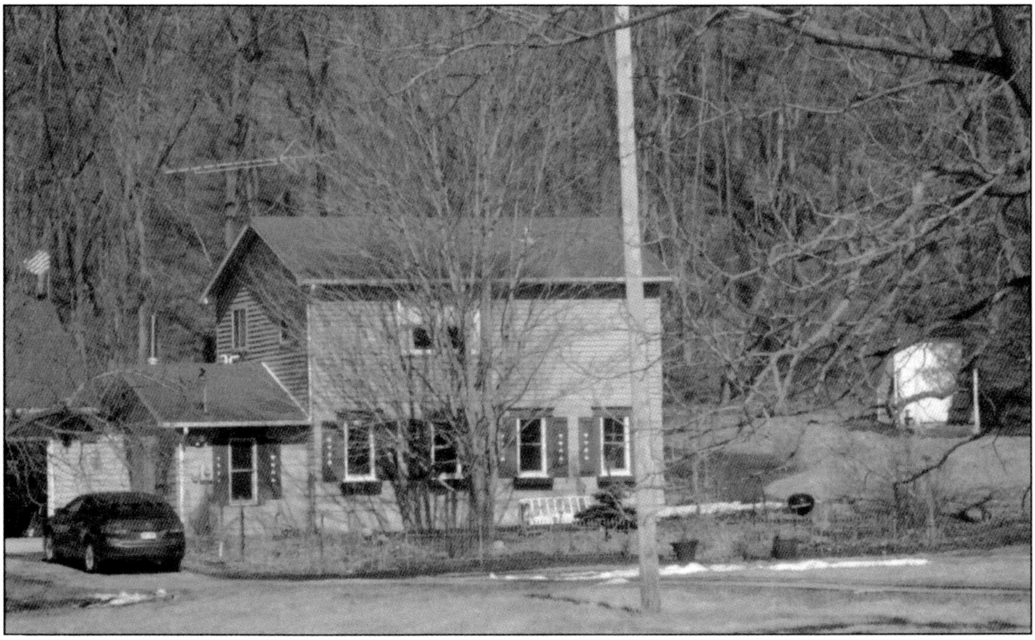

Through this ordeal, the Amish decided to build their own school. The Amish went to the Wisconsin Department of Public Instruction and found a sympathetic ear in Archie Buchmiller. Buchmiller helped the Amish meet the Wisconsin regulations necessary for a legal school. Today, the schoolhouse serves as a private residence.

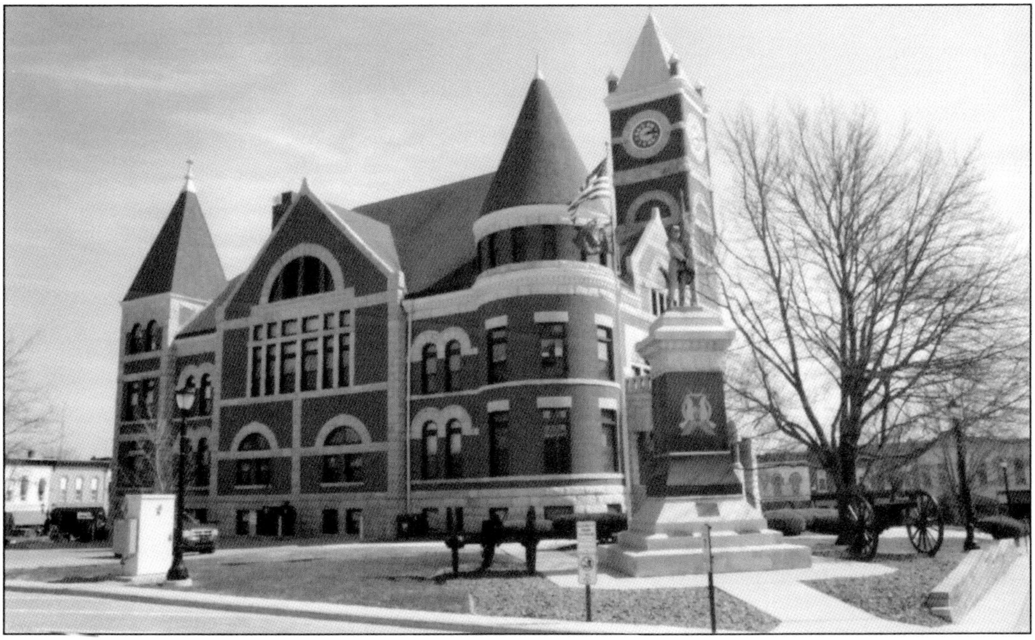

The Green County Courthouse is where, in December 1968, the first two trials of the Amish farmers were heard. The first case was charged in Green County court and heard by Green County judge Roger Elmer. The second trial was also held here, but in circuit court, with Judge Arthur Luebke presiding. Both cases found the three Amish guilty. Each of the Amish defendants was fined $5, which they readily paid.

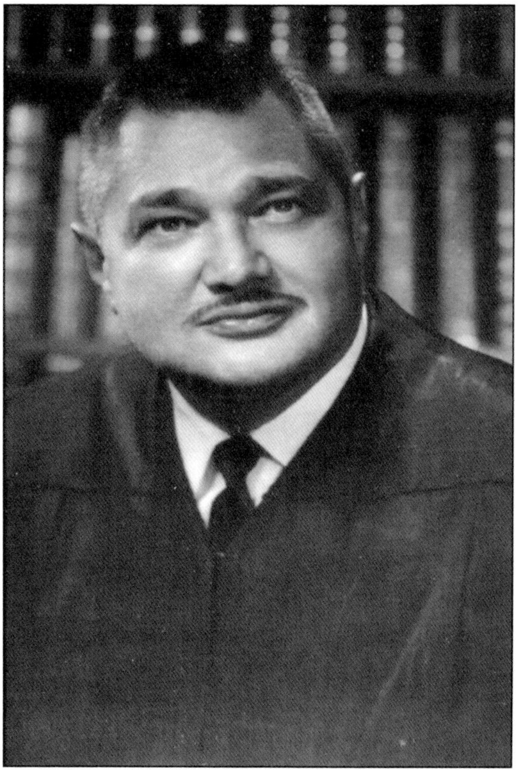

Green County judge Roger Elmer heard the first case filed against Jonas Yoder and Wallace Miller, both Amish, and Adin Yutzy, a Mennonite. All three defendants were found guilty. Elmer was eloquent in his words at the end of the trial, saying, "The State should know no heresy. It should condone no new Salem Witch trials." Much was at stake in this case, which would be the most important and far-reaching case in Judge Elmer's legal career.

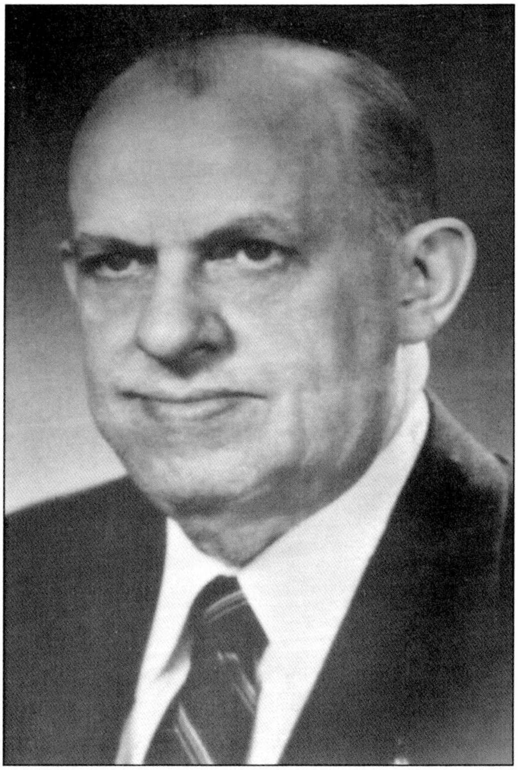

Green County Circuit Court judge Arthur Luebke heard the second case against the three Amish defendants in October 1969 and found them guilty and levied a $5 fine against each defendant. Luebke concurred with Judge Elmer that the Amish "were a sect admired and respected by all who know them for the integrity, rugged self-reliance, high moral character and ability to support and care for their brothers."

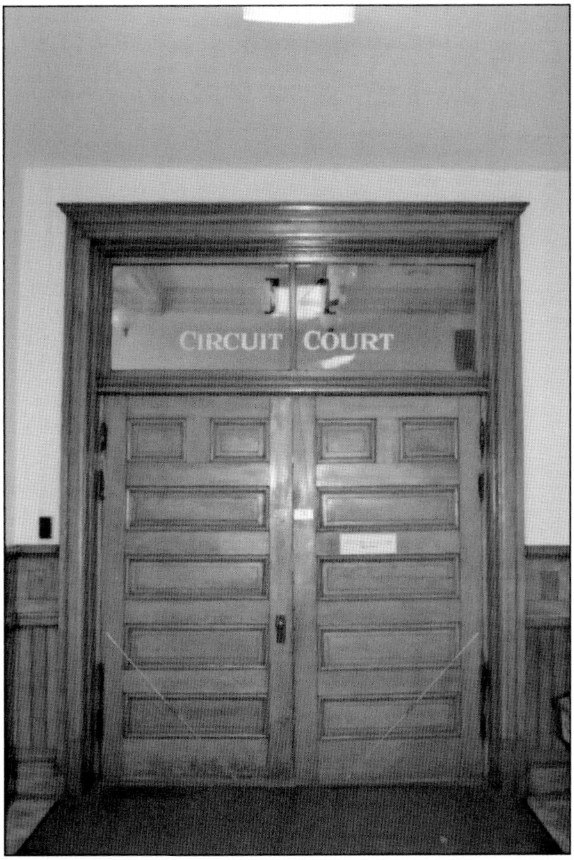

Tom Eckerle, a lawyer from Madison, Wisconsin, had just opened his law firm when contacted by Don Rush, legal counsel for the Wisconsin Catholic Conference, asking if Eckerle would be willing to represent a religious freedom group from Pennsylvania willing to pay the legal fees to defend the New Glarus Amish. He quickly accepted the offer. This is the Green County courtroom where Eckerle's most famous court case, Yoder v. Wisconsin, began.

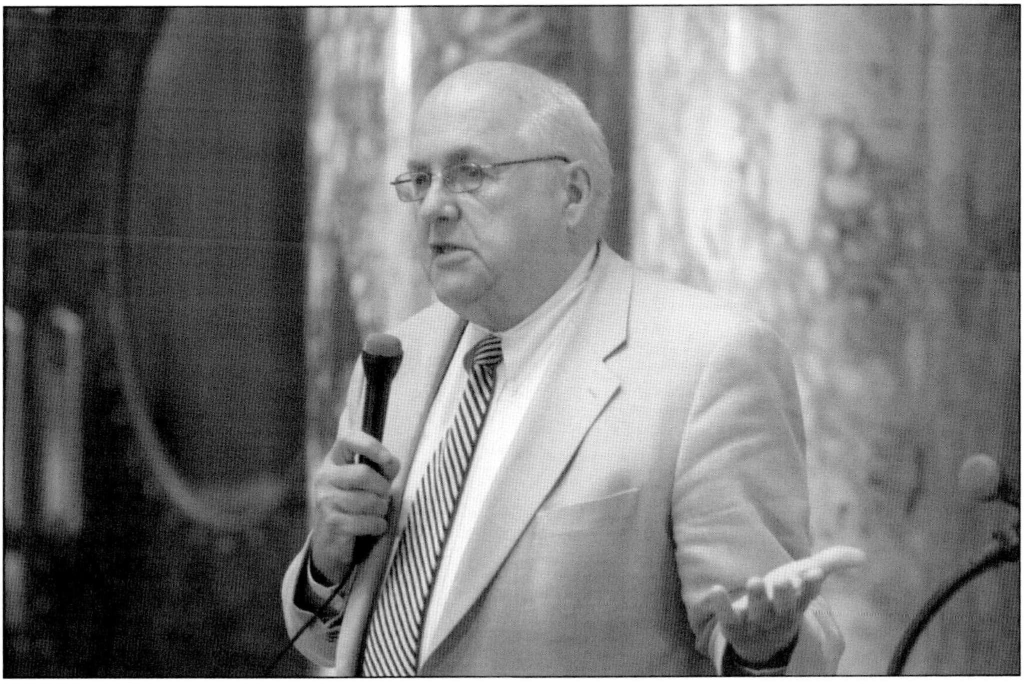

Wisconsin State Assembly representative Frederick Kessler (pictured) and assembly representative Kenneth Merkel worked together to author and sponsor a law exempting the Amish from the state's compulsory school-attendance-to-age-16 law. The law failed to pass. (Fred Kessler.)

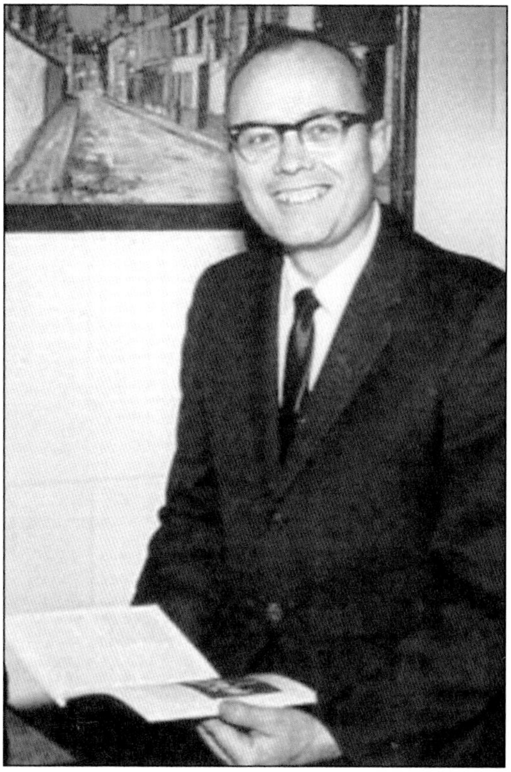

Kenneth Glewen, New Glarus school administrator, filed charges against the local Amish. Glewen worked with the Amish and the courts to see if a settlement could be worked out, but one did not happen. The groundwork was laid for the Yoder v. Wisconsin case.

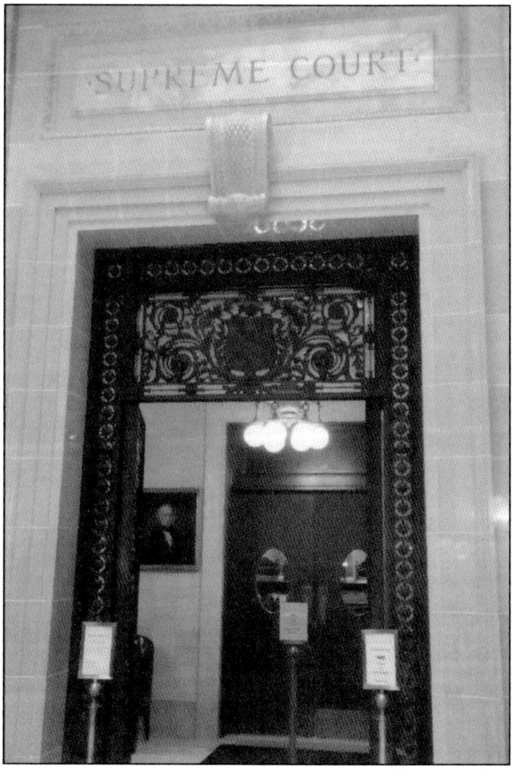

The Wisconsin Supreme Court on December 1, 1970, heard oral arguments in Yoder v. Wisconsin. The Amish men's lawyer, William Ball, presented his opening statement, "The destruction of a way of life is involved here." On January 1971, the Wisconsin Supreme Court handed down a 6-1 vote in favor of the Amish. (Rep. Sondy Pope.)

Eight

The Evolution from Agriculture to a Tourist Economy

A January 15, 1962, announcement that the largest employer, the New Glarus Pet Milk plant, would be closing its doors after 52 years of operations sent shock waves through the area. This loss of Pet Milk brought an end to the jobs of approximately 80 people.

People were worried and anxious about what would happen to New Glarus and the surrounding area. A public meeting was called and much discussion was held. Many asked the question, "What do we do now?" There were already underpinnings of a tentative tourism industry. Annual events such as the Wilhelm Tell Pageant on Labor Day weekend, the Swiss Volksfest, the Swiss Historical Village, and the Chalet of the Golden Fleece each drew thousands of visitors each season; however, this was not sufficient to sustain a strong economy. Wieser's Upright Swiss Embroidery factory also brought in many customers and visitors as well. Many of those customers, after making purchases at the embroidery factory, also visited other attractions in New Glarus. This meeting called for exploring the idea of trying to expand the tourism business to a more year-round development of tourism.

There were already some tentative steps by merchants to "Swissify" front facades of their businesses. Gody Schuetz purchased a downtown café in the late 1950s, remodeling it by adding a beautiful Swiss facade and interior. Schuetz purchased the former Eagle's Club and remodeled the interior to replicate a Swiss cheese factory, which he renamed the Glarner Stube.

Robbi Schneider, newly arrived from Switzerland, purchased and renovated the New Glarus Hotel. Schneider became very instrumental in promoting the Swiss culture in New Glarus. A world-class yodeler and Swiss flag thrower, he taught yodeling and flag throwing to the youth of New Glarus. Schneider had approximately 35 young people participating in Swiss flag throwing and yodeling classes.

In an effort to keep the Swiss motif, the Village of New Glarus enacted a Swiss Design ordinance to make modifications in the downtown area conform to the Swiss theme. New Glarus has several buildings listed in the National Register of Historic Places: the Blumer House; New Glarus Grade School; the 1887 Chicago, Milwaukee, St. Paul, and Pacific Railroad depot; and the 1886 New Glarus Town Hall. Entry into the National Register of Historic Places of the Chalet of the Golden Fleece is expected in November 2014.

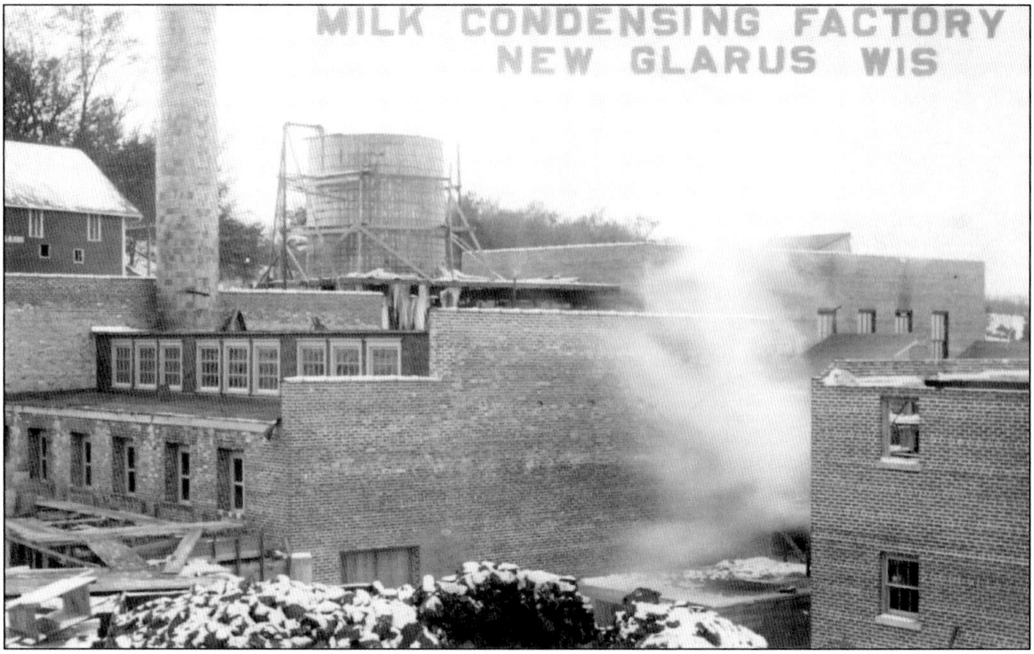

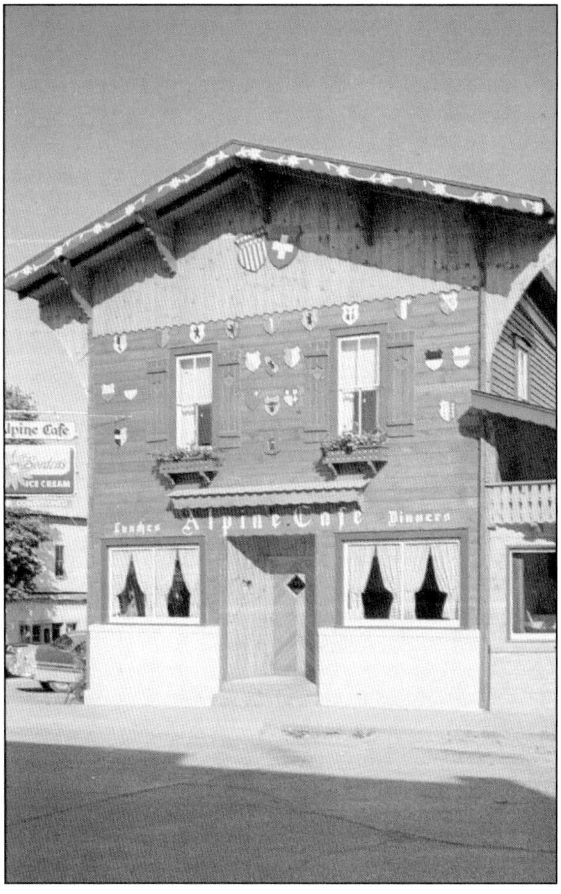

On November 1, 1910, Helvetia Condensing Company began operations in New Glarus and eventually became Pet Milk. Pet was an employer of many area men and women. On January 15, 1962, the announcement that Pet Milk would be closing sent shock waves through the community.

In 1955, Gottfried "Gody" Schuetz and his mother opened the Alpine Café at the corner of First Street and Fifth Avenue. A native of Switzerland, Gody remodeled the interior of the building and put a beautiful Swiss facade on the front and began offering Swiss food.

The top photograph of the interior of the Alpine Café shows the intimate dining room with its knotty pine paneling and a collection of Swiss clocks on the wall. In earlier years, this dining room served as an insurance, legal, and newspaper office. The bottom photograph shows the main dining room. The chairs on the left were handmade by an area Swiss craftsman.

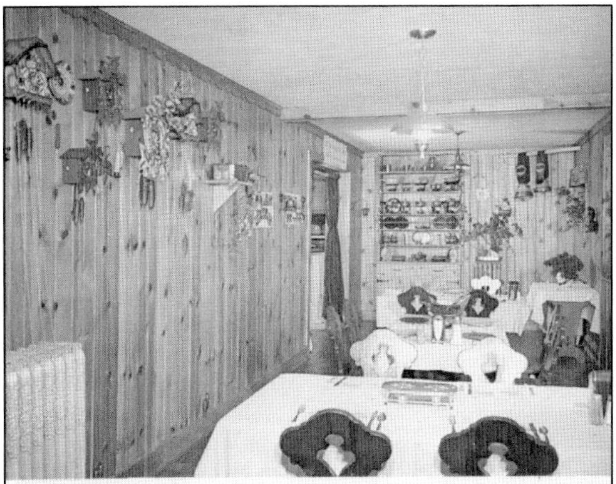

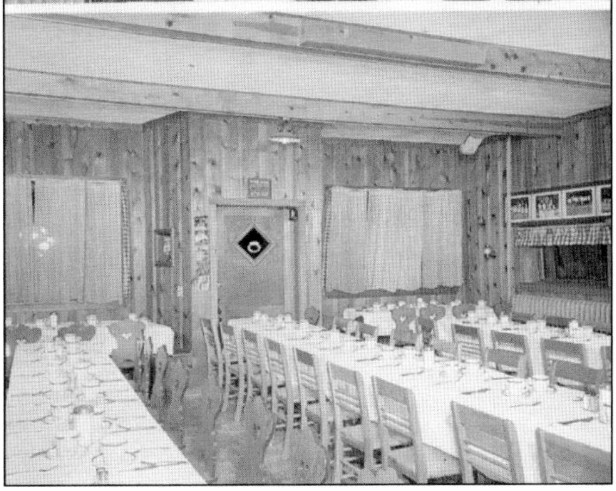

The building on the left shows a newer rendition of the Alpine Café. Over the past three decades, several owners have operated the business. Fred and Margaret Ryser, who own the adjacent tavern, also operated the Alpine Café. They merged the two businesses. The building on the left is now the Primrose Winery.

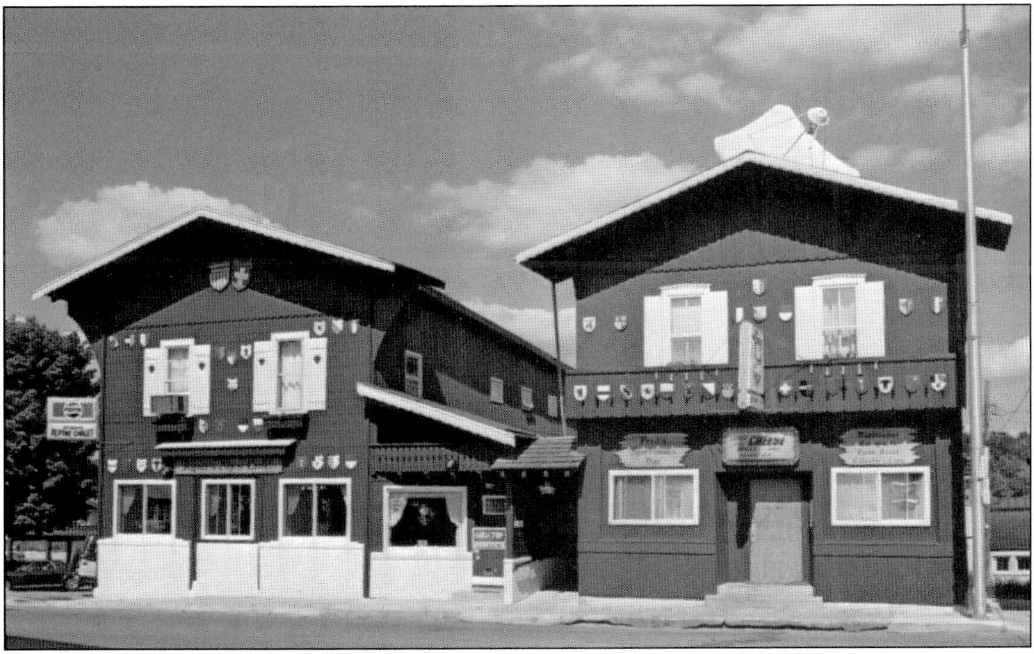

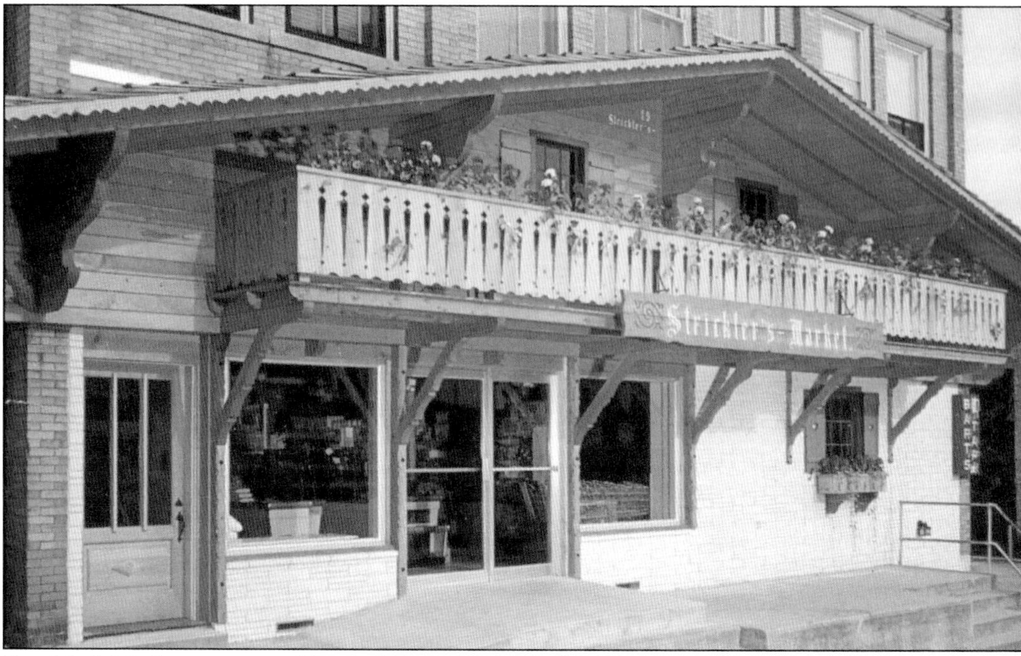

Strickler's Market was one of the early businesses to adapt the Swiss theme. Owner Butch Strickler is well known as one of the largest donors to University of Wisconsin sports through his Butch's Bologna Bash. The right side of the building used to serve as the New Glarus post office. Myron Bartle operated a tavern in the basement of the building.

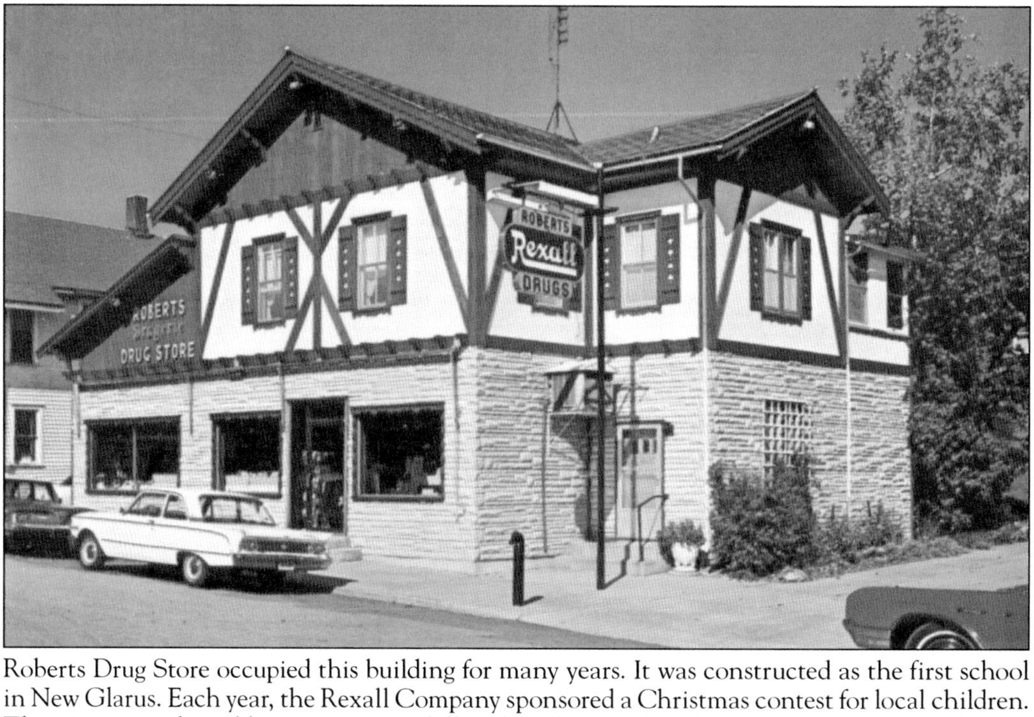

Roberts Drug Store occupied this building for many years. It was constructed as the first school in New Glarus. Each year, the Rexall Company sponsored a Christmas contest for local children. The winning girl would get a very nice doll and the boy an electric train. Roberts's specialty was square ice cream cones. (Fagan collection.)

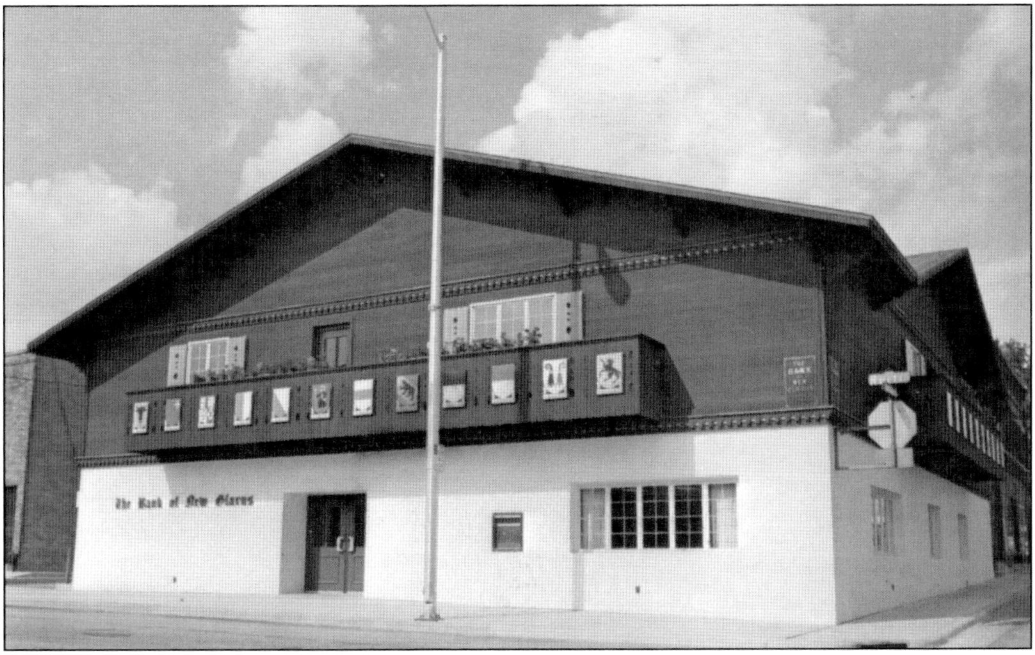

The Bank of New Glarus opened in June 1970 and held a grand opening on August 23 to show off the new Swiss-style building. The bronze plaque on the far right side of the upper story of the building was the sign on the first Bank of New Glarus on this site.

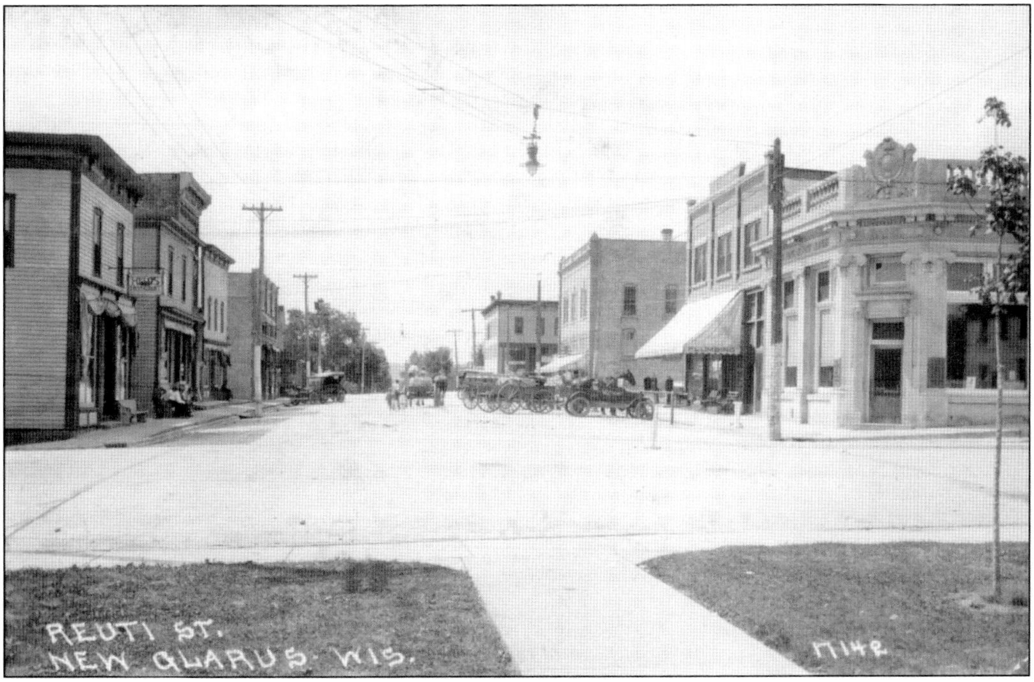

This 1927 postcard shows the intersection of Fifth Avenue and First Street. The building on the left corner is the Alpine Café. Next to it is the Sportsmen's Bar. The building on the right in the foreground is an earlier Bank of New Glarus. Next to it is the Hoesly Hardware building, which was torn down to build the current Bank of New Glarus.

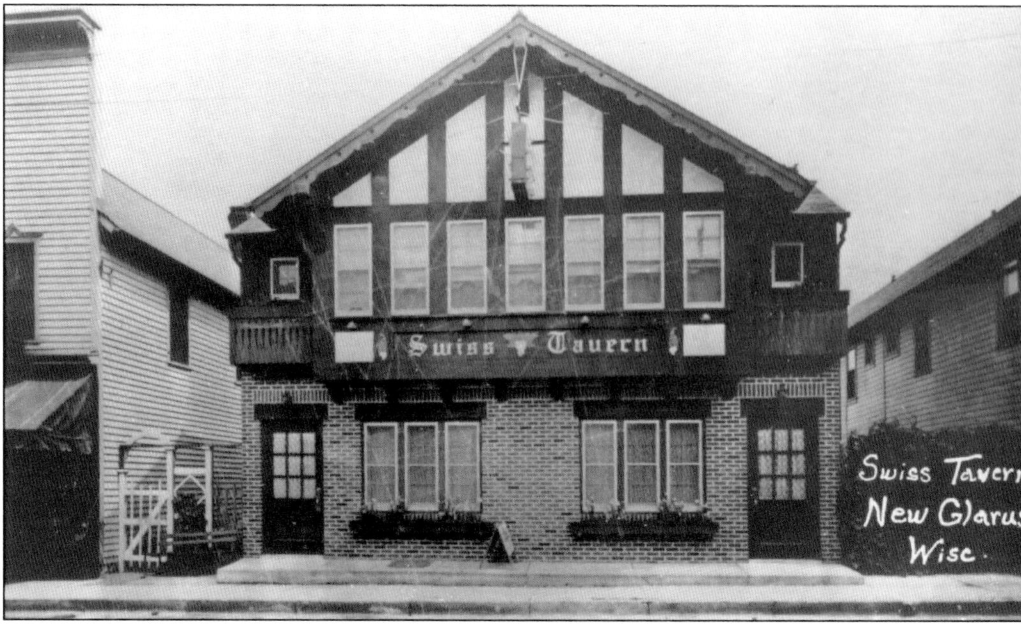

Bigler's Swiss Tavern was the first Swiss-style building constructed in New Glarus. Fred Bigler, a bricklayer from Switzerland, did all the masonry work on the building. He and his wife, Marie, operated the tavern for many years.

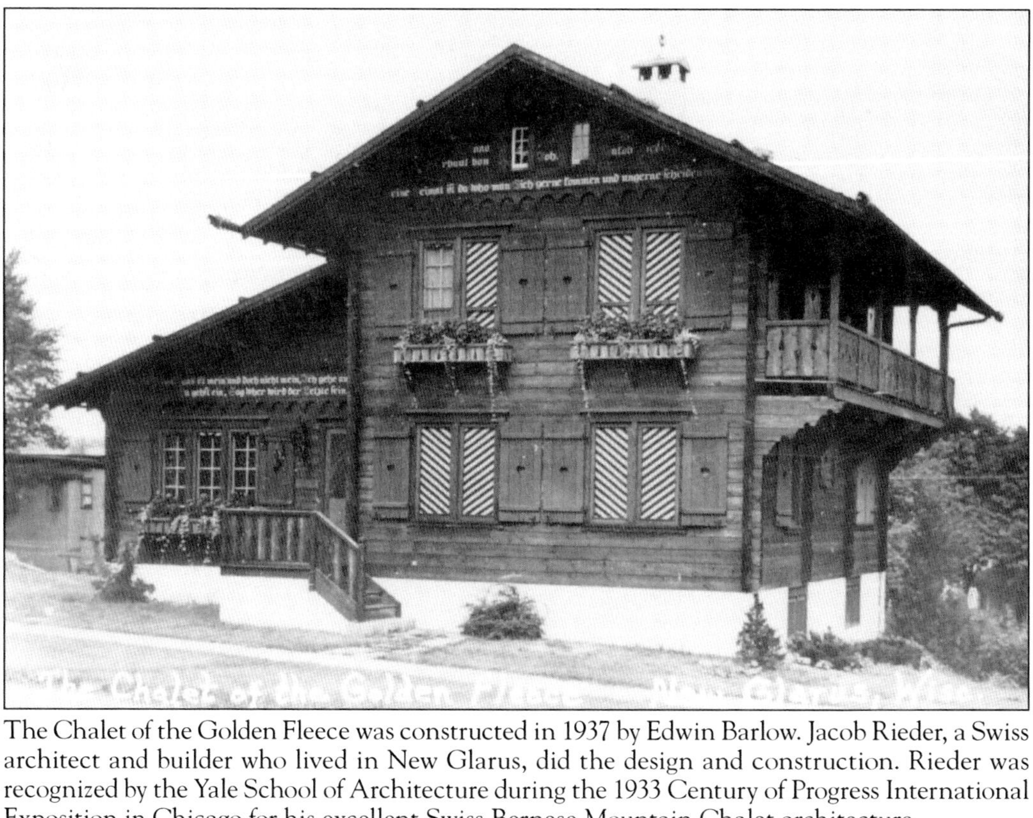

The Chalet of the Golden Fleece was constructed in 1937 by Edwin Barlow. Jacob Rieder, a Swiss architect and builder who lived in New Glarus, did the design and construction. Rieder was recognized by the Yale School of Architecture during the 1933 Century of Progress International Exposition in Chicago for his excellent Swiss Bernese Mountain Chalet architecture.

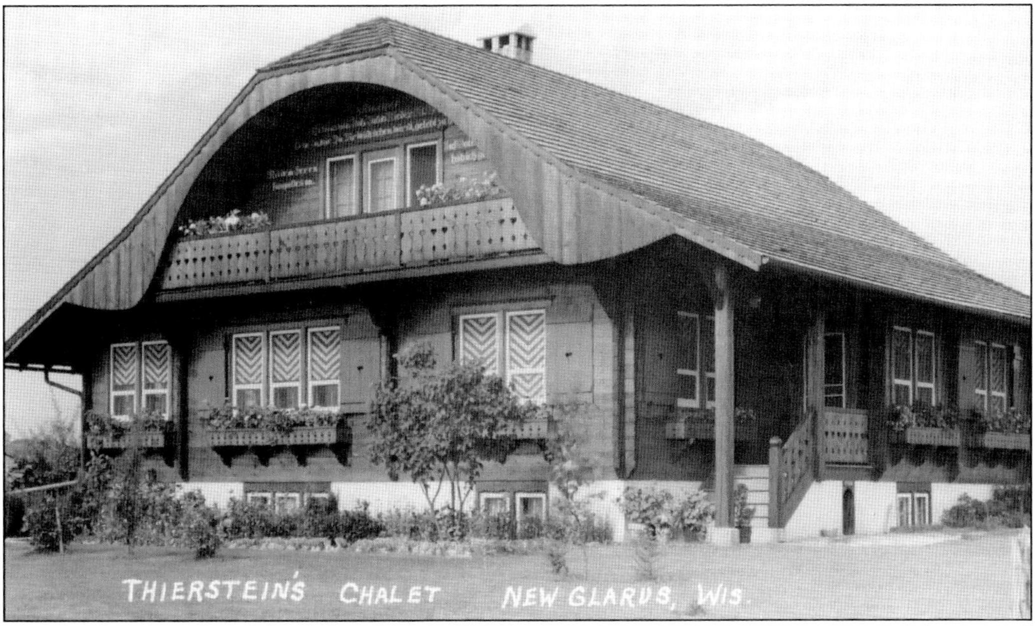

Jacob Rieder built this beautiful residence for Ernest Thierstein, a Swiss immigrant who owned and operated the 4 Corners Tavern in New Glarus for years. Thierstein's dog would walk around the bar picking up empty beer bottles and taking them behind the bar, where the dog would carefully drop the bottles into a bottle chute to the basement.

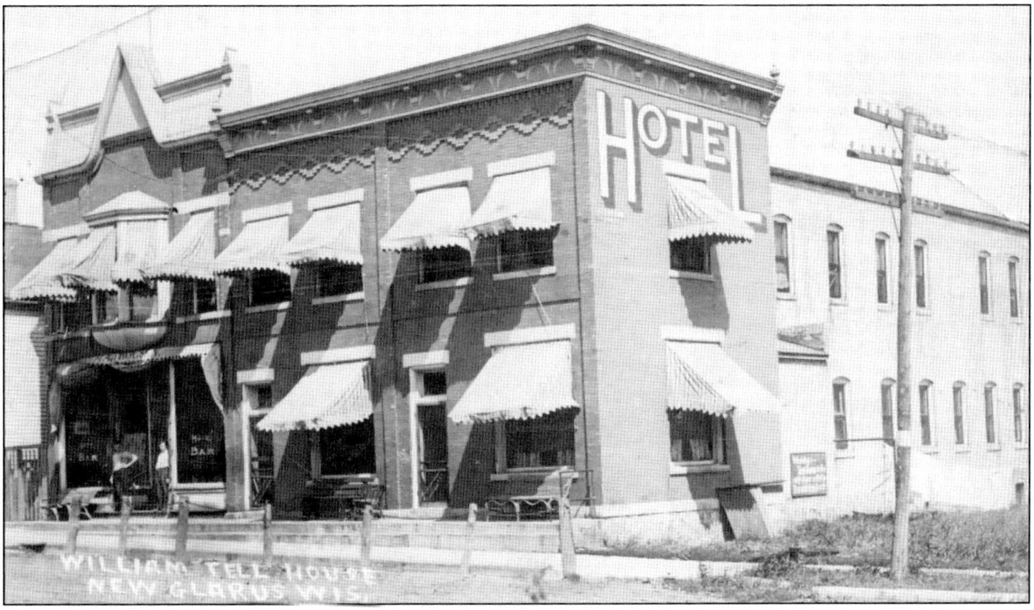

This is an early photograph of the Wilhelm Tell Hotel. A dance hall was added later. In winter, area cheese makers would hold Swiss wrestling matches in the dance hall.

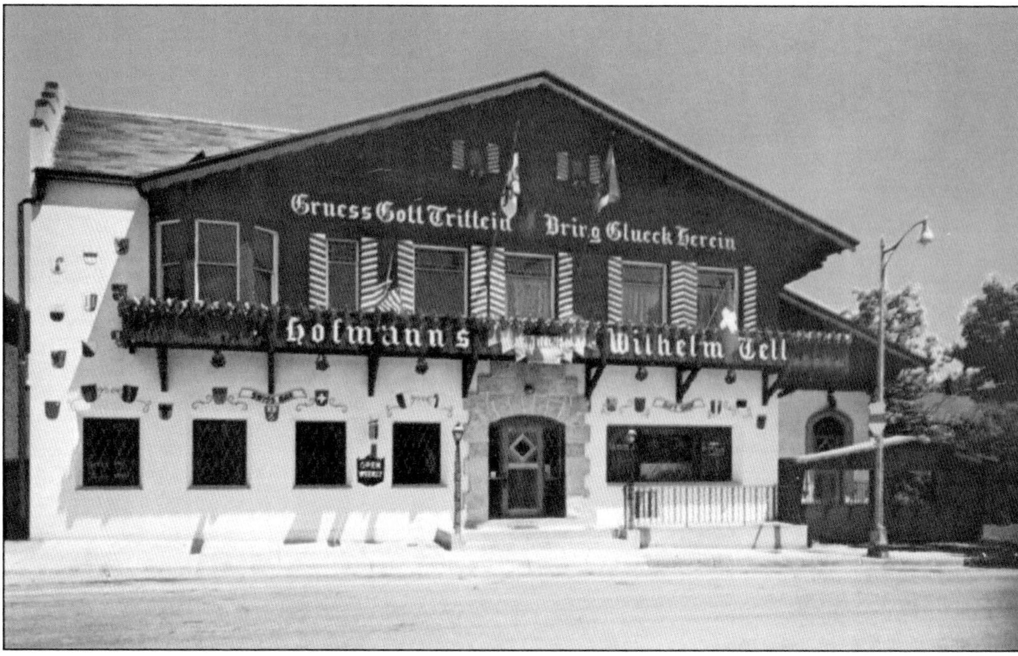

The Karl Hoffmann family purchased the Wilhelm Tell in 1964 and completed a major remodeling of the building utilizing the Swiss motif.

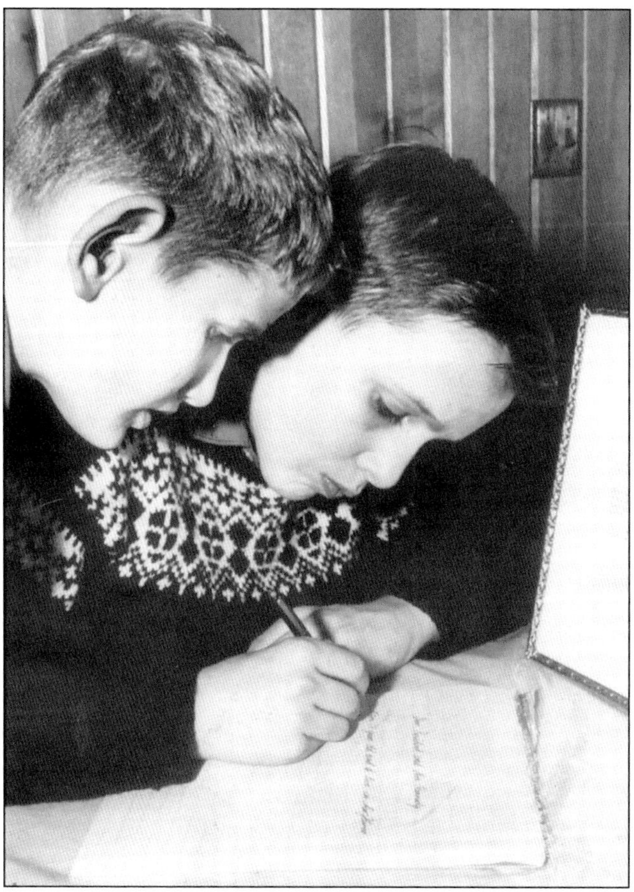

Karl (left) and Hans Hoffmann, ages 13 and 11, are writing a letter to President Kennedy inviting him to the Hoffmann's home for a meal of Wiener Schnitzel. President Kennedy's staff responded, "We will keep your offer in mind should an appropriate occasion arise."

The Zweifel Jewelry and Gift store has gone through two major renovations. The first, in the early 1970s, is shown here. The second floor was removed and a more Swiss-like gable roof was installed. Earlier in the life of the building, the first floor held New Glarus Cleaners, Dr. Earl Hicks MD, and local dentist Dr. Brauchle.

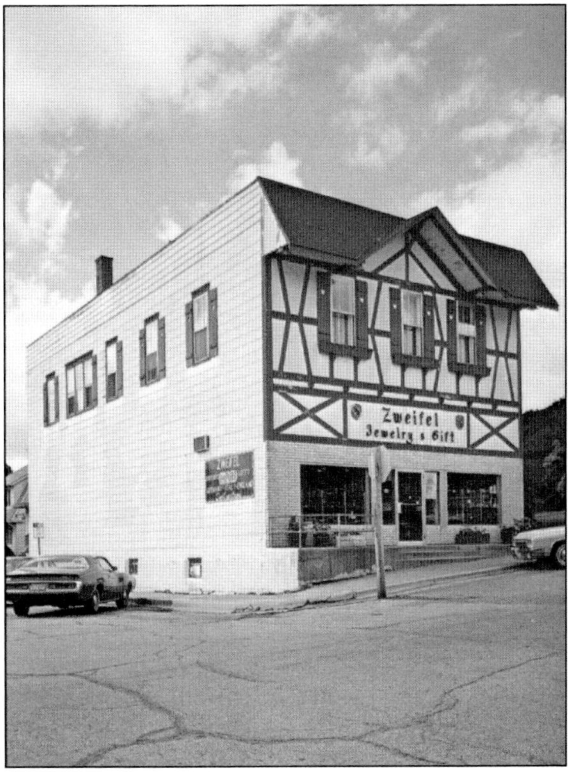

Ken and Beverly Blum owned and operated the Cities Service station, known as Ken's City Service, offering auto and tire repair. In the early 1960s, the Blum's purchased a popcorn wagon, which they set up in front of the gas station. In 2013, Ken and Beverly's daughter Sherry opened a popcorn wagon near the Sugar River State Trail. (Ken Blum.)

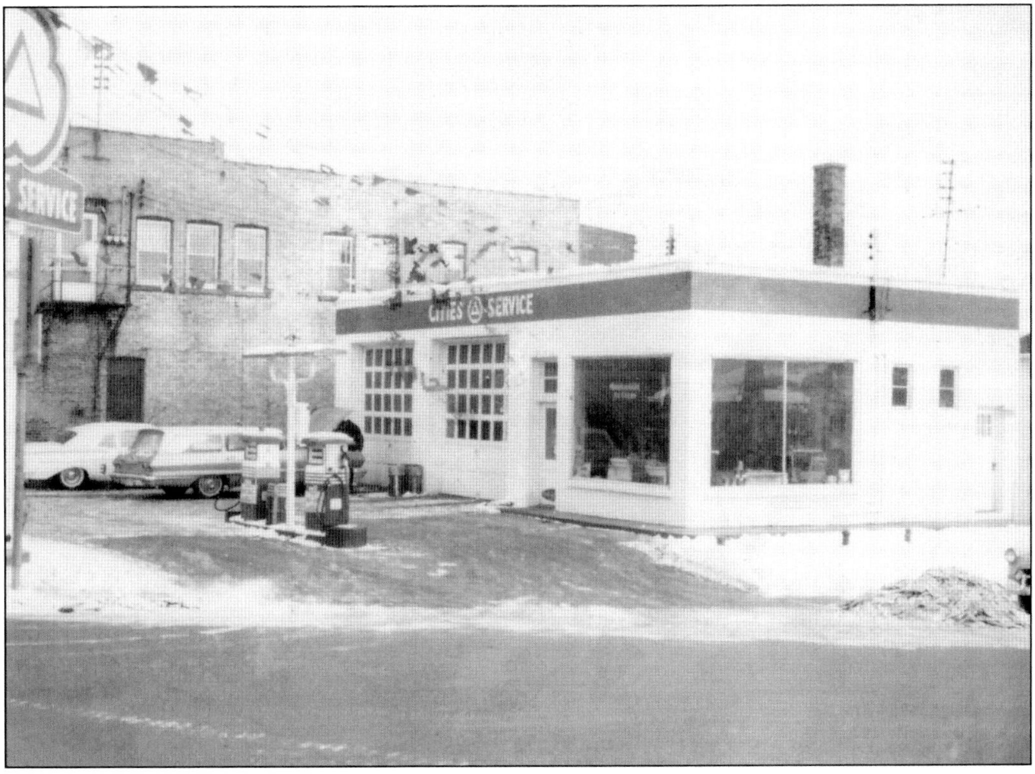

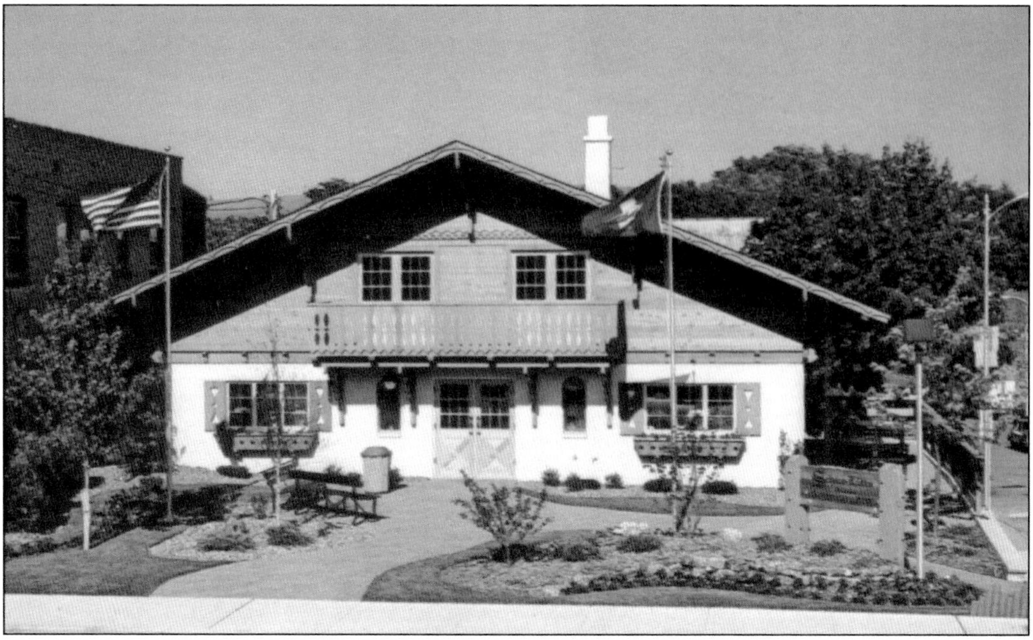

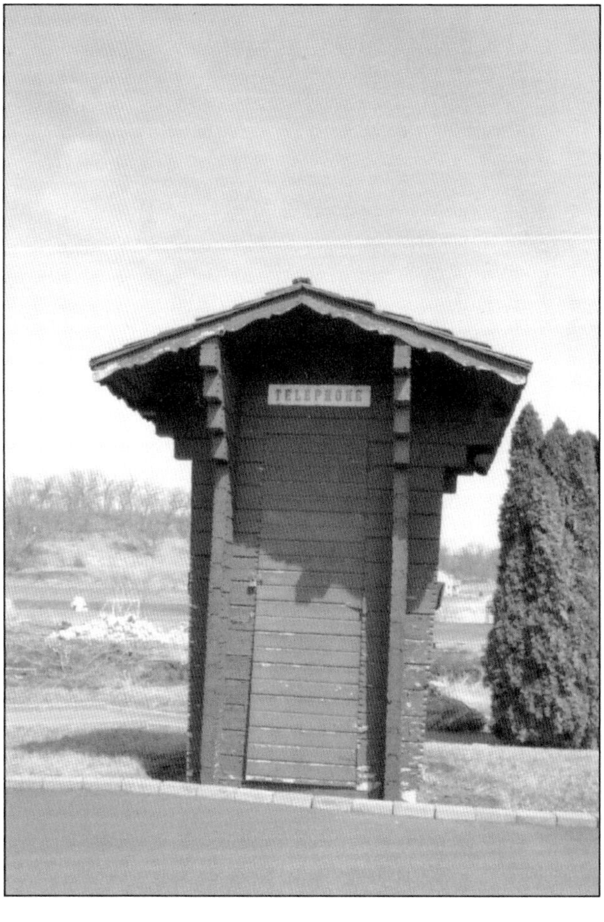

A local investment club purchased the Cities Service gas station and did a total remodel of the building, utilizing a Swiss motif, the result of which was the Schoco-Laden. The Schoco-Laden opened in 1981. (Chuck Phillipson.)

Even the telephone booths in New Glarus utilized the Swiss architecture theme. Robbie Schneider, former owner of the New Glarus Hotel, was instrumental in getting these phone booths built.

Nine

Around Town

This final chapter is a collection of various photographs that do not neatly fit into any other chapter. But, within this chapter, the reader will find a very broad overview of what is and was New Glarus.

As this book was being completed, a revival of Second Street has been visible with all of the storefronts once again occupied, breathing new life into the main street. Recent news of a market and café offering locally grown foods opening up soon brings with it yet more hope for the future of not only the small rural community but the entire area.

In 1845, those of Swiss ancestry were the new residents of the Little Sugar River Valley. Today, as the numbers of families with Swiss names thin by attrition and the surnames are being replaced by those of many different ethnicities, locals see not despair but hope for the future.

This transition has been an interesting and exciting one. Change can be difficult to cope with, but in the end it serves the entire community, giving it a greater worldview, and that makes it a richer place to live.

So, this book ends where it started, with the prophetic words of the Oglala Sioux holy man telling of the story of the power of the circle. New Glarus began as a wheat-farming community, and over the past 170 years, it has returned once again to growing wheat.

Black Elk concludes, "Even the seasons form a great circle in their changing, and always come back again to where they were. The life of a man is a circle from childhood to childhood, and so it is in everything where the power moves." Our new childhood as a community is once again beginning.

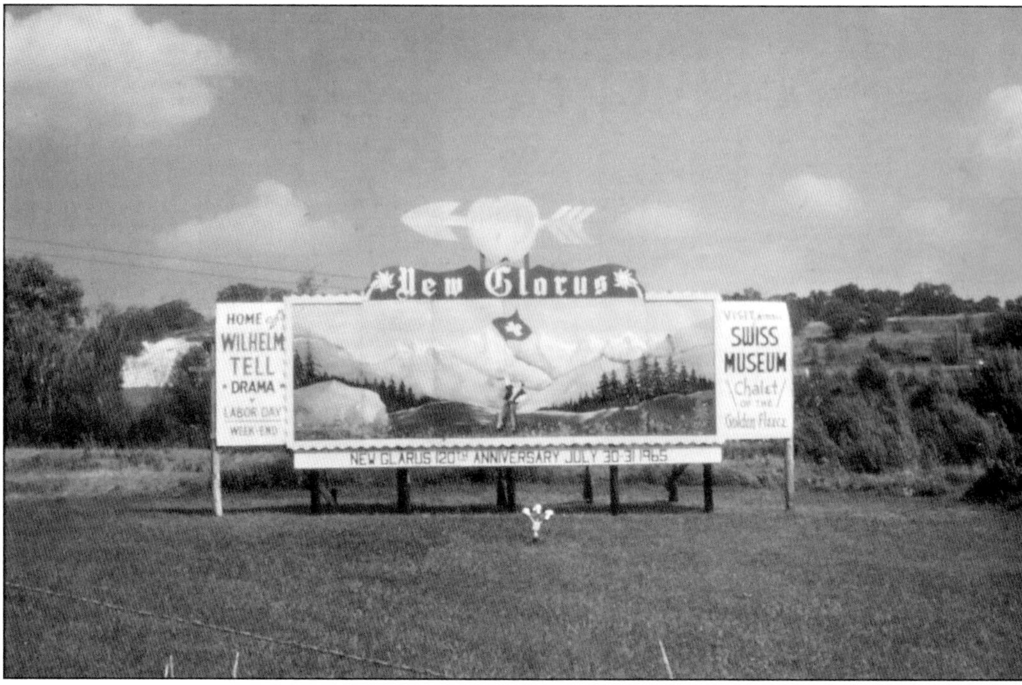

Welcome to New Glarus. This sign painted by Paul Grossenbacher invited tourists to New Glarus for many years as they headed north. In many ways, this sign told the story of New Glarus during the 10 seconds motorists had it in their line of sight.

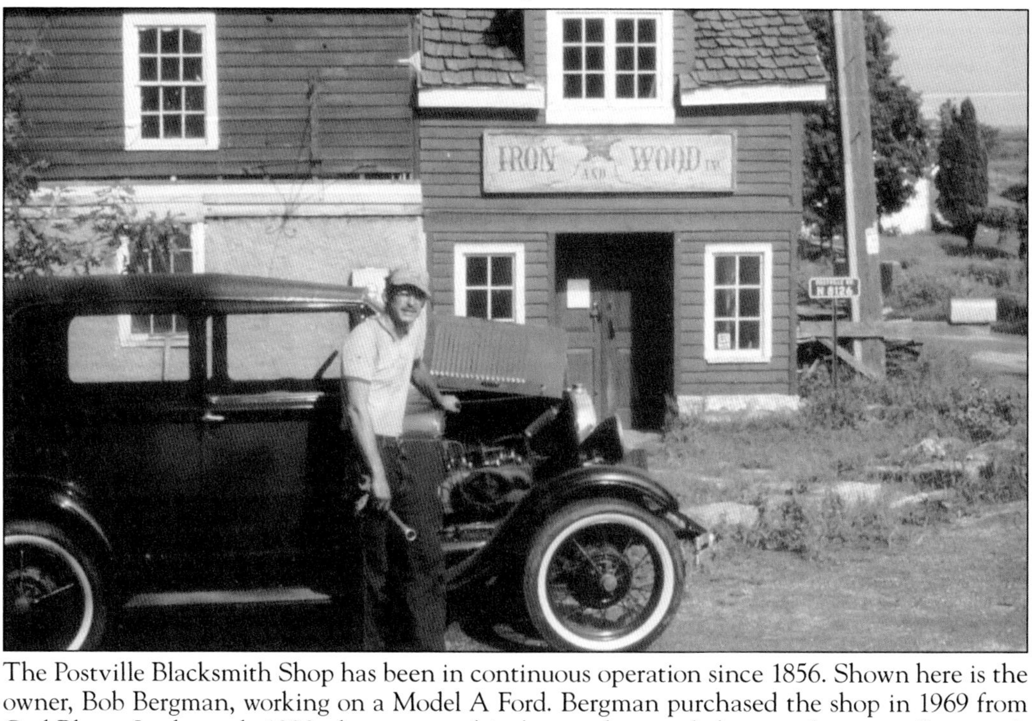

The Postville Blacksmith Shop has been in continuous operation since 1856. Shown here is the owner, Bob Bergman, working on a Model A Ford. Bergman purchased the shop in 1969 from Carl Blaser. In the early 1990s, he outgrew this shop and expanded across the street. Bergman's ornamental ironwork takes him across the United States for commissioned jobs.

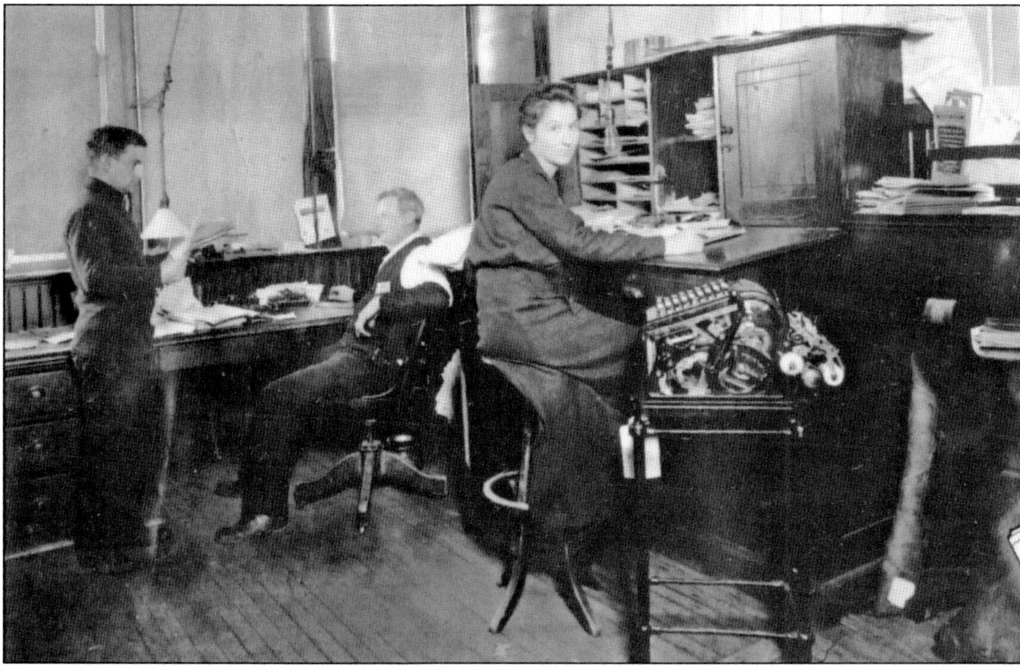

The Milwaukee Road railroad abandoned service to New Glarus in 1972. This photograph shows the interior of the depot agents-and-operators room. The woman sitting at the desk probably is the bookkeeper for the depot. The lower half of the desk she is working at is still in the depot. The two men in the bay window are telegraph operators. (Robert Luchsinger.)

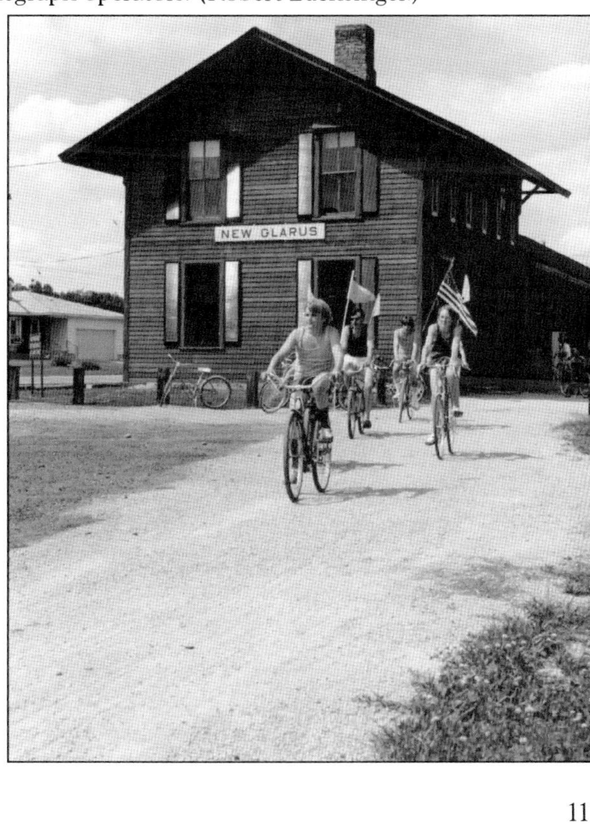

The Wisconsin Department of Natural Resources purchased the 23-mile railroad right-of-way from Brodhead to New Glarus on July 27, 1972. Work began immediately to remove the ties and rails and convert the right-of-way to what would become the Sugar River State Trail. The trail drew many people to New Glarus each weekend for biking or snowmobiling.

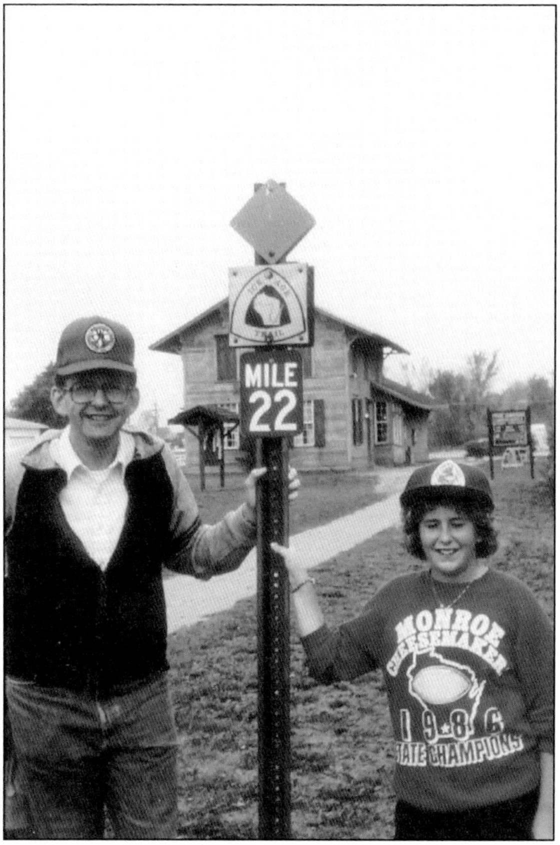

Pictured are state representative Dave Deininger and his daughter Emilie participating in the annual Ice Age National Scenic Trail Hike-A-Thon. The New Glarus depot, shown in the background, has been fully restored and is listed in the National Register of Historic Places.

Peggy O'Neill, a primate researcher for the University of Wisconsin Primate Center, brought her monkeys to her rural New Glarus property in the last years of the 1980s for a summer research project. One of her monkeys, Eric, escaped and was on the lam for several weeks. Each day, there were news updates on the latest Eric sighting.

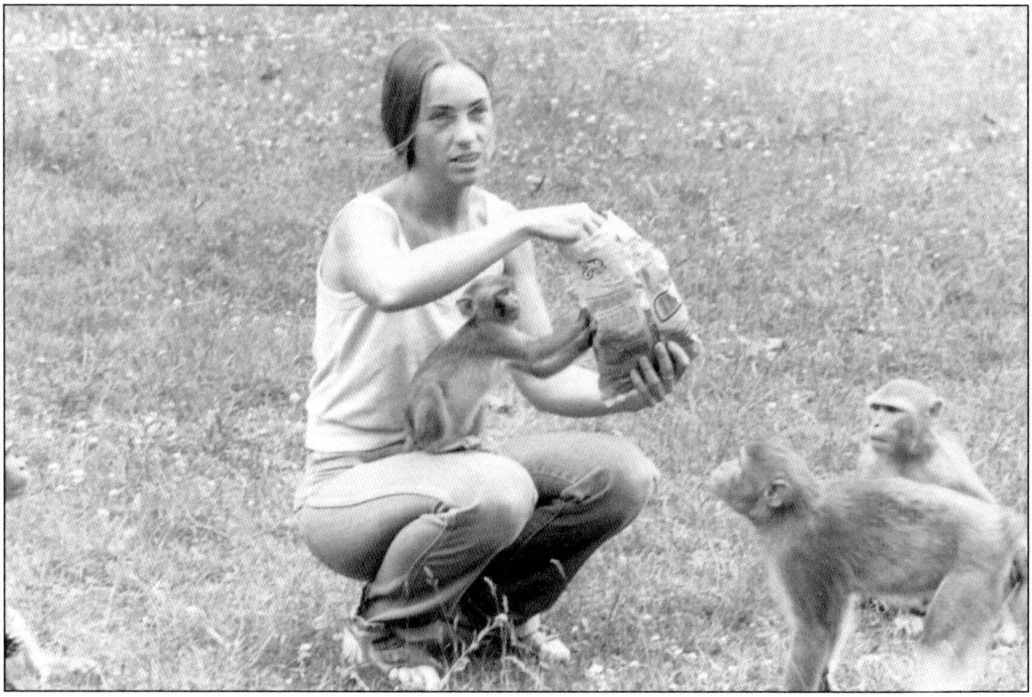

Robert "Bobby Dent" Smith lived in Jimtown, near New Glarus, where he operated the Montrose Store. Bobby came to New Glarus on Friday or Saturday nights in his Model A Ford. Each Sunday morning, a group of regulars would stop at his store for Dr. Pepper and conversation. A robbery attempt and beating left him nearly dead, but he survived and lived for several years above his store.

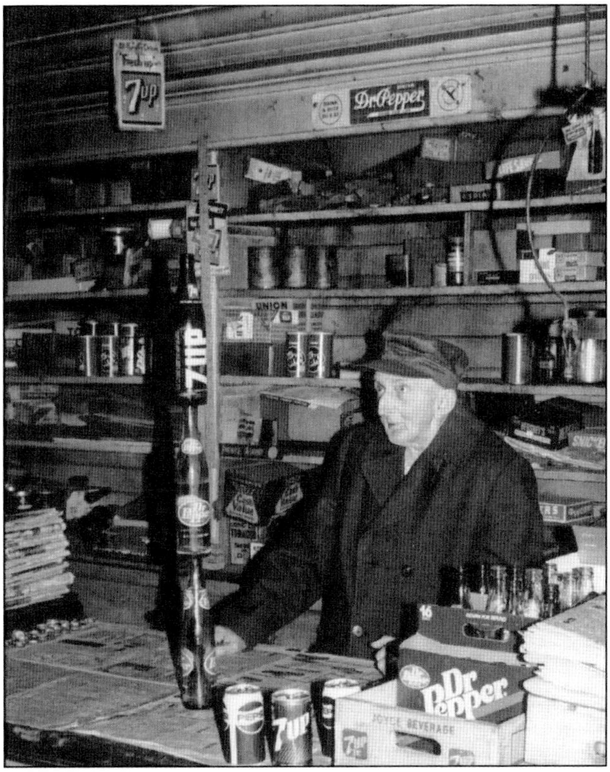

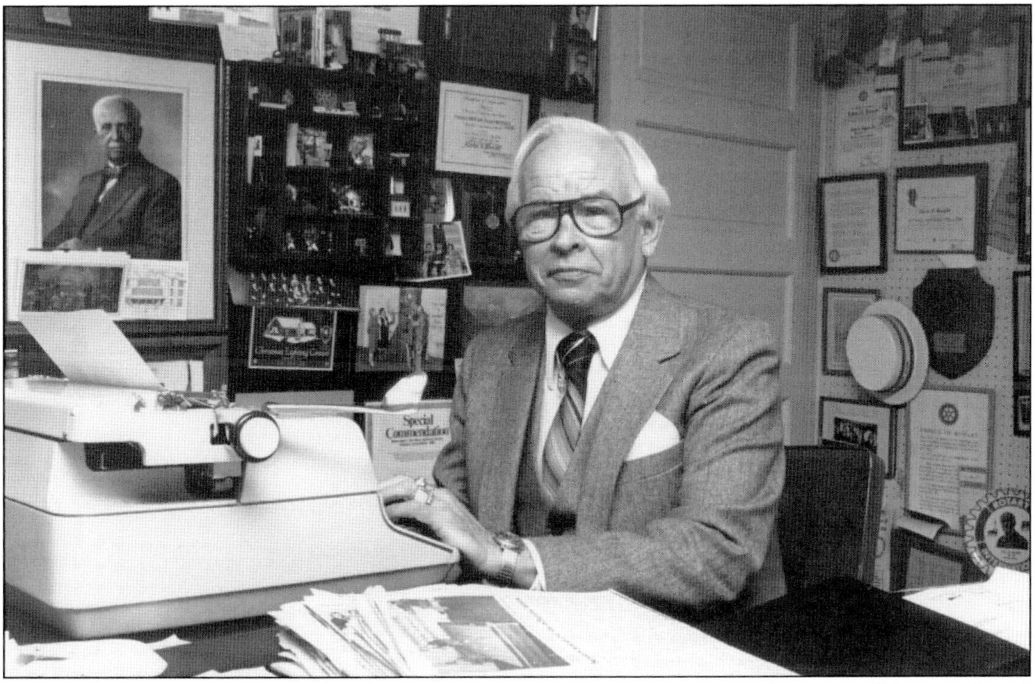

Alvin Streiff, a New Glarus native, wrote a column for many years, "Alvin Streiff Remembers," for the *New Glarus Post* newspaper. His 78 columns reflected on the daily lives of the people he came into contact with while growing up in New Glarus. (New Glarus Historical Society.)

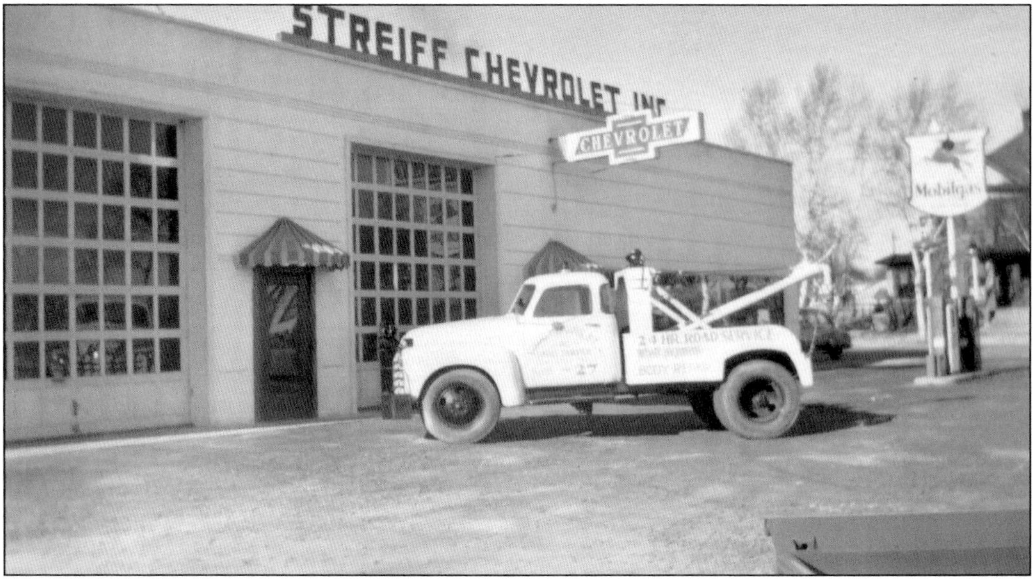

Fred Streiff built and moved his Chevrolet dealership into this building in 1950. In 1951, Streiff partnered with Delmar Kubly and Ed Richert. Streiff also built a roadside diner and motel, Streiff's Waffle Shop, next door. The restaurant became a popular hangout for high school students.

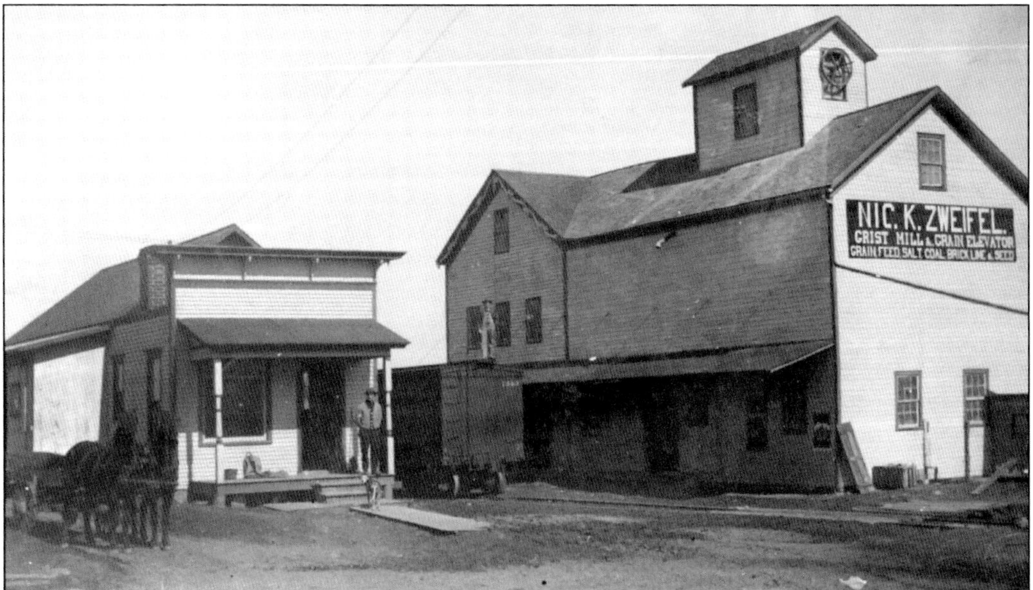

This mill was built in 1851 by Joshua Wild. Wild operated it for several years before selling it to David Klassy. The mill has had many owners, including Nic Zweifel. For many years, it operated as the New Glarus Feed and Fuel Coop. The building was demolished in 2012. (New Glarus Historical Society.)

Walking through New Glarus, one will notice a very interesting Swiss Folk painting, *Bauernmalerei*, on some of the buildings. Much of the work was done by Jakob Bodenmann of Alton, Switzerland, and Janeen Babler. Babler went to Switzerland to learn the art of Swiss Folk painting from Bodenmann. (Janeen Babler.)

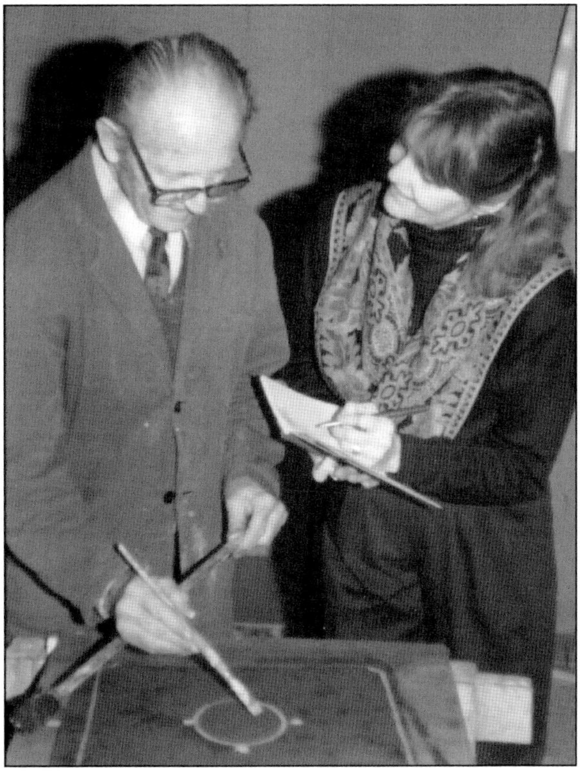

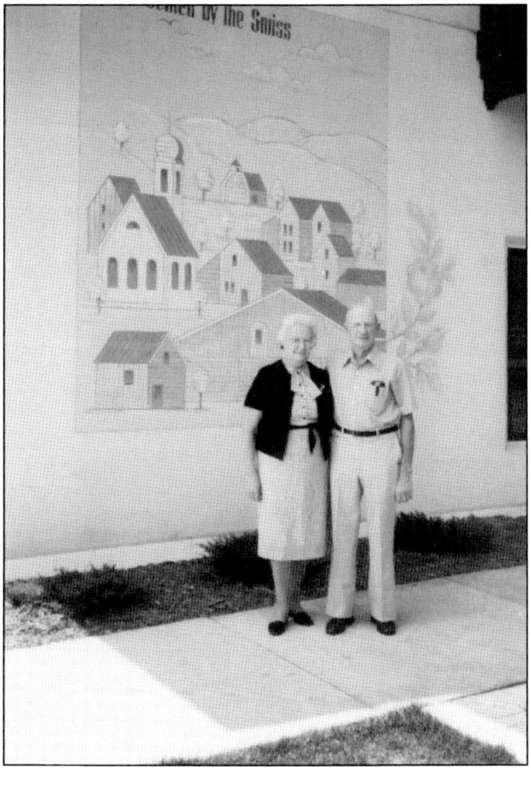

Frank and Elda Schiesser are standing in front of a *Bauernmalerei* painted on the east wall of the New Glarus Village Hall. Their daughter Linda commissioned Swiss Folk artist Jakob Bodenmann to do this folk painting to honor all that Elda and Frank had done for the community over many decades of dedicated volunteerism. (Schiesser collection.)

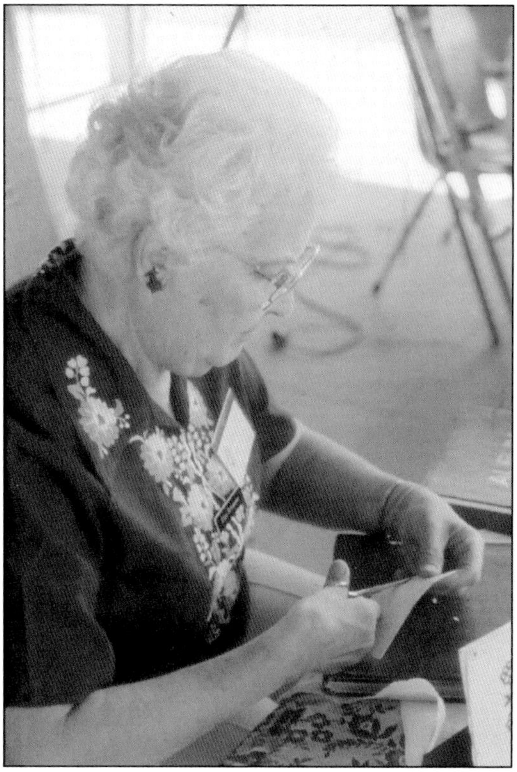

Elda Schiesser, on a 1985 trip to Switzerland, purchased a book on Scherenschnitte, (scissor paper cutting), a form of Swiss folk art. This art form requires small, specialty scissors, which make very intricate cuts in the paper to create the design. Her work has been on display at art shows in both the United States and Switzerland. In 2002, one of her works was used on the White House Christmas tree. At age 96, Elda is still actively cutting several days each week. (Schiesser collection.)

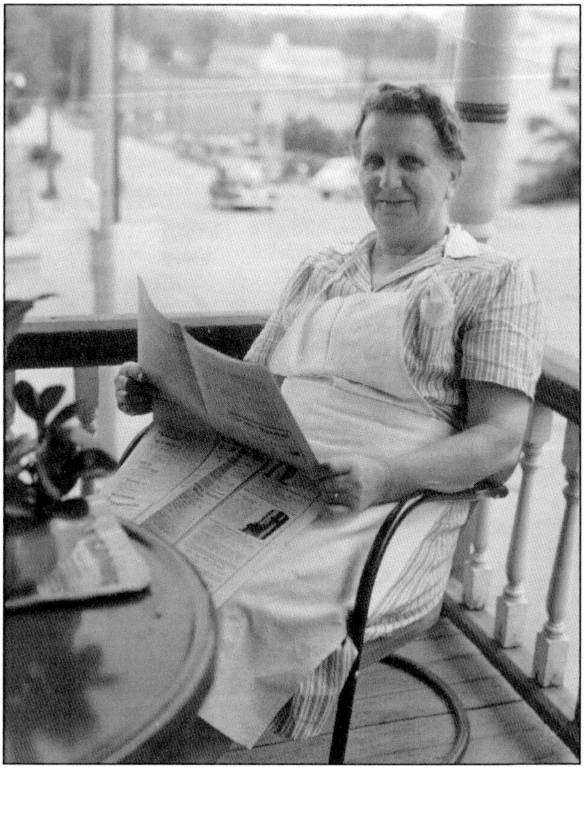

Marie Lienhardt, co-owner of the New Glarus Hotel, is taking a few minutes to catch up on the news of the day. The Lienhardt family owned the New Glarus Hotel for a number of years. During their ownership, they opened up a theater in what is now main dining room of the hotel. Former hotel owner Robbi Schneider expanded the hotel into the former theater. (Al Lienhardt.)

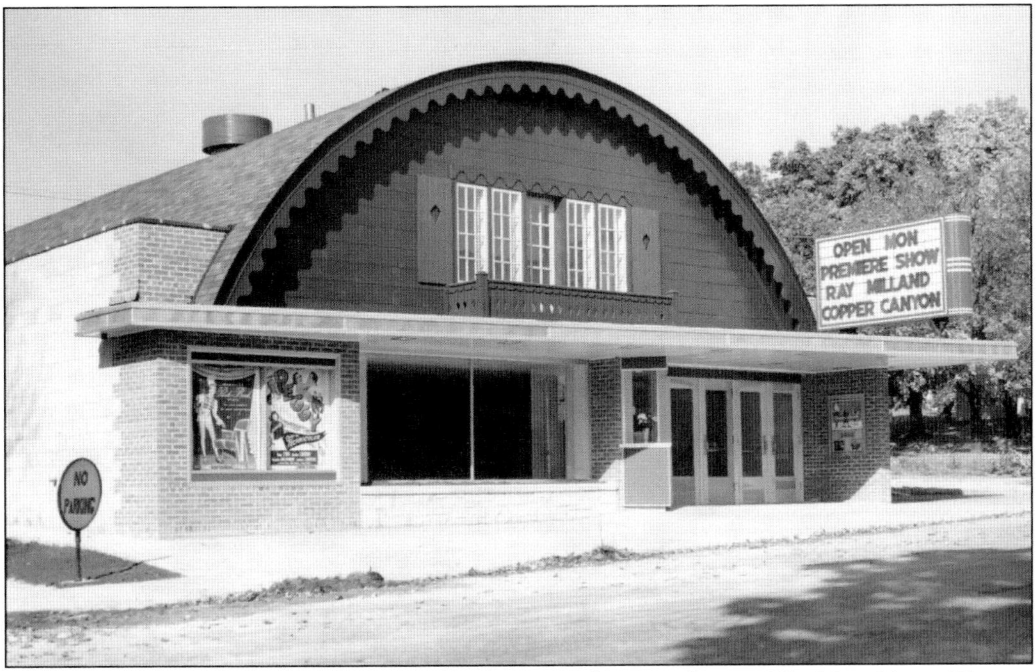

It is October 1950, and Fred Lienhardt is about to open his new theater. The New Glarus Theater was advertised as "Southern Wisconsin's most comfortable theater." The Swiss Chalet–style theater was designed by Myles Belongia of Milwaukee. Presidential candidate John F. Kennedy made a Wisconsin primary election speech to a packed theater in April 1960. (Al Lienhardt.)

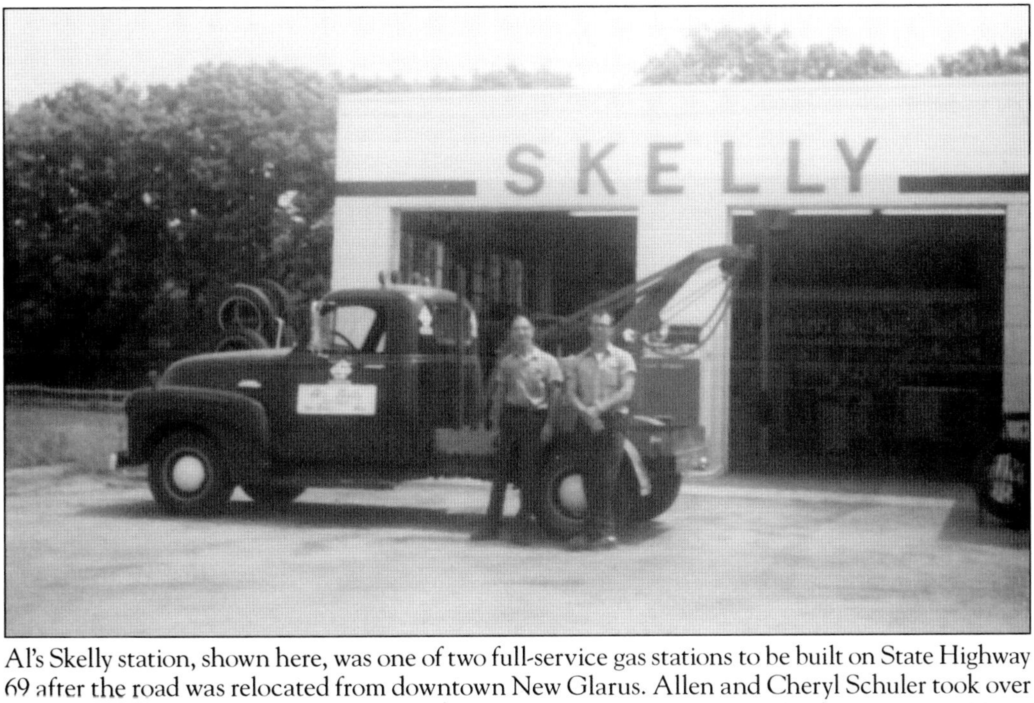

Al's Skelly station, shown here, was one of two full-service gas stations to be built on State Highway 69 after the road was relocated from downtown New Glarus. Allen and Cheryl Schuler took over the business created by the Rufenacht and Rupnow Oil Company. Posing for the camera are Vince Schuler (left) and Al Schuler. (Cheryl Schuler.)

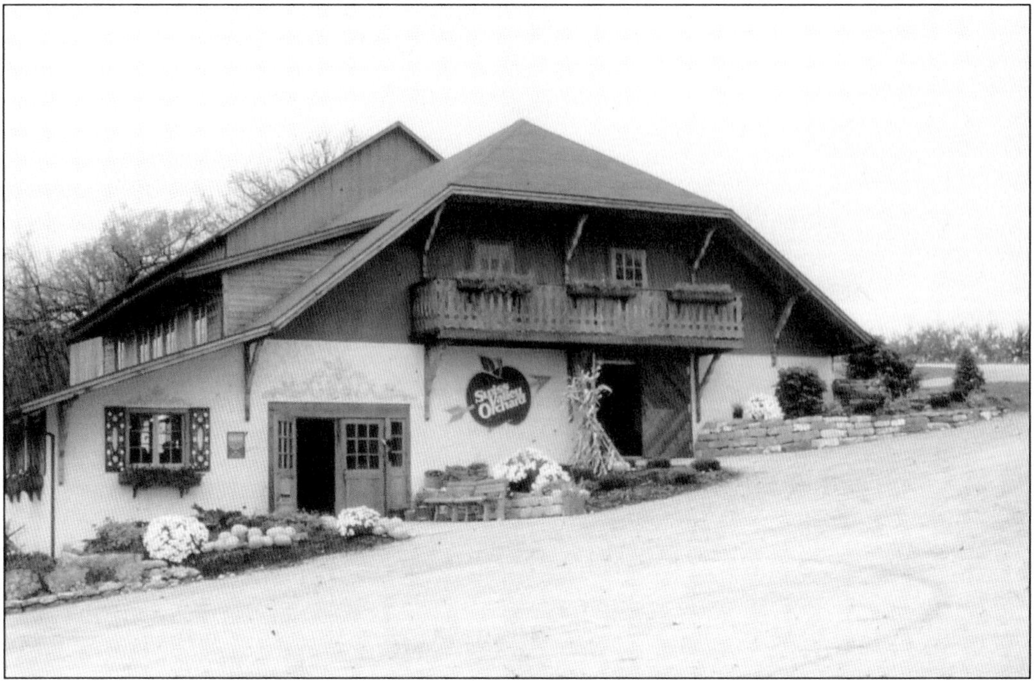

Swiss Valley Orchard was a family project of the Paul Roehrig family. The orchard grew to be the most poplar orchard in southern Wisconsin. The farm was one of the five original Amish farms in New Glarus.

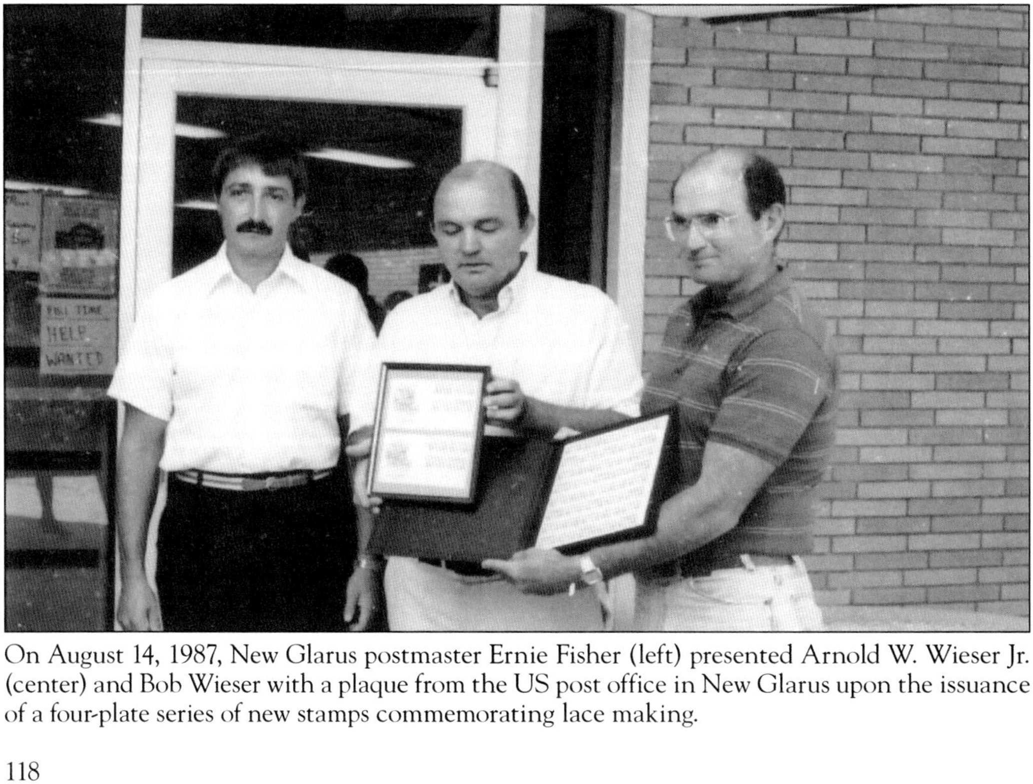

On August 14, 1987, New Glarus postmaster Ernie Fisher (left) presented Arnold W. Wieser Jr. (center) and Bob Wieser with a plaque from the US post office in New Glarus upon the issuance of a four-plate series of new stamps commemorating lace making.

The ties between New Glarus and Switzerland have always been strong and continuous through the years. This Friday, April 13, 1956, gathering at Edwin Barlow's Chalet of the Golden Fleece brought together members of the Swiss Consulate and a number of people in New Glarus.

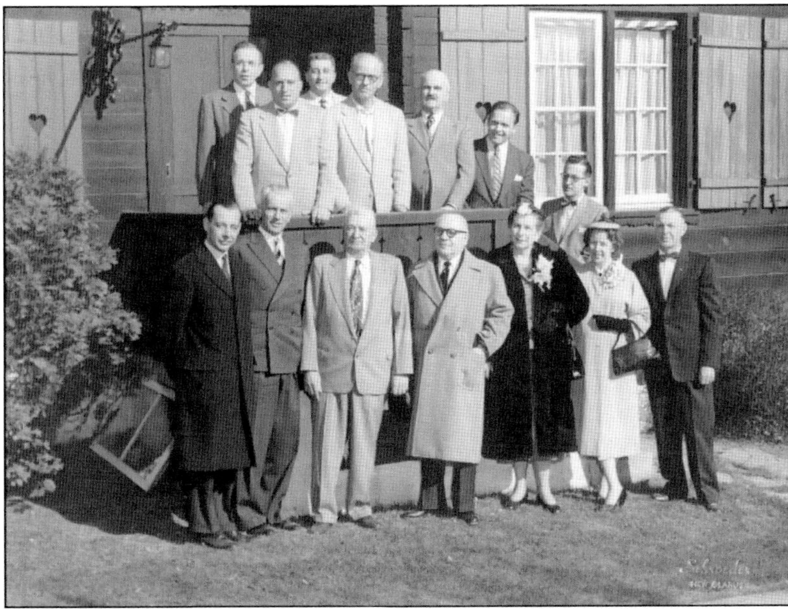

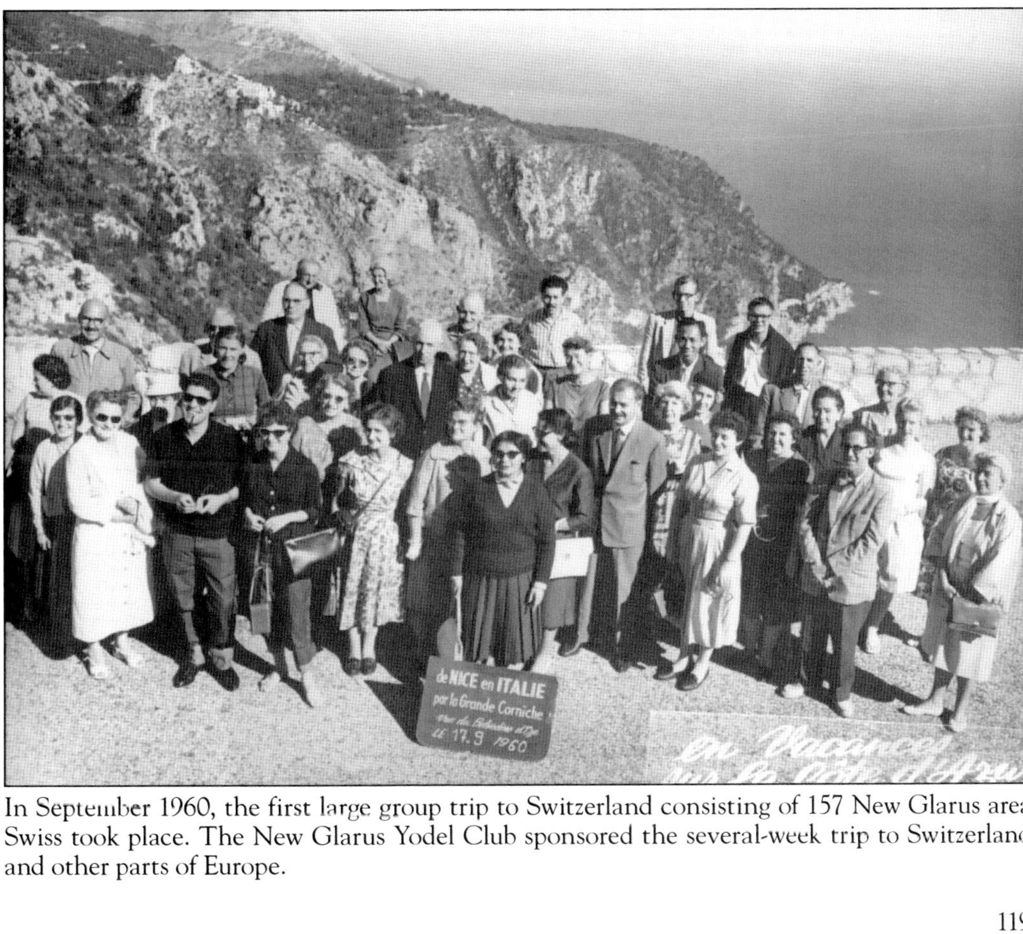

In September 1960, the first large group trip to Switzerland consisting of 157 New Glarus area Swiss took place. The New Glarus Yodel Club sponsored the several-week trip to Switzerland and other parts of Europe.

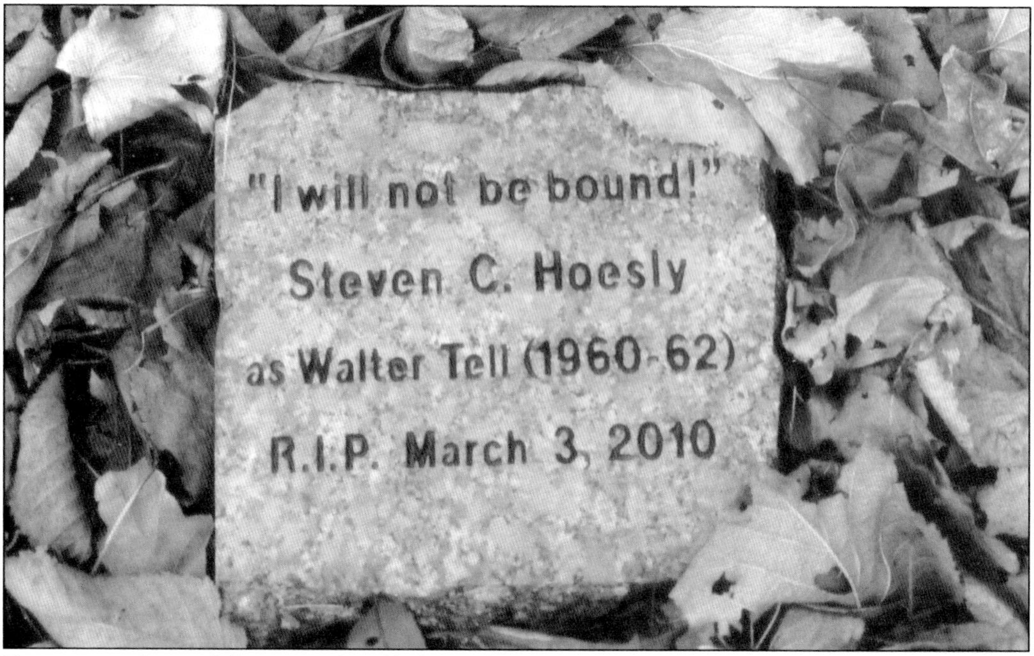

Former members of the annual Wilhelm Tell Pageant never fully leave their time in the Tell play behind them. Steven Hoesly played numerous parts in the play, including Tell's son. After Steve's passing, his relatives placed this small memorial store where he stood when Wilhelm Tell shot the apple off his head.

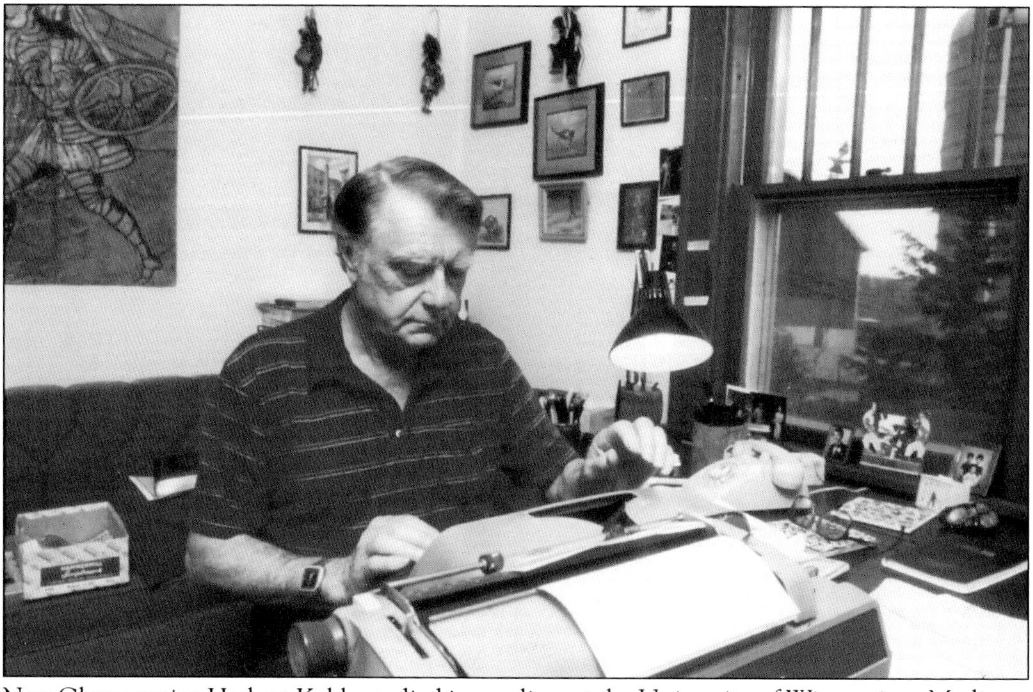

New Glarus native Herbert Kubly studied journalism at the University of Wisconsin—Madison. Kubly won the 1956 National Book Award for the best nonfiction book of the year, *American in Italy*. Kubly's friend John F. Kennedy presented the award. (Kubly family.)

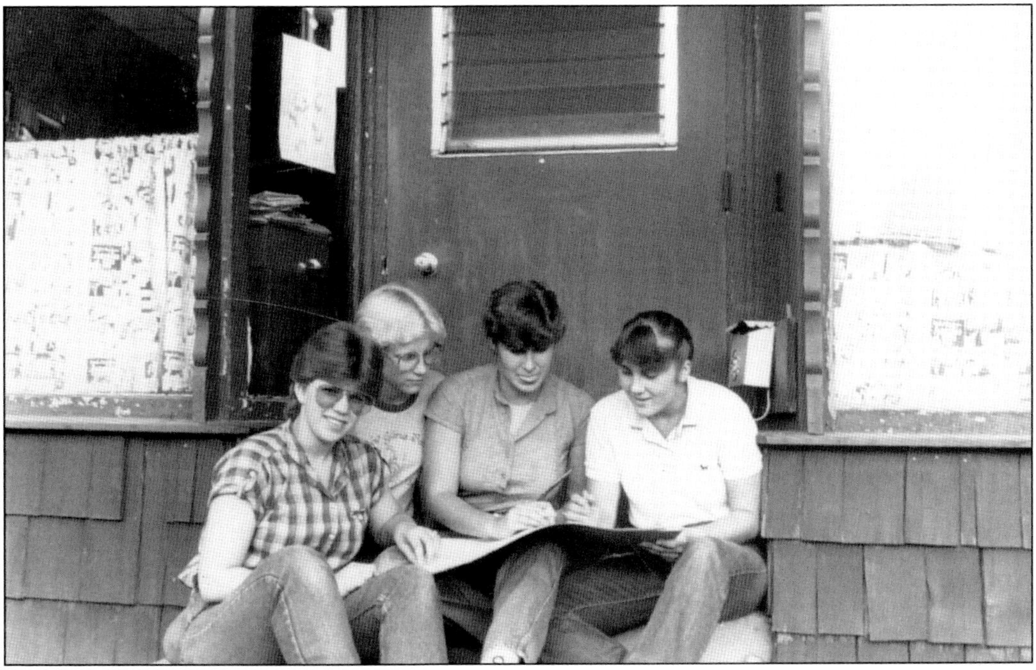

In 1983, frustrated by a lack of press freedom with the official high school newspaper, the *Old Guard*, this group of four budding journalists launched its own school newspaper, the *Gazette*. Pictured from left to right are Julie Hefty, Wendy Steffen, Catherine Capellaro, and Lisa Thompson.

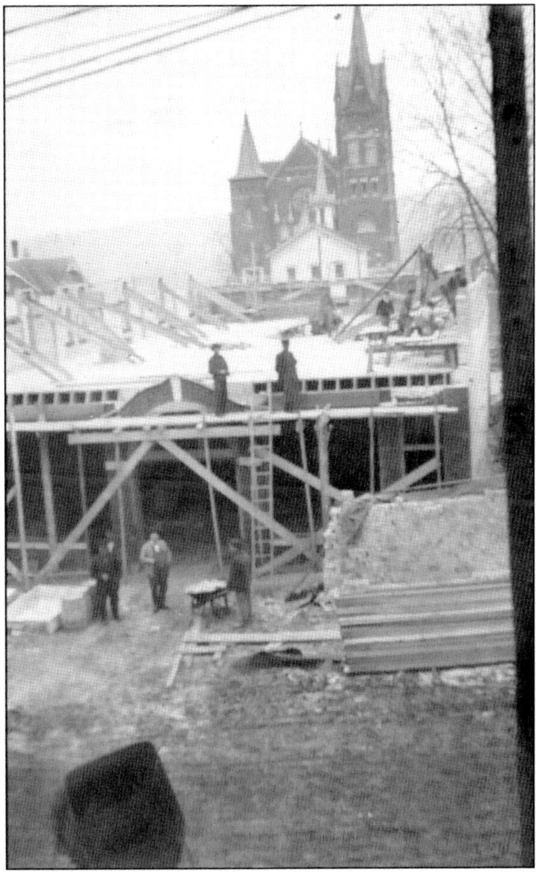

Nic Zweifel, after having sold his gristmill and grain elevator, became a car dealer for Buick, Pontiac, and GMC trucks. To accommodate his new business, he constructed this building. The second floor of the garage had an owner's apartment and Masonic hall. (New Glarus Historical Society.)

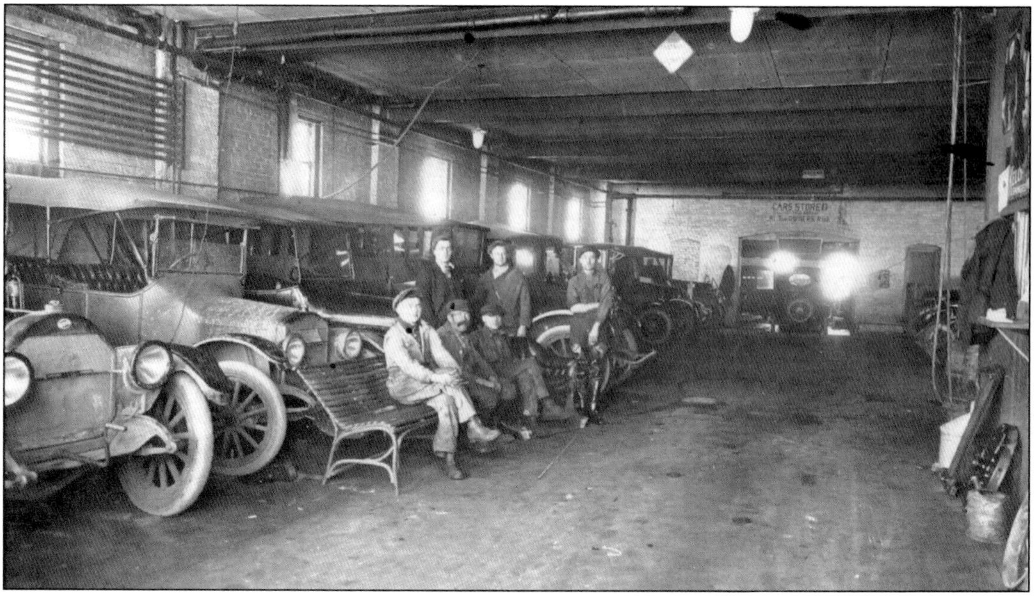

Zweifel's Garage mechanics pose here in front of a row of new cars. The sign about the door toward the back of the building states, "Cars Stored in this garage, At the Owner's Risk." This building is now Grace Church, located at 416 Second Street. (New Glarus Historical Society.)

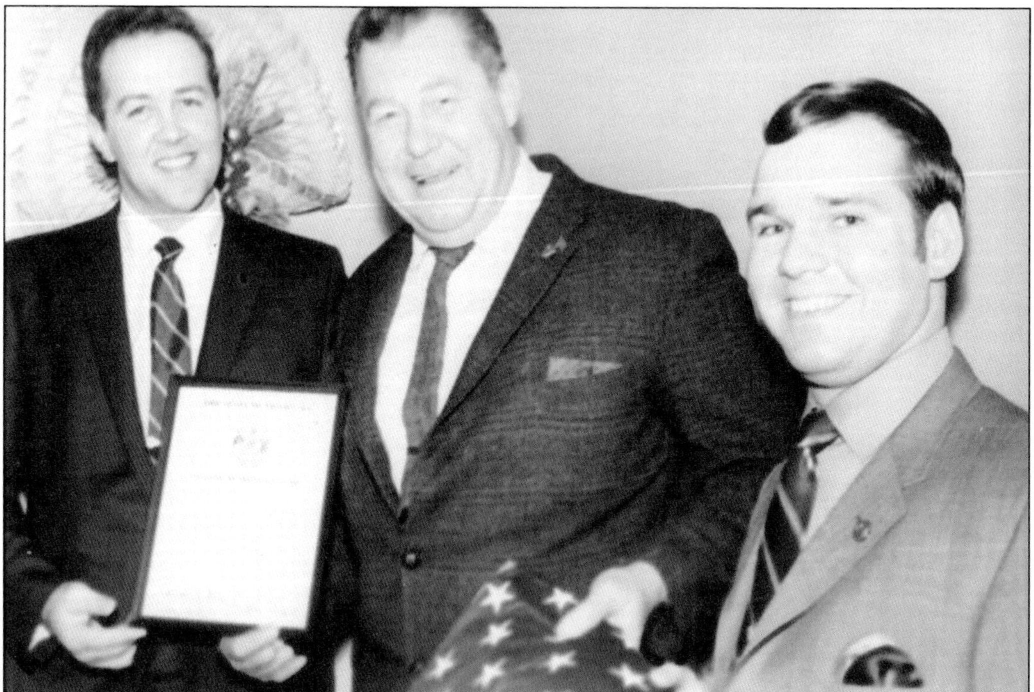

The New Glarus Jaycees were very active in civic affairs in New Glarus through the many community service projects they took on. This photograph shows Steve Jeglum of Blanchardville, on the left, accepting the Blanchardville Jaycees charter, which is being presented by State senator Gordon Roselip. Jim Haldiman, New Glarus Jaycees president, is shown on the right accepting an American flag from Senator Roselip.

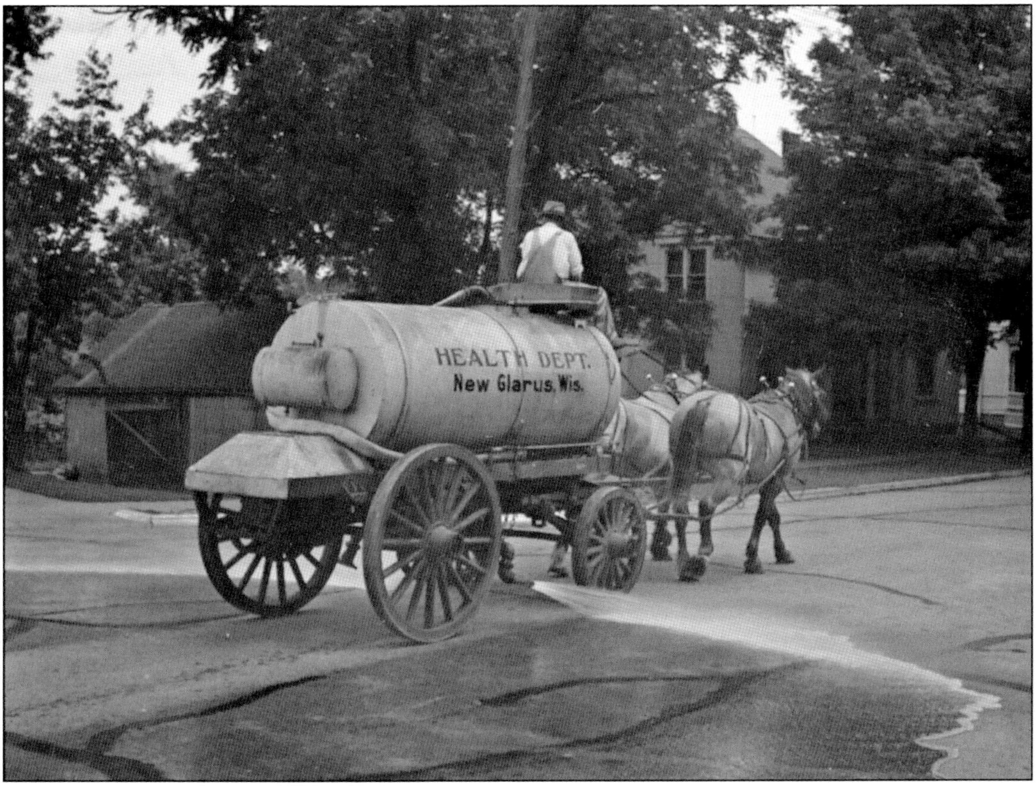

This street washer has a very interesting history. The federal government, in 1935 as a part of the New Deal, created the Farm Security Administration to combat rural poverty. A part of this program was to document life in rural America. FSA photographer Russell Lee took this photograph in July 1937. (Library of Congress.)

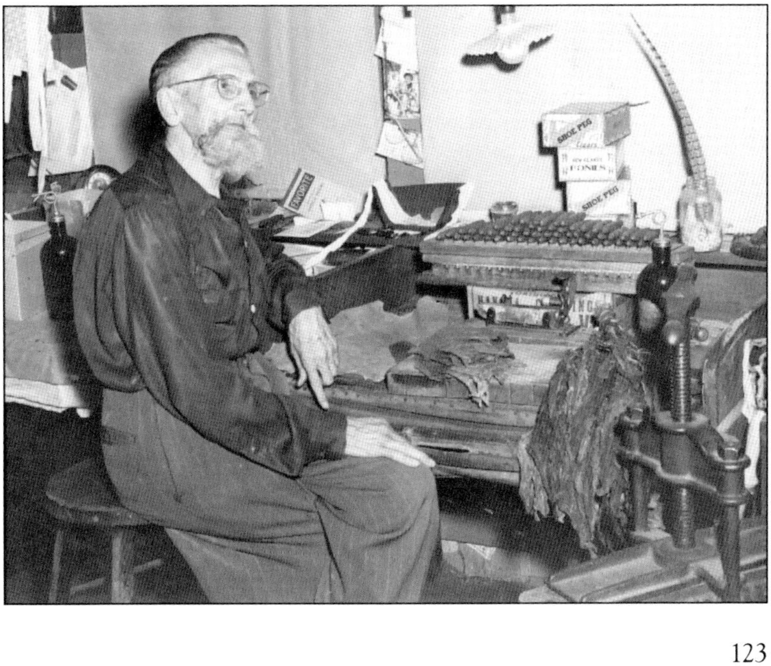

Sam Luchsinger, a New Glarus native, was an early New Glarus photographer. A number of his photographs appear in this book. Sam is shown here in his cigar-making shop. The cigar boxes represent a few of the brands of cigars he made. His 1855 home (a log cabin) is undergoing a major historic restoration. (New Glarus Historical Society.)

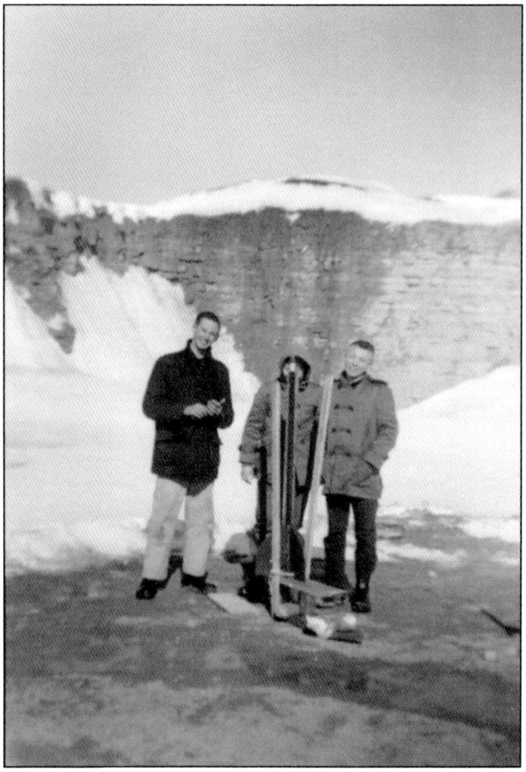

These three budding rocket scientists began their amateur rocketry in the basements of their parents' homes. The three mad scientists shown here are, from left to right, Ralph Bethke Jr., Kim Tschudy, and Byron Arnes on a February day as they were about to launch a four-foot-high rocket. The ground shook as the rocket lifted off and exploded 10 feet into its test flight.

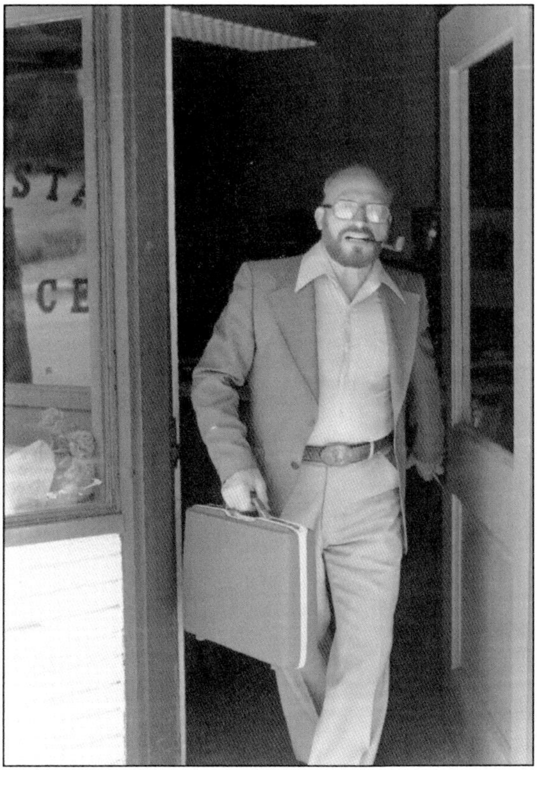

Ed Willi, a longtime New Glarus attorney and veteran of many years in the cast of the Wilhelm Tell play, is enjoying a few minutes of relaxation before he is to go on stage in his role of Baron von Attinghausen. Ed played the part for 48 years until six weeks before his death.

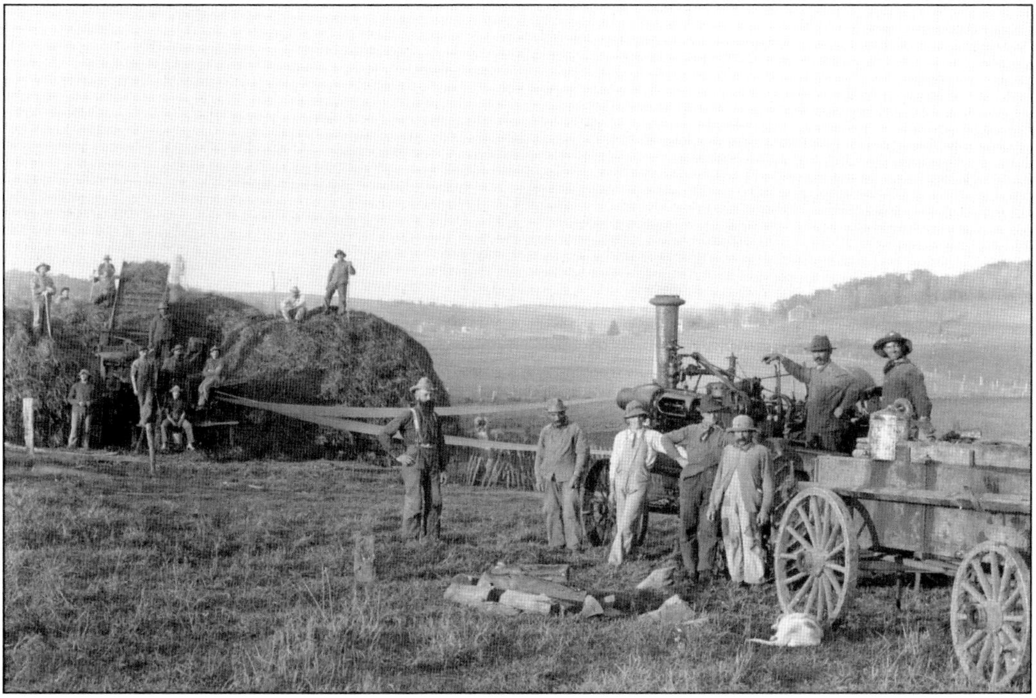

This large straw pile is a badge of pride for this group of farmers. They came from several neighborhood farms to share the work that took a couple of days as they threshed the oats from several fields just south of New Glarus. Threshing was hard and dirty work. (Jane Greene.)

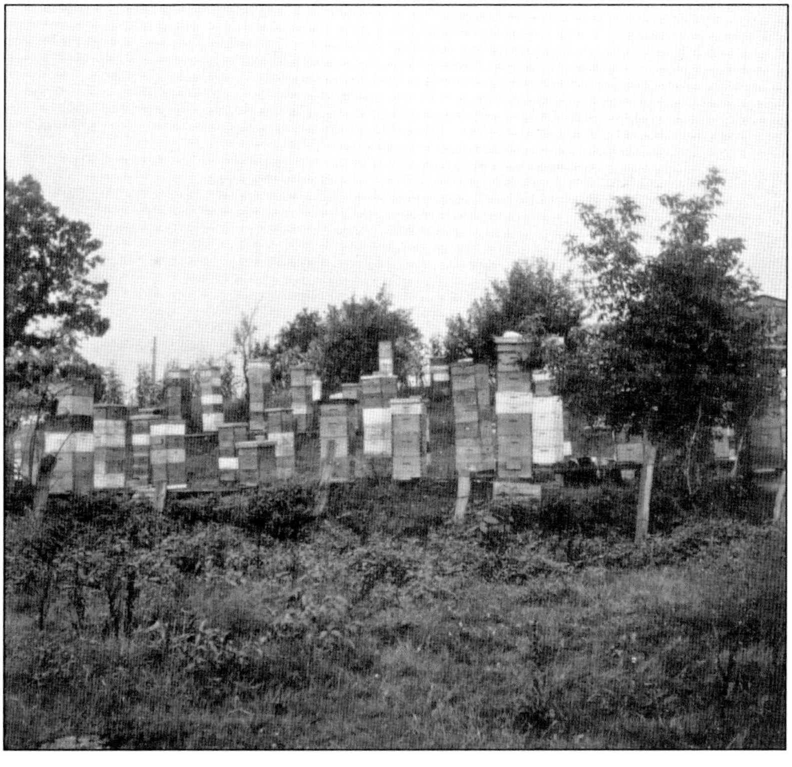

Karl Schenkel was one of a number of people engaged in one-person businesses they operated out of their homes. Schenkel operated a fairly large apiary near his home. (Charlie Schenkel.)

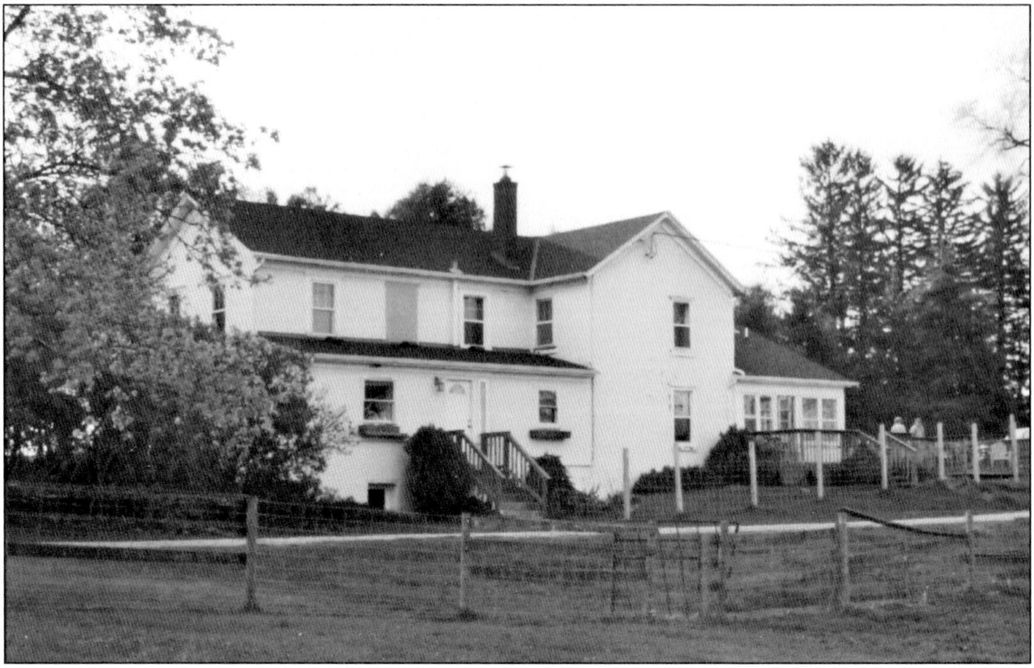

Many former dairy farms in the area have been broken up with a farmer purchasing the cropland and a second buyer purchasing the buildings and a few acres, similar to the very earliest farms. Often, these small farms are being used for small-scale agriculture. The Lazy Dog Farm is a bed-and-breakfast, using sustainable organic practices for vegetable and meat production.

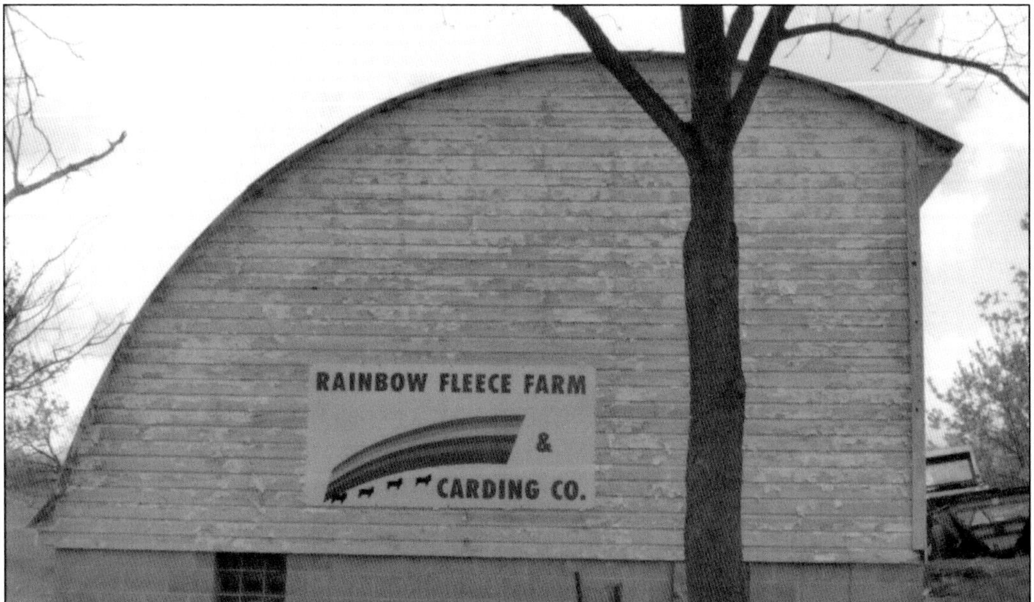

Rainbow Fleece Farm owner Patty Reedy has been in business on this farm since the early 1980s. Since the beginning of the farm, Reedy has expanded her business numerous times to reflect the needs of her customers. She specializes in very fine-wool breed of sheep. The farm also has a custom wool carding shop and sales area.

It is March 2011, and John Ott is calling the trucking company, telling them how many animals are to be picked up at the Farmers Cooperative Stock Company. This was the stockyard's last day after being in business for 97 years. Kent Duerst, in the foreground, is the third of four generations of his family to sell livestock here.

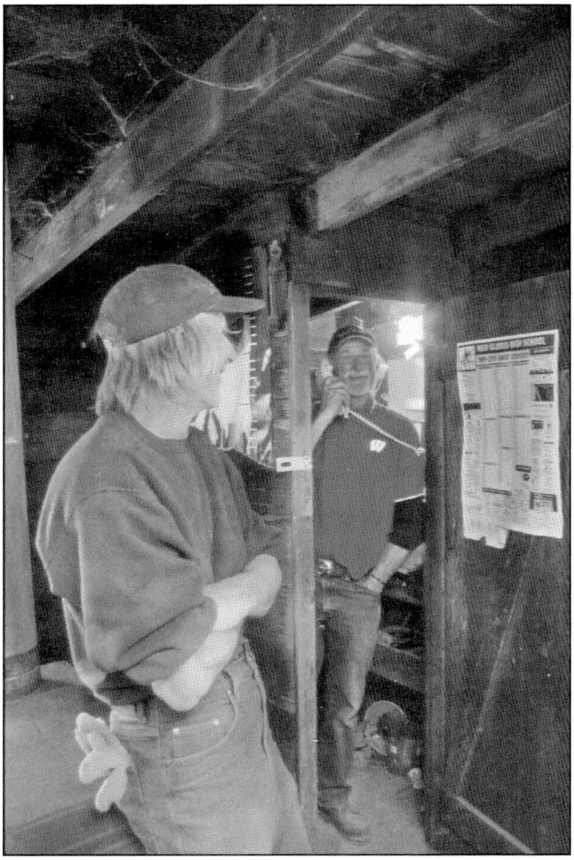

In 1863, wheat farming was the lifeblood of New Glarus's agricultural economy. By 1880, dairying replaced wheat farming. This is a 2013 photograph of a 34-foot-wide combine that has just finished combing this wheat field. It has taken 170 years for the circle of life to close once again and begin anew.

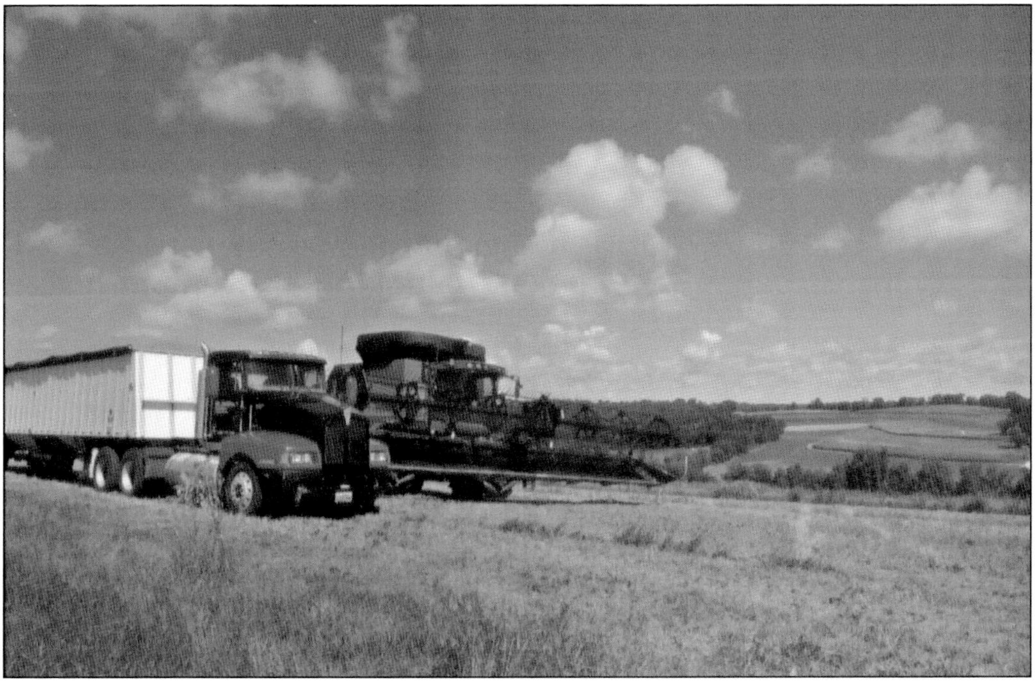